W9-AFV-788

NO BORDERS

TRANSLATED FROM THE SPANISH BY **PATRICIA J. DUNCAN**

NO BORDERS

A JOURNALIST'S SEARCH FOR HOME

JORGE RAMOS

rayo *An Imprint of* HarperCollins*Publishers*

HarperCollins books may be purchased for educational, business, or
sales promotional use. For information, please write: Special Markets Department, HarperCollins Publishers Inc., 10 East 53rd
Street, New York, NY 10022.

FIRST EDITION

DESIGNED BY **SHUBHANI SARKAR**

Printed on acid-free paper

Library of Congress Cataloging-in-Publication Data is available
upon request.

ISBN 0-06-621414-9

02 03 04 05 06 DIX/RRD 10 9 8 7 6 5 4 3 2 1

FOR MY CHILDREN, **PAOLA** AND **NICOLÁS** . . .

SO THEY CAN LEARN A LITTLE MORE ABOUT ME

We shall not cease from exploration
And the end of all our exploring
Will be to arrive where we started
And know the place for the first time.
—T. S. ELIOT

. . . each day I long for home, long for the sight of
home.
—HOMER (THE ODYSSEY)

What other occupation allows one to live history at
the very same moment it is occurring and also to be
a direct witness to it?
Journalism is an extraordinary and terrible privilege.
—ORIANA FALLACI (INTERVIEW WITH HISTORY)

Yes we can.
—CÉSAR CHÁVEZ

QUOTES VII

ACKNOWLEDGMENTS XI

PROLOGUE 1

ONE | **MY HOUSE**

MY HOUSE 7

THE FIRST OPPORTUNITY 46

TWO | **THE AMERICAN EXPERIENCE**

FREE IN LOS ANGELES 65

THE FIGHT FOR THE NEWS 84

LIVING WITH AN ACCENT 103

NEWS OF THE RECONQUEST: THE FUTURE OF
SPANISH-LANGUAGE MEDIA IN THE UNITED
STATES 116

CONTENTS

THREE | **GOING GLOBAL**

WAR AND LOVE 145

GROUND ZERO 184

AN (INQUISITIVE OR PREGUNTÓN)
JOURNALIST IN LATIN AMERICA 210

FOUR | **THE ETERNAL RETURN**

MÉXICO ME DUELE 247

CUBA OF THE NORTH 268

GRAY HAIR, AIRPLANES, TRIPS
AND SMELLS 283

THE ETERNAL RETURN 296

ACKNOWLEDGMENTS

A book is a victory.

—PABLO NERUDA (ODE TO THE BOOK II)

I don't know what it's like to write calmly. This book came together in the midst of interruptions, trips, changing homes, contract revisions, translations, soccer games and the demands put on my time from my other jobs as television news anchor, radio commentator, newspaper columnist and Internet contributor. Considering all this, the mere fact that I finished it is a victory in itself. Hence, the quote from Neruda.

What I regret most about writing this book is the time it stole from my son, Nicolás. My first thanks go to him. Nicolás is three years old, and he has brought new life into the house; his toys, his new words, his energy and his wonderful amazement at all things new fill every corner of the house. Sometimes Nicolás would sit patiently with me, watching TV while I wrote. Those who say that writing is a lonely occupation are mistaken. In my case I wrote these memoirs to background music that included songs from *Barney, Sesame Street* and the *Teletubbies,* and under the glare of the restless eyes of

Nicolás, who waited for the happy moment when I would turn off the lousy computer so we could horse around. Even though you can't read yet, thank you, Nicolás. I want you to know how much I liked the way you sang the ABC's in English as I recalled my childhood years. You were a great help in putting me in touch with that little boy in Mexico who my aunts would call *"ejote verde"* (string bean), and who I ceased to be so long ago.

My daughter, Paola, has kept me young with her dreams and adventures, and she has kept me awake after eleven o'clock at night. Without you, Paoli, I would be behind the times.

Lisa, my wife, opened the spaces I needed in my already limited and busy family schedule in order to write. Thank you for understanding, and forgive me for the constant distractions. I hope this book captures the result of so many mental absences. Your love and your joy have been the greatest gift in my life.

This book is extremely unfair to my siblings, Alejandro, Eduardo, Gerardo and Lourdes, and to my parents, Lourdes and Jorge. It is impossible for me to recall my life without them; after all, we were inseparable for the first twenty-five years of my life in Mexico. They were my compasses. However, what I am relating herein are very personal impressions about the history that we shared. Surely my siblings and parents may have seen these experiences in a different light. But thanks to them I have never felt lonely, no matter where I've been.

I can't say enough about Patsy Loris, who knows my work better than anyone. She spots my good and bad moods from a distance and criticizes what she doesn't like with an irresistible smile. Without her, my career as a television journalist would not have taken off quite so easily. Many of the events and interviews I describe here I either lived through with her or they were a result of her invaluable collaboration. First and foremost, however, she is my friend.

Univision has been extraordinarily generous to me. Workwise, I am like the Japanese employees of old who worked for the same company their entire lives. I have been with Univision since 1984, and still counting. Univision bought my ticket to witness history, and then it lent me the stage to tell what I saw. Their support of my work and understanding of my many journalistic concerns are priceless. A special thanks to Jerry Perenchio, Ray Rodríguez, Frank Pirozzi and Alina Falcón.

Tony Hernández and Gustavo Pombo of the Latino Broadcasting Company (LBC) have been extremely generous for allowing me to explore on radio several of the topics that I cover in this book. My voice, my real voice, was first heard on the radio thanks to Tony and Gustavo.

Rosaura Rodríguez encouraged me to write my first book, and since the day we met she has not lost track of me. Along with Patsy, she read the first draft of this book. She knows how to listen like a magician, and she is an incorrigible freethinker. Her piercing observations have kept me honest with myself.

It may surprise my childhood friends Gloria Meckel and Benjamín Beckhart to receive a mention here. "What did I have to do with this book?" they might wonder. "A lot," I would reply. We have lived parallel lives since high school, and they are my confidants. They help me change course when I am flying low, and like skilled air traffic controllers, they are always there at the most critical moments. Because of them, too, I do not feel lonely. They heard many of the stories in this book long ago.

Ever since I met her at a summer camp in Cuernavaca, Mexico, Kela Terán has been the greatest example of what it means to love life. Sometimes I felt that without her energy the world would come to a stop. No illness has been able to stop her, and her enormous, solid faith is still something I do not comprehend. Thank you for the encouragement, Kelita.

Bill Adler, my agent, sent me a very tempting letter full of possibilities. He didn't know me, but was up to the challenge. That letter would eventually prove to be a springboard for me, allowing me to jump from Spanish to my first two books in English.

Rene Alegría of HarperCollins was quick to seize the idea of showing the rest of America what an immigrant journalist or a journalist immigrant does and what he thinks. He has guided me in this editorial adventure gently but firmly. When I handed René the first draft of the book, he returned it to me with hundreds of comments and some words of advice:

"Now write all that you are holding back." Thanks to his intuition and his almost psychological ability to analyze, not to mention his sharp eye, I discovered things about myself that I had hardly thought about before. René opened the doors that I wanted to keep shut.

My very intense yet gentle conversations with Teresa Rioné left their mark, from the very beginning, on what I have written herein. She opened pathways to feelings that I didn't even know existed. These pages represent the times that she was there and those that she wasn't: some of them tender, and some of them very difficult to handle. As far as they concern me, they were all of the essence.

Dennis Farney will never know what his article in the *Wall Street Journal* meant for my career in the United States. Thanks to him, I decided to write this book.

Lastly, the chapter about the war against terrorism was written in memory of those journalists who died in Afghanistan in 2001, when I was covering the conflict: Johanne Sutton, Pierre Billaud, Volker Handloik, Harry Burton, Maria Grazia Cutuli, Julio Fuentes, Aziz Haidari and Ulf Stormberg.

NO BORDERS

I do not feel at home. Never. Anywhere.

Anyone who watches me anchoring the evening news, dressed in a suit and tie, might think that I have it made and that I'm not missing out on anything. But in fact I have yet to find a place where I belong, either tangible or emotional.

I have lived in the United States for almost twenty years, and I still feel like an immigrant. In fact, if one day I decided to make the United States my permanent residence, I suspect I would die feeling like an immigrant. It is an idea that makes me shudder.

Being an immigrant inevitably implies feeling of out place. No, it does not necessarily mean feeling discriminated against in another country. It is knowing, as the song by Facundo Cabral goes, *"que no soy de aquí ni soy de allá."* It means having the awareness that you will never feel completely at peace, because you are far from the country where you were born. However, when you return to that country, you find it changed, strange and different from the one you left.

In Miami, where I live, I am a Mexican. In other words, I am a member of a minority in the midst of another minority, the Cuban American minority, which itself exists in the midst of another minority, the Latino minority. In Mexico, I am the one who left, the Americanized one, and even—some may say—the traitor. The neutral form of Spanish that I use is understood throughout Latin America, but it infuriates my relatives and childhood friends. And when I speak English, anyone can tell that I am dogged by a long-standing accent that is beyond repair. I'm criticized for not speaking the standard form of Spanish approved by the Royal Academy of the Spanish Language (my Spanish is peppered with Spanglish), and for enunciating all the vowels when I say "Shakespeare" or "Beatles." And sometimes, they ask me where am I from. I was born in Mexico, but my children are American. I lived twenty-five years in Mexico and have lived twenty in the United States. What am I, a Latino, a Hispanic, a Latin American immigrant or a Mexican? It's not that I suffer from an identity crisis. Not at all. I know myself very well. What I don't know is in which world I belong. But maybe I belong, a little bit, in all of them.

I am an exiled *light:* I was not forced to flee a dictatorship but decided, on my own will, to leave a political system and a society that suffocated me. It was a personal decision. Nobody forced me to leave for the United States. But I did not get there; I stayed on the road.

I live without a home and without borders.

These are very interesting and good times to be a citizen of the world and a journalist. Not having defined borders has given me the flexibility and perspective a journalist needs to see things and analyze them. Not having a home, however, compels me—like Ulysses in Homer's *Odyssey*—to think constantly about going back.

The journey has changed me. I am not the same person who left Mexico on January 2, 1983. At the same time, I am exactly who I was and what I wanted to be. The past and the land—Mexico—continue to beckon me, but the United States and its obsession with what is new has taught me to look ahead and to reinvent myself. I have done just that, yet being comfortable with the notion that change is good has taken a lot out of me.

Now, the obvious question is, "Why write my memoirs at the age of forty-four when, ideally, half my life lies ahead?" I come from a part of the world where only the wise, the old, the rich and the powerful write their memoirs. And I am not wise, old, rich or powerful. But the simplest answer I can give as to why is because I have something to say and to share. Millions share this road in this country. In a sense, I am surrounded by wanderers.

Looking back at my life has also been an extraordinary exercise. It has allowed me to organize it, to recapture memories that I barely knew I had and to give direction to what still lies ahead.

I must admit, however, that the opportunity to write these memoirs halfway down the road—or, rather, as I travel on the road—has brought me great personal pleasure. In many instances, remembering has been like living it all over again. For someone who left so much behind—friends, houses, family and love—remembering is to not lose one's way, but rather reexperience it, and in some ways enjoy it all through a more mature point of view.

I also write because I am frustrated with television. After so many years of anchoring the news and not being allowed to give my own opinion, I have loads of things stuck in my throat. How can you explain a war, the death of an immigrant or the fall of the Berlin Wall in two minutes?

Writing has freed me and has given me a new voice. After the publication of my first book in English, *The Other Face of America*, I suddenly and unintentionally became an advocate for immigrants, for the use of the Spanish language in the United States and for Latinos in general. It's interesting that both people who know me and my television audience have generally accepted the notion that I should verbalize my opinions outside of the evening news, and in some cases, that I do so in a very direct manner without any pretense of journalistic objectivity. It's obvious that hosting the evening news or reporting a newsworthy event does not mean that one doesn't have one's own opinion. In fact, I sometimes think that many people who see me on television—especially immigrants, such as I—expect me to come to their defense. This book is about them as much as it is about me.

It's by way of this book that I am trying to both find inner peace and a home that I can call my own.

WHO ARE WE: what we remember or what we are hiding?

Both.

"There are many people who would prefer to forget or even to expunge from their lives certain events and certain experiences, those knots in the large net of experience that ultimately bind together all people who find themselves caught in the same web of time," wrote Pramoedya Ananta Toer, the Indonesian writer and politician, in his memoirs. In this book I have not wanted to forget or expunge the knots that bind my life. My intention, rather, is to reveal the driving forces that have brought me to where I am today.

The process has been somewhat strange. I have spent close to two years digging into my memories, searching for what defines me. In the process, I recaptured a part of my life that would otherwise have been lost for my children and me. When I was young, I was impressed by Marcel Proust's quest to recover lost time. His quest is also mine.

Living without borders has its advantages. In my case it implies being tied to two countries. The experience, therefore, is much richer and also means being able to talk about my professional life without nationalistic, partisan, religious or sectarian concerns. I don't have to please anyone.

In fact, never before have I spoken about such personal matters so candidly or written so freely. Doing so has relieved me of a great burden. Actors, I maintain, explore other lives through their theater or movie roles. Journalists, on the other hand, can only live one, but it vibrates with great intensity. An intensity that at times leave me mystified and energized. As life should be.

ONE | MY HOUSE

MY HOUSE

I wanted only to try to live in accordance with the
promptings that came from my true self.
Why was that so very difficult?

—HERMANN HESSE

The past is indestructible.

—JORGE LUIS BORGES

"What do you dream about?" journalist Dennis Farney asked me. "I dream about my house," I replied,
"my house in Mexico." Farney's front-page article
for the *Wall Street Journal* was published prior to the
2000 presidential elections, and it introduced me to
many non-Spanish-speaking Americans who would
otherwise never have heard of me. The article, however, did not include my response about my house.
Fortunately, politics—not my dreams—dominated
the country.

Unlike my days, which are filled with news of
wars, violence, assassinations and coup d'états, and
the constant traveling and stressful, unstructured
schedules, my dreams are almost boring. They are
my refuge. Those dreams, in fact, are a desperate
search for balance. For someone whose profession—

journalism, what else?—does not allow him to be certain in the morning where he's going to be sleeping that night, dreaming is an escape. One day I woke up in Los Angeles and I went to bed amid the ruins of a city in Mexico that had just been devastated by an earthquake; another day I woke up in Miami and went to sleep opposite a Berlin wall that was falling to pieces; one morning I opened my eyes in Madrid, and only exhaustion drove me to collapse in a rickety bed just a few feet from the bombing in Kosovo.

These are the reasons I live without tranquility, without inner peace, and why in my mind I often escape to the house in Mexico, to that house where I lived most of my childhood and adolescence and which still represents stability and serenity. That is my real home, my only home.

Sometimes I dream I am walking calmly from one side of that two-story house to the other. I climb the stairs as if I were floating to the room I share with my brother Alejandro, and I glance over at my other brothers Eduardo and Gerardo, who are playing in their bedroom behind an arch that never had a door. I smile without opening my mouth. I hear my sister, Lourdes, placing her dolls on the high, white, squeaky bed. I leave my room and see the small bathroom with its blue tiles; it's open, the sink is stained with toothpaste, the hamper of dirty clothes overflowing and the lid is thrown on the floor. The television is on in the background, but no one is watching it. A few steps away is my parents' room, its giant bed covered with a green and gold bedspread. I never did find out how many meters long that bed was! I look out the window and there is the garden, a bit neglected but still green, which my father waters when he comes home from work. My mother is downstairs in the kitchen. On the left side of the kitchen there is an enormous stainless steel counter with five glasses of chocolate milk lined up. It is the metal plank that my father brought home from one of his construction jobs. The stoves emit a white, rich and comforting steam; it's coming from the pressure cooker for the *frijoles*. The tomato sauce for the cheese stew is simmering next to it, and in the center of the stove is a pile of tortillas, puffed up by the warm air. I cross the kitchen, go out to the patio and smell the clean white sheets that are hanging in the sun. When I get to this point, I almost always wake up. Sometimes I open my eyes ever so slowly, trying to return to the dream. When I am successful, I see myself playing soccer with my brothers in the garden or hanging from a green handrail next to a tree that never bore any avocadoes. I can't always return to my dream. It doesn't matter; I was in my house. I am calm. I know where I come from.

I come from that house on 10 Hacienda de Piedras Negras Street. Bosque de Echegaray, Estado de México: I can still remember my phone number. Really. 560-51-20. I might forget many things, but not that address and my telephone number. If I were to forget them. I would lose my center; I wouldn't know where to go when I get lost, when I am confused, when the world seems too big for me.

When I return to Mexico I like to go by the house and look at it from afar. The last time I went, it still had a green gate and a red roof. Interestingly enough, that same house—located just a few feet from a noisy superhighway and smothered by pollution, surrounded by a hardware store, a hospital and a homeopathic pharmacy—produced a wonderful internal peace in me.

I have often been on the verge of getting out of the car, ringing the yellowish bell and asking whoever lived there—my parents sold the house and moved to an apartment—to let me in to see the house. I admit that I have felt like climbing over the gate the way I used to when I was a child and had forgotten the key. That movement, that metallic rattle, reminds me of those days when nothing—not even a gate—could stop me.

Terrible things could have occurred in that house. I can still remember down to the last detail the secret plans I had to throw myself from the roof into the imaginary pool in the middle of the yard—a five-meter free fall at least—and the dreams I had of putting lots of *chinampinas,* which were really small amounts of gunpowder, on the soles of my shoes so I could fly like Batman or Superman. For lack of a few pesos, I didn't break my neck or burn my feet.

Truthfully, I don't really need to see that house. I have it recorded inside. I lived there for twenty years. In contrast, the next twenty years I lived in at least sixteen different houses, apartments or hotels.

Almost everything about me has its origin, its reason for being, in the time I lived in that house. For example, sleeping next to a highway for such a long time has caused me to have a serious aversion to noise. Now that I can choose where I live, it would never occur to me to buy or rent a home where you can hear cars go by. I can still recall, with a mixture of excitement and fear, when the sirens of the new patrol cars and ambulances sounded like flying saucers to me. For several nights I slept with a camera next to the bed so I could photograph the aliens who were coming to visit me. I quickly lost the extraordinary tolerance for noise I had during those two decades as soon as I was able to make a choice. Back then, it would never have occurred to me to complain.

Many of the things that I was forced to eat as a child—meat with gristle, cabbage, broccoli, cauliflower, tapioca soup—are now absent from my diet. When I turned forty, I promised myself that I wouldn't do anything that I didn't want to do. (A little late, I suppose.) Back then, neither my brothers nor I would dare protest, or rather, we protested but we had to eat what was on our plate anyway. "Try it and then tell me if you like it or not," my mother would always say.

Just as there are now foods that I refuse to eat almost automatically, there are others that I try to eat whenever I need an emotional boost. The noodle soup and *filete frito* in butter accompanied by slices of avocado that my grandmother Raquel would make for us on Sundays—a real luxury in those days for a family that had to tighten its belt as much as ours—are flavors that even today transport me to a world far from mine but one that is utterly safe.

Despite the financial limitations, once or twice a year my parents would take us out to a nice restaurant, "so we could learn how to behave at the table," they told us. My *mamá* assures me today that it was much more often, but to me it didn't seem so. What I learned was to eat what we almost never had at home: shrimp.

My notion of what it means to live well seems to be tied to shrimp. In the early seventies, shrimp were extremely expensive in Mexico. They usually came from the Gulf coast, so they had to be shipped frozen to the capital city. They were transported along the same route—Veracruz to Mexico City—that the Aztecs used to supply fresh fish for the emperor's diet. For example, I became aware that if I ordered shrimp in a restaurant, neither one of my parents would order the same so that the check wouldn't get too big. Only people with lots of money or power could afford to eat shrimp . . . or so I thought. And in those days, when pesos were hard to get, a shrimp cocktail with avocado or an order of shrimp in garlic sauce was a real luxury for a family of our means. You had to savor each shrimp individually. You would never even think of filling your stomach with the few shrimp that there were on the table. "When I grow up." I began to think, "one day I will eat only shrimp until I can't eat any more." Many years had to come and go before I was able to afford myself such a luxury. Many years.

In the end, my taste for shrimp turned into sort of an obsession. I associated having shrimp with either a party or the celebration of an important event. My mother and my aunts would make a wonderful shrimp stew for Christmas or New Year's, and we only had shrimp in the house when we had guests. The few times when all my siblings and I were able to have shrimp at home, we knew that it had something to do with a special event, or that my *papi* had landed a new construction contract. I still find that smell that remains on your fingers after cleaning shrimp a delight.

SOMETIMES WE WOULD GO to the movies. One time, however, I almost suffocated, and due to that tragic experience we stopped going to the movies. I was eating some sugar-covered lemon candies as we watched the beginning of *2001: A Space Odyssey* when one of the candies got stuck in my throat. It got stuck right when the monkey in the movie threw a bone into the air. I remember the moment perfectly.

My siblings and I were seated in the row in front of my parents. Desperate, I turned around and said to my father, "I can't breathe." At first they didn't hear me since I could barely get the words out. I repeated them as best I could. "I can't breathe." I must have been eight or nine years old. My *papá* carried me to the back of the movie theater. Then he picked me up by the feet with my head hanging down, almost touching the floor. As he shook me, forcefully, I practically stopped breathing, and I went limp like a rag doll.

I remember that my anguish disappeared for a moment, and with my eyes half open several scenes from my short life came to mind just like the stories of people who are about to die. Violent coughing and an intensely painful burning in my throat, however, broke the strange sense of calm of one who is resigned to the inevitable.

My *papá* laid me on the ground and I was able to breathe in some air, the first in a couple of minutes. The lemon candy coated with tart sugar never came out. All the shaking had caused me to swallow it. My *papá* and other adults who were worried about what was happening gave me some water. After the scare was over, we went back to our seats to finish watching the movie. My *mamá* took the bag of candies from me and put it away forever. I haven't eaten that kind of candy since. I was so young; I had never thought about death, but I was very close to it. Years later, in Los Angeles, I went to see the same movie just to see the scene where the monkey throws a bone into the air. I watched it with my sweaty hands stuck to the seat. When the bone fell to the ground, I left the theater. I had to remind myself that I could live through that moment and live, one more time.

At around that time, we took a trip to Acapulco that also almost ended in tragedy. As my parents were getting comfortable in their beach chairs at the seashore, I got into the water and I began playing with a boy who was a little older than I. In those days, I thought that I was indestructible, and despite the incident at the movies, I didn't have a clear idea of what it meant to die. Well, the boy said: "If you're brave, follow me," and I wasn't about to stay behind. I began following him out to sea until the waves started to cover me and I could not touch bottom. I barely knew how to swim, and I swallowed a lot of seawater; I couldn't even yell out for help. That's when I lost my courage. I struggled to get back to the beach, and when I finally reached the shore, terrified, I realized that my parents hadn't noticed that I had gone. These events are how, before the age of ten, death became a tangible reality for me: with a piece of candy and the waters of the Pacific.

With the exception of those dramatic experiences, outings were real celebrations. We would put on our finest clothes, slick back our hair with gel and race toward *Papá*, who would have come home early from work for the occasion. Whenever the Ramos family entered a restaurant or mass on Sundays it never failed to attract attention; we were five well-behaved blond kids—four boys and a girl.

The tumultuous entrances, however, always made me a bit anxious, especially when we would go to Sunday mass at the church in Polanco. I liked being the first or the last to enter, but it bothered me to enter in a single pack, for people would stare at us. Being stared at was more than just a matter of race, although we were five young blond-haired green-eyed children, and that is why my grandfather called the boys *"pollitos"* and my sister *"polla."* We attracted attention because we were all only one year apart from one another. The incline in height from the oldest to the youngest was perfect. Furthermore, it was a period of time when we were dressed almost identically. That was until I became aware of it and I started to pick my own clothes. Now, though, I understand that, with so many siblings, I was looking, unsuccessfully, for a way to stand out. I am the oldest, and it mustn't have been easy to see a new sibling take a little more of my parents' and relatives' attention away from me each year. The story goes that my father was looking for a girl and he didn't stop until he found her. My three brothers and I are irrefutable proof of that.

The distancing from my siblings that I longed for finally happened when I was sent to kindergarten. But I didn't like the experience. It caused me a great deal of pain. I still remember that horrible sensation caused by the separation from my mother. The image is still vivid: I am standing in the school's courtyard, crying, alone, as I can see my mother leave through the gates of the main door. That was the first time that I felt different.

I obviously never fully appreciated how wonderful it was to have so many siblings until I left them to live abroad. The earliest childhood memory that I recall is of me playing with my siblings with toy soldiers that I called *"señoritos."* Every time I remember this, I feel happy. Later on, the soccer games, the games of hide and seek, and even the fistfights were organized with ease. Alejandro, Eduardo, Gerardo and I had an osmosis-like childhood; their experiences were mine, and my experiences, I'm sure, were theirs. When I was a child I never imagined my life without them, and interestingly, after I left Mexico to live in the United States, and now years later, I still feel the same about them. Nowadays we are all in our forties, but it's funny that when we're all together we don't make a big fuss about it; it's as if we just woke up in our house on Piedras Negras Street. What would be surprising is if one of us were missing.

I spent most of my early days with my four brothers—first at school, and later playing in the street—while Lourdes, my sister, went to another school and had another group of friends. She remained in a world apart until, as the years passed, she began to integrate into our eminently male existence.

My relationship with Lourdes has played a pivotal role in my life. We are more alike than either one of us wants to admit: we are both shy, we both avoid publicity and having to speak in public. But ironically, we both ended up being television journalists, she in Mexico and I in the United States. We both hold very strong beliefs, some of which are written in stone. It's not easy (or very pleasant) to argue with us. We also share a highly developed degree of self-consciousness; it has helped us avoid missing our footing in life.

Whatever we didn't share as children, we have more than made up for as adults. It's not just sibling love that we feel for one another. It goes much further than that. We call one another almost every day, and we keep ourselves informed—in extraordinary detail—about both our public and private lives. I can never say this enough: Lourdes is my main critic and she never lets me get away with anything. When she doesn't like one of my articles or news reports, or my clothes, she lets me know immediately, with such honesty that if I didn't know how much she loves me, it would hurt. And when I talk to her about my future projects or my desire to get involved in politics, she is the one who quickly brings me down to earth. Nobody speaks to me like she does. Nobody. And nobody loves me in the unique way that she does, either.

My aunts and uncles and grandparents who we would see religiously—Saturdays at the Avaloses and Sundays at the Ramoses—used to call me *"el ejote verde,"* or string bean; there was no better way to describe me in my early years. I was skinny, asthmatic and had a greenish tint to my skin. My head was too big and bony for my body. Many people said to my mother, "Poor Yuyú, such an ugly child."

The photographs from that time, mostly in black and white, show me looking sad, or in the best of cases, very serious. I don't remember having felt that way though; I was a very loved child. I didn't like being so skinny, however, and as soon as I entered high school I decided to do something about it. A friend of mine had changed his physique dramatically by following the exercises of Charles Atlas. I had no difficulty getting the money I needed and I ordered the exercise regimen that would end my life as a string bean forever, just as the advertisements in the comic books that I devoured promised. For three months I followed Mister Atlas's exercises to the letter, and to my surprise I developed muscles in my arms and abdomen that I never knew existed. Although it may have been frivolous, this had an enormous impact on my self-image. It showed me, for the first time, that I could be the architect not only of my stomach muscles, but of my own destiny too.

Regardless, my siblings never called me "Charles Atlas." Instead, they nicknamed me "Pote." Nowadays, no one in the family can tell me what exactly "Pote" means nor who gave me this nickname. I think that it comes from *"potrillo"* (Spanish for "colt"), since I was always running around. No matter what it means, they still call me "Pote."

Another nickname that my mother gave me, and that thankfully did not stick, was *"Inutilito Ramos"* ("Little Useless Ramos"). In fact, I have always had an almost physical inability to fix things. Hammering nails or fixing a simple problem with an electric appliance was a virtually impossible task for me to do. I never understood why my friends would get so excited when they took a look at a car's engine, and much less when they fixed it.

I am the exact opposite of a handyman. My inability to fix anything is still part of my life. Everyone at home, including my children, knows that if something breaks down, I'm the last person to call. It's very hard for me to program a VCR, to figure out how to leave a message on my answering machine, to make my cellular phone work in a city other than Miami or to operate the most simple of computer programs. I am always—and I mean always!—asking someone how to do the simplest things in life. And now as a reporter, it seems to me to be a magic trick how my interviews and reports travel from any part of the world via satellite back to the studio in Miami. I admit that without the experienced, patient and creative producers at Univision I would have no chance as an anchorman or a correspondent.

A pair of computers has replaced my old typewriter, on which I wrote with bare fingers my excessively long thesis at the Iberoamerican University of Mexico. But computers, which have simplified my life tremendously, are helpful to me for the only thing that interests me: writing. All the other programs are a terrible waste.

It's true, surfing the Internet has saved me from spending countless hours in archives and libraries. But this doesn't erase my obvious clumsiness when it comes to manual skills or my pathetic inability to decipher even the most simple of mechanical processes.

It was obvious from childhood that I was not going to be an engineer, and that's why I worked on my other personality traits—such as writing and debating—that would allow me to compensate for my lack of understanding of the machines that surround me. I suppose that deep down inside I will always be "Little Useless Ramos."

At school I was a leader, at home I always had someone to play with, and in the street I took part in an unending Olympiad centered on, what else, soccer games. *"Vamos a echarnos un fut,"* was the battle cry. When we got home from school, my brothers and I would cry, "maaaaaa" to be sure that she was home, and after that wonderful confirmation we would eat something—I ate bread most of the time—do our homework, and then fly out the door to play in the street. My knees, always bruised and covered with scabs, were proof of my street life.

That street was the extension of my house. I can't imagine my children having that experience today. In the house next door there were four sisters who everyone wanted to pair off with the Ramos brothers. Our first encounter, however, was a very early lesson in sexual education that resulted in the surprising discovery that the two oldest were not exactly like Alex and me. We went into a room, and without much further ado, all four of us lowered our pants. We didn't even laugh; we just stood there in absolute silence. I suppose we were in shock. Upon realizing that my brother and I had plenty of something that our female neighbors did not have, I divided the world between men and women for the first time. It goes without saying that after this anatomical exploration, our unsupervised visits to our neighbor's house came to an end: I never did find out who told, but I know it wasn't me.

That first encounter with sex only fed my curiosity. We were not used to discussing these topics at home, so instead, the whole issue was shrouded in silence. I couldn't talk to my friends about it either. I didn't want them to find out about what we had done, although I never felt guilty. What did impact me from that first sexual encounter was the realization that sex is closely related to eyesight, a realization that shaped more sexual experiences as an adult than I'd like to admit.

Sergio and Alejandro Aceves lived two houses down from us, and they were the only ones on the entire block who had a pool. That instantly made them as popular as the little store on the corner where we would buy all kinds of sweets: *chamois*, *zansitos*, exploding chewing gum and *tamarindos*. When the Aceveses went swimming, my brothers and I would climb up the wall surrounding their property so they would see us, hoping they would feel some pity and thereby extend an invitation to go swimming. It was healthy envy.

Piff and Sassa Plaza read as many books as their father smoked cigarettes. When they weren't reading, however, they participated in *"fut,"* roller skating races and games of hide-and-seek. Of all the stories of the block there is one that stands out: the day Leandrito, Piff and Sassa's father, left home. His wife was an imposing, authoritative but warmhearted French woman who we called *Oui Mamá*, because when she told her children to do something, that is how they responded. One day, Leandrito said, "I'll be right back, I'm going to buy cigarettes," and Leandrito, many kilos lighter and several centimeters shorter than *Oui Mamá*, never came back.

It was very traumatizing for me just to think that someday my father would disappear and never return. Leandrito's departure was funny to me then. At that time I never thought of the sadness that Leandrito's actions caused my friends Sassa and Piff. But I understood very well that an important part of being a father was simply being there, always there, always strong. (This ideal would be seriously put to the test when I, as a father, had to be separated from my daughter, Paola.)

Our friends on the block also included the Hallivis—Luciano was the first one on the block to own a car, and Beto was the good-looking one of the group; the Mier y Teráns, who were involved with the very conservative Catholic organization of the Opus Dei and were overly protective of the first girl I liked; the Del Valles, who organized some incredible parties; the Prietos, my cousins and a countless number of relatives, hangers-on and acquaintances who would join in our games and adventures every afternoon and weekend. We were proud to be *"los de Piedra Negra,"* and I would have loved for my children to have grown up in a neighborhood like that.

We used to spend hours sitting in Luciano's car listening to music and talking about school and our plans for the future. But we only listened to music with English-language lyrics. In the early seventies, Mexico was extremely influenced by the following dichotomy: anything that came from outside Mexico was good, and anything Mexican was, in the best of cases, questionable. This was especially felt with music. That's why radio stations spent hours airing contests to see which one of the most popular groups of the moment—the Beatles and the Monkees—would get the most telephone votes from listeners. We used to listen to a radio station called "La Pantera" ("The Panther"), which never played a single song in Spanish. That was my first introduction to the United States; from afar and through the waves of a radio station that called the group from Liverpool *"Beet-*les."

No one could have imagined a world without trade barriers in the mid-seventies, since economic protectionism was the rule in Latin America. There was even an objective to create a block of the southern and developing countries that could face up to the giant of the north in cultural, business and political arenas. Mexican Pres. Luis Echeverría—whose hands were still bloodied from the massacre of students of Tlatelolco in 1968 that took place under his watch as minister of the interior and from the repression that was a hallmark of his regime—wanted to create a new information and cultural order that would oppose American influence. But the more that Mexico tried to close itself off from the United States, the more my friends and I were attracted to American clothes, music and amusement parks like Disneyland. We loved everything American.

Mamá was always busy with something in the house; with five children, she had barely finished serving a meal when she was already preparing the next one, sweeping, sewing, making the beds or washing and ironing. In her rare spare time she liked to read; she was not fond of television. My best memory of her, however, is that every time I would ask her something or want to talk, she would lower her book or stop her chores to listen to me. I can't really remember a time when she said, "I don't have time right now." She always had it and still does.

My *mamá* lost her mother to cancer two days before her fifteenth birthday, and it still bothers her that she was not allowed to be with her at the moment she died, supposedly to protect her from emotional trauma. That is why when my father had an emergency operation for a brain lesion at the Mayo Clinic in Rochester, my mama insisted on my being there. My father could have died in the operating room, and my mama wanted to give me the opportunity to be near him in the end, even though it would be painful. She did not want to do to my siblings or me what her family did to her.

She grew up in a very traditional family, surrounded by unmarried aunts. My grandfather Miguel, who would later open his mind enthusiastically to the ideas of a changing world, did not have the foresight then to allow his daughter to study for anything other than a secretarial career. She still recalls that when she received her degree and asked her father to help her look for a job, he replied, "Why are you going to look for a job if you don't need it?" And that was that.

Marriage was the only legitimate road for this restless woman who had not yet garnered the courage to challenge the norms of the time, which was to have one child after the other. Contraceptives? What contraceptives? "No one told me about that," she recalls. Yuyú—as she was called since she was a little girl—kept reading, though, and questioning the role she was relegated to play. There were always books on her night table.

One afternoon, when I went in to the kitchen after our daily soccer scrimmage, she stopped me at the door and asked, "Do you believe in happiness?" The question surprised me, not just because I was ten years old and no one had ever asked me about such esoteric matters, but because I had always assumed my mother was happy. "Happiness," she said, without waiting for my response, "is in a moment; it's not permanent." In my soccer-player mind, the idea of happiness shot right by me like a ball by the goal. Years later I understood that that was the moment in which my mother rebelled against the life she had been dealt.

The tension with my father grew, and the day she refused to make hot chocolate for him for dinner I knew that something dramatic was happening and that a big change was coming.

Hot chocolate was what my father had drunk since he was a child, and it required a great deal of time and skill to prepare. You had to melt a bar of chocolate in boiling milk, and then, making sure it didn't curdle or turn into cream, beat it until it was foamy; not so much so that it would spill over the side of the cup and not so little that it would be lost in the liquid. Dozens of times I watched my father give the hot chocolate back to my mother because it was not well made. Only my maternal grandmother was capable of the precise degree of beating required, and my mother would work up a sweat trying to emulate such perfection, until one day my mother grew tired of the routine and said to Papá: "I'm not going to make chocolate anymore; now you can do it." From that day on, my *papá*, aware of the technical impossibility of making the hot chocolate himself, began to drink *café con leche* that he himself would prepare on the stove.

That was my mother's first rebellious act, and at that time it seemed unforeseen and, frankly, revolutionary. Other events, less dramatic than refusing to make the hot chocolate, followed, until one day, when we were at the university—my sister, Lourdes, was entering her first year at the communications school, and I was about to graduate—I bumped into my mother in the hallways of the university. "What are you doing here?" I was about to ask, but it would only have been a rhetorical exercise. It was a deeply emotional moment when my mother, with her mysterious eyes, said to me: "I finally was able to do it." "How are you doing, Ma?" I asked her, as though I were the adult and she the teenager. And in her response—"Really, really well"—there was much more understanding than in any of our previous conversations. Walking together, as students, down the same hallway in the same university, is an image I'll never forget.

At home Mamá had solemnly informed us, before the sulking face of my father, that she was going back to school. Because she had never finished preparatory school, she could not officially register at the university. That, however, did not stop her from taking several courses in history, literature and psychology at the same university and at the same time as her children. My *mamá* grew up with us, her children, and that bond, a more pure respect than between mother and son, has remained the cornerstone of our relationship.

For years I thought—and still do—about those brief yet striking encounters with my mother in the university. It was as though she wanted to recoup the youth that she had lost locked up in a house where her aunts only cared about cooking, embroidery, television soap operas and the latest gossip from the beauty parlor. The most wonderful thing of all was that the first conversation I had with my mother about the idea of happiness expanded into much more complicated themes: Freud, Marx, Nietzsche and any other renowned (and dead) European that came our way. Both she and I were obsessed with one thing: giving meaning to our lives. My mother had given meaning to her life through her children, but she wanted more. It's exactly that same desire to go beyond the conventional wishes of an average middle-class family—a good house, trips, fashionable clothes, the latest model car—that I learned from my mother during our conversations. I never wanted the same things that my classmates wanted. To begin with, I didn't have the means that they did, especially during my college years. But I was looking for something that would make my life whole. That same search took my mother all the way to college, at an age when some women only think of living vicariously through their husbands.

With this act, my mother completed her liberation. From that moment on, she was going to choose her life, and that is how it's been ever since. Yuyú—whose aunts did not allow her to be with her mother when she was dying, whose father prevented her from continuing her studies and finding a job, whose husband and children temporarily held back her intellectual development—could finally say that she, and no one else, was responsible for her actions. That's why I have always seen the characteristics of a silent heroine in my mother.

My mother's newfound liberation, as you can imagine, did not sit well with my *papá*. He came from a well-to-do family from the north of Mexico: Ramos Arizpe, Coahuila, to be more exact; the Ramoses of Ramos Arizpe. He studied architecture in a country where the priority was not building houses or buildings but rather surviving, so he always had to fight hard to make a good life for a family with five children. In return, I suppose he was expecting a family like the one he had, where authority was never questioned. His father was unyielding, and his maternal grandfather was a general in the Mexican army. Therefore, my father was used to a strict and unwavering form of authority. That's what he expected from us too. And that is where destiny played a trick on him.

The roles at home were well defined. My mother was the one who lent emotional support and my father the one who imposed discipline, although those who really got to know him knew that deep down my father was a softie. He was full of affection, but he lacked the ability to express it.

As the oldest child, I sat on his right at the dinner table, and naturally that pleased me. When I was small, his presence commanded respect: well dressed, with stylish ties, a thick, perfectly trimmed mustache and an unforgettable smell of cigarettes mixed with lotion. He would buy a new car every two years—except when times were bad and we had to scrimp—and he had a notable record collection of American instrumental music. His car and his music were his refuge.

I don't remember playing with him much, maybe because he didn't have time or because it was not part of the world from which he came. His presence, however, made its mark on me. For years I sincerely believed that he was perfect; that he didn't make mistakes, that he earned more money than anyone, that his car was better than my friend's father's car and that he could kick the ball better than Pelé . . . until one day we played soccer together.

For me soccer was trial by fire, it is what divided the world; on the one hand were those who knew how to play, and on the other . . . everyone else. At school they would call me "Borjita Ramos" after the goalie on the Mexican national team named Enrique Borja. My father, however, did not look anything like Borja or Pelé. One afternoon at my maternal grandfather's house, I asked my father to kick the ball so that I could play goalie and try to stop it; but he didn't hit the ball. His black shoe missed the ball badly by a few centimeters. I have the image engraved in my mind. For him the incident was unimportant, but for me it was devastating. When he went inside and I was alone in the yard, I began to cry. The image of my father as Superman was shattered. No, Papá wasn't perfect.

This seemingly unimportant event played a pivotal role in my life. It was at that moment when I painfully realized that I didn't want to be like him nor did I want my life to be a carbon copy of his. The same person, who for years had been an example, suddenly became—all because of a stupid soccer match—someone who could not meet a child's expectations. I would ask myself, as if it were the most important thing in the world: "How could he have not hit the ball? How couldn't he?" After that, I began seeing my father in a more critical light, and with some distance between us. I finally got over the whole soccer ball incident when I broke away from expected norms and then defined my own idea of what a father should be.

If my father would've played soccer better, I am sure that our relationship would have gotten stronger over the years. But instead, from that moment on, I tried to find more ways of distancing myself from him, until we practically stopped playing together. Now that I have two children, one of my major concerns is growing too old to play soccer with them. My daughter, Paola, is a great basketball player, and she runs pretty fast, but she still can't beat me. Not yet, that is. I also expect to offer my son, Nicolás, fierce competition when he decides which sport he will play, although I don't hide the fact that it would make me very proud if it were on a soccer field where we could measure our physical prowess. Nicolás was born on June 14, 1998, the same day that three memorable soccer matches were held in France during the World Cup competitions. Was that a coincidence? And just in case I will have to play with Nicolás someday, every Saturday I play soccer religiously. When Nicolás wants to play, I hope to be ready.

AS WITH ALL FIRSTBORNS, it fell to me to pave the way and test the limits that my parents had set. I never had any academic problems; I didn't need to study much to get good grades. The challenges to my father's authority came along later, with adolescence.

The sex education I received from my father lasted about three minutes; that is exactly how long it took to get from our house to the closest shopping center. He got me into the car, put on a serious face and then let out, "If you ever want to be with a woman, let me know." The Ray Conniff Orchestra played in the background. The conversation went no further. Nowadays, advice like that sounds absurd, even comical, but I'm sure that in the early seventies in Mexico a father talking about sex to his son was a great advance (and a result of pressure from my mother). Decades later, comparing notes, my brothers and I laugh uncontrollably when we realize that we all received the same quick, concise sex education class—in my father's car at the entrance to the mall. Today I remember it as a wonderful gesture and effort from someone for whom the world was changing too rapidly.

I suppose that in this short conversation with my father there was a hidden offer to take me to a prostitute, if I wanted him to. I couldn't. First of all, it would embarrass me in front of my father; we had never spoken about sex before, and the first time we do so, he offers—in a veiled way—to take me to a "Date House," as they were called back then. I didn't feel comfortable enough with him to discuss those things. Still, the offer didn't shock me. In certain circles in Mexico, it is culturally acceptable for fathers to help initiate their son's sexuality with a prostitute.

This was also a lesson on how Mexican culture controlled the lives of millions of young women, known as "family oriented girls," for whom any sexual contact before marriage was prohibited or terribly criticized.

The second reason why the idea of being with a prostitute repulsed me is that while I was a teenager, I had a very intense relationship with my girlfriend, so I saw no reason to leave her for some unknown person. I learned very little from that first and only talk about sex that I had with my father. In retrospect though, his offer taught me plenty, but it taught me nothing about sex.

I probably learned more from the *Playboy* magazines we were allowed to read when we went to the barbershop with my father. The shop was in Polanco, one of the nicest areas in Mexico City, and the ritual was always the same; you would sit down, they would offer you something to drink, and then the barber would throw a porn magazine on your lap. All that happened—I am sure of it—with the full complicity of my father. It was another way of giving my brothers and me a lesson on sex: with women you don't know it's all right, with friends, it's not. It's not surprising, then, that when I told my papá I was going to Acapulco with Kuas, my girl-friend, he hit the roof. "If you really love her," Papá told me, "respect her and don't go away with her." Those were the days when one of my friends, whose nickname was *"Perro,"* had his sexual initiation with a prostitute his father had arranged for him at a bordello. I was not willing to have that kind of sexual life; the idea of having a "sacred girlfriend" on the one hand, and a whore on the other did not convince me.

I went with Kuas to a gynecologist, who patiently informed us of the available contraceptive methods and gave us wonderful advice that is still valid today, "The worst thing you can do is have sexual relations with one person while thinking about another." Then we left for Acapulco, happy. The trip was crammed full of mishaps. The car broke down on the high-way, I ran into a jellyfish while I was waterskiing and the stinging lasted for days, and we had no money left for dinner the last night because of the expense of repairing the car. The feeling of freedom and independence, though, was incredible. It is a feeling I must still satisfy.

My relationship with Kuas lasted, on and off, about eight years, and together we experienced that first great love of youth that leaves its mark forever. The trip to Acapulco bound me to her in such a permanent way and, ironically, wound up marking my break with my father. I did the exact opposite of what he wanted, and things had turned out very well.

I also discovered the wonderful freedom afforded by hotels. A hotel room's four walls gave us the freedom that we were just beginning to discover and a level of privacy that we could never enjoy in her house or mine. Kuas's mother always had a well-tuned ear for very prolonged silences, and in my house, with three brothers, a sister, a mother who was always home, even a small kiss would have been caught by somebody . . . and then followed by jokes at my expense or embarrassing questions. Therefore, hotel rooms in Cuernavaca, Acapulco and Bajío became oases. They were mine, only mine, and nobody could bother us there. Interestingly, these experiences were my first taste of total independence and freedom. Something as simple as a hotel room became a symbol of the life that I wanted to lead. (Now I understand how this symbolism has reached an extreme when in my life as a journalist I have had to—many times against my will—make my semipermanent home in hotels.)

I met Kuas in high school, and she charmed both my brother Alejandro and me. She was a nice, intelligent, friendly and very open-minded blonde with guaranteed willpower. We used to talk about philosophy, we listened to music and we connected very well on both the physical and emotional levels. We had more than enough time to get to know one another. Our relationship was so equal that I became—without thinking about it—an ardent feminist. In those days, I never thought that our relationship would leave its mark on me for the rest of my life, and that the way that I would effectively connect with women depended to a large degree on how the relationship compared to that first wonderful one.

Our relationship began in the most normal way. After many conversations at school, one night during a party I decided to ask her to be my girlfriend. I must've said the right thing, something like: "Do you want to be my girlfriend?" And she responded with a soft yes. We danced then to a Stevie Wonder song—which quickly became "our song"—in an open-air patio, where she put her arms around my neck, and put her head on my shoulder.

At these kinds of parties, we would wait for the slow songs by the musical group Bread so that we could dance with our girlfriends or with the girls that we liked. This was the only chance that you had to touch her waist or feel her body close to yours. But invariably, and right in front of the worried faces of the parents who organized the party, after one or two slow songs, came the lightning rod music of Chicago, which by then was leading the Beatles and the Monkees on the Mexican charts. A disappointment on many levels.

Kuas was also the first and only woman that I serenaded with mariachis—I brought them to her—one day before she left to study abroad in England for a year. But of course, with joy came pain. The party went on so late into the night that my parents went to get me at Kuas's house, so I had to face the sadness of having to say good-bye to my girlfriend quickly, because if not, I would have had to face the humiliation of having my parents take me home by force in front of everyone. The following morning, I cut school to go to the airport to give her one last hug. My parents never found out.

Kuas's trip to Europe, after the sudden and disconcerting death of her brother Daniel from leukemia, made me feel the pain of separation for the first time. And the phone didn't help either. Long distance calls were so expensive, that I was only able to make one, on March 1, her birthday.

But letters did indeed go back and forth. As a matter of fact, I still have some of them. Furthermore, every time that I write, I keep right in front of the copy of the *Oxford Advanced Learner's Dictionary of Current English* that she used while in Great Britain.

It's odd that such young people—I was about seventeen years old and she was a bit younger—would have gone out for eight years. But we were in an experimental and adventurous phase that we thought was better shared than constantly changing partners as our friends and classmates did. We would have had our first sexual relationship if it had not been for a cheerful American woman from Chicago who would visit Mexico City to (momentarily) forget about her husband. During one of my breakups with Kuas, I ended up having sex with a woman from America's heartland.

I think Kuas forgave me, or better yet, she accepted the fact that with just one escapade in bed, I had ruined our dream of beginning our sexual lives together. But this event was very symptomatic. Although Kuas and I had a wonderful relationship, I felt trapped by Mexican rhythms and traditions, and I didn't want to be married with children at the age of twenty-five. I wanted to see the world, I wanted to travel and see beyond the traditional society into which I was born.

In the end, my desire to explore and free myself of what asphyxiated me in Mexico—tradition, expectations, social pressures—was more powerful that anything that tied me to Mexico: Kuas, my family, my friends, the cuisine, soccer . . .

Kuas visited me a couple of times after I left to live in Los Angeles, but nothing was the same. She always knew why I had left Mexico, what I had fled from, and as soon as we started seeing other people, our old teenage wish to end up together someday, faded away.

MY PATERNAL GRANDFATHER, Gilberto, was an authoritative figure, like many of the successful men of his time in the early twentieth century. He was a lawyer, owner of a wonderful ranch with nuts, oranges and avocadoes in Ramos Arizpe, Cohauila, and he did not accept dissension in his house. My father tried to impose the same system in his. At first it made sense: it was the only system he knew and with five children it was important to establish discipline. The times in which I grew up and chose a career, however, were much freer than those of my grandfather, so I had only two choices; accept the rules of my father or rebel. I chose the second.

I did not really know what I wanted to study, but I knew all too well what I did not want: something traditional. In those days, I took a notorious interest in body language—I discussed the idea of personal space (that imaginary bubble that surrounds all human beings) enthusiastically with the "niñas" who would flirt with me—and the only career that had anything to do with that was communications. Besides, I had such a good time in restaurants when I would tell my female friends that touching their hair was an unequivocal sign of sexual interest and that the way one placed the salt shaker, glass and plates on a table could indicate emotional rejection or acceptance. Yes, dining with me then was a joke, but still, what I thought then about physicality, communication and the subconscious has helped me tremendously as a journalist.

When I explained to my father that I wanted to study communications, he replied, "And what are you going to do with that?" For him, the only legitimate university careers to be in were law (like his father and brother), medicine (like his brother-in-law), engineering (like his friends) or architecture (like his). I'm sure he thought that his son was making a mistake and jeopardizing his future. He wanted—what else?—the best for me, and I had simply gone astray and wasn't listening.

My mother reminded me of an incident that happened when I was an adolescent. I entered the living room and, without mincing words told my father, more as a provocation than a conviction, that I didn't believe in God. My problems with God, I can now see, had much more to do with his supposed and imperfect representatives on earth than with a problem of faith. But at the same time, I was rebelling against my father's religiousness. Instead of listening and trying to reason with me, my father got up, furious, and punched the kitchen wall. He broke his hand, naturally— which required a cast—and I think something much more profound broke too: his son had gone hopelessly astray. This event, coupled with the serious disagreements that I was having at the time with the priests who ran my school, made me break from Catholicism for good.

Perhaps I have emphasized the tension with my father too much and not the calm, pleasant times, which were the norm, but it was those confrontations, caused by his best intentions and his love, that made me who I am today. As a matter of fact, I think that having my dog, Sunset, and my cat, Lola, in my current home comes from a desire to go against my father's wishes, since he did not allow pets at home when I was a child. Oddly enough, once I left home, our relationship became much closer. When he no longer felt he had to impose his authority on me, he let go emotionally and became an affectionate, proud and supportive father.

He came to the United States several times to visit me, with a surprisingly open, almost adventurous attitude. When a genetic defect caused a brain hemorrhage and his diet of cigarettes and fried eggs brought about several heart attacks, he spent many of his afternoons watching my sister and me on TV. (The wonders of satellite TV!) "The children are coming on!" he would shout to Mamá, before Lourdes gave her newscast from London and I mine from the United States. It was exciting for me knowing that every afternoon my father was watching the news. I worked hard not to make a mistake reading the TelePrompTer, and I wore ties that I know he would have liked. Sometimes, after the newscast, I would call to ask him what he thought of the news that day. The truth is, though, that he never watched the news for the news itself but rather to see me.

I was fortunate that we were able to reconcile long before he died, and I remember two heartfelt hugs we exchanged the last time I saw him in the apartment he had recently bought in Mexico City. He was wearing a sweater and he was standing, despite how hard it was for him to walk. I hugged him and then went to the door, but I couldn't say good-bye. I turned around and hugged him again. It was as if we both knew that those hugs would be the last. The loss of that man with a mustache who couldn't kick a soccer ball, who would have preferred to be a magician to an architect and who instilled in us his taste for elevator music every time we got into his car, has left a terrible void in me. I miss his smell of tobacco and cigarettes so much, and that fragile look, like a frightened boy, that he sometimes had.

When I shared my feelings of loss with Chilean writer Isabel Allende, who had just suffered the loss of her daughter, Paula, she sent me a note (in February 1995, a few weeks after my father's death) that contained one of the best pieces of advice I have ever received: "The deceased who are most loved never disappear completely. Paula is a sweet presence in my life, just as my grandparents are, Granny, and so many other benevolent spirits. Your father is part of you now, you carry him in your memory, in your genes and many of the gestures you make, but they are his."

I am still startled today when I find myself imitating one of my father's gestures. The other day I was driving my car with the windows closed, listening to music, and I turned the volume way up—just like my *papá*. I also realize that I have the most intimate conversations with my daughter, Paola, in my car when she is, how shall I say, captive and unable to escape. Even in the most trivial matters, though, like eating only chocolate or vanilla ice cream, the noise I make when I yawn, buying sugarloaf in the evening before going home or trying to catch mosquitoes on the fly with one hand, I am like him. That, I recognize, is what my *papá* used to do. It brightens my day, for I realize that Isabel was right and I am not alone. My father is with me in my gestures, my memory and my belly.

My grandparents are also with me. Tolerance, passion for history and reading, and their tireless gift for listening are traits of my grandfather Miguel that I try—not always successfully—to imitate. Even in the simplest things I mimic my family. I almost always have avocadoes on hand in my house, just as they were at my grandfather Miguel's house. The way he would cut them and serve them, like the most treasured dish, is very much like my father's ritual, which I now perform. From my grandfather I learned how to identify ripe avocadoes from hard ones, to accelerate the ripening process by wrapping them in newspaper and to make a hole in the top part of oranges to then suck the juice out noisily and happily on hot days, just like he used to do when we would visit his ranch in Ramos Arizpe. While there are things from my father and grandfather that I will carry with me my whole life, I never wanted to be their carbon copy.

THE REBELLIOUS SPIRIT that I developed at home was reinforced at school. I went to a school in the outskirts of Mexico City, the Colegio Tepeyac, which would later change its name to the Centro Escolar del Lago (C.E.L.). Throughout kindergarten, grammar school, high school and two years of preparatory studies, I was subjected to the disciplinary abuses (and prejudices) of the Benedictine priests in charge of my education.

The most fun, of course, were the long recesses when we could play soccer, run in the open field and torture some poor classmate with the cruel punishment of a wedgie—pulling up on the elastic of one's underpants.

I also learned some of the most important lessons of my life during those recesses. I can still remember, with regret, how in the middle of a basketball game, one of the biggest bullies in the school yanked on my brother Alejandro's hair. I am still ashamed I didn't defend him at the time. I wish I had acted more quickly and more decisively. On the other hand, shortly after that incident I found the courage to tell that stupid kid that he had picked on *my* brother and not to let it happen again; it never did. I learned one of the main lessons for survival: always protect your family and don't allow anybody to hurt you, ever.

Speaking of survival, one of the most vivid memories I have from my school days is a trip we took to the Churubsco Studios. What was intended to be a visit to learn about the film industry turned into a real tragedy when we came upon a lion cub. He was tied up but out of his cage, as he was being used in one of the movies that was being filmed. We never thought that the animal could be dangerous; he was eating and was the perfect picture of tenderness and innocence.

One of our classmates, Ander, however, went over to pet him, and the cub stood up on his back legs and viciously attacked his head and neck. They both fell to the ground as the cub continued to attack Ander while no one did anything to stop it. We were in shock. We couldn't believe what was happening in front of our eyes. Then, one of our classmates, Eduardo Fuentes, in a display of unusual courage, went over to the lion and gave him several strong kicks in the stomach until he opened his mouth and let Ander go. Ander was rushed to the hospital, on the verge of losing an ear. The trip was over.

And so was my innocence about death.

Until then, I had never thought that my classmates or I could die. Death had never been a part of my life education. I thought that I was immortal, like the Batman and Superman characters that were such a part of my childhood. But with the lion's attack on Ander all that changed. Death was now a possibility. And what if I died before going to confession? The notion of never seeing my family or friends again sent shivers down my spine.

On a more human level, I discovered that I was vulnerable. Lalo

Fuentes had saved Ander from the lion's jaws, not me. I didn't have the quick thinking or courage that Lalo did. I would've wanted to save Ander, but I froze and chickened out. Perhaps that was a normal response under the circumstances. But this didn't go along with my childhood belief that death could not get me, and that there was nothing that I couldn't do.

The daily routine was not as exciting as that adventure. I was never a particularly diligent student, but I got good grades. In fact, I bragged to my friends about not studying and getting a nine or a ten (A or B) on exams. There was no homework or presentation to the class that I couldn't talk my way through. It was never hard for me to talk my way out of a jam, and my friends can still recall a presentation I had to give on the discovery of America in which I spoke about everything except the subject assigned. Of course I passed the course.

Almost everyone had nicknames. There was "Sope" and "Tortilla" (because they were dark), "Chino," "Cuco," my good friends "Lalo" and "Perro" (the toughest and most loyal one of all), and "Huevo," who liked to change into his shorts for gym class in the last row of class, without the teachers catching him.

I also remember a nun who wore dark glasses so we couldn't tell who she was looking at. She often caught us throwing papers at our neighbor's head or copying on the monthly quizzes. I have disliked dark glasses ever since, and I am annoyed by those who do not remove them when they are speaking to you.

Later on Benjamín Beckhart and Gloria Meckell came to the school, and to this day we are still friends. With Benjamin and Gloria I have always had a very intense intellectual relationship and an affection that has stood the test of time; our philosophical conversations probably marked their destinies and mine. None of us wanted to go through life unnoticed, and I believe that insofar as our capabilities would allow, we were all successful: Gloria as a brilliant lawyer, Benjamín as a tough businessman and I as a journalist.

Several decades later, they are still my confidants, and I consult them before every important decision. Even today I don't dare take a significant step without knowing I have their support. They are far away—Benjamín lives in Mexico City and Gloria in Dallas—but they are always with me. Always.

The competitiveness that I felt, especially toward Benjamín, almost disappeared. But I must admit that when they went off to study at an American college, and I didn't, I was full of (good) envy. Nevertheless, in one way or another, and years later, they eased my transition from Mexico to the United States. When we get together we can say the harshest things to one another without being offended, since we know deep down that our friendship has survived the tests of time. But I have also been honest to myself. I can never lie to Gloria or Benjamín; they would know right away by the look in my eye or the tone of my voice. Also, in some way, the three of us have achieved the levels of success that we said we would when we were merely ambitious teenagers. But we can't say the same of all our classmates. And we also recall things that we can't forget, such as some of our old teachers.

The *"Garapiñado"* was our math teacher who had a bad case of acne, and it was into his class that the seniors brought a cow one day. Miss Nora taught us literature. She had no nickname, maybe out of appreciation for the emotional discussions and intense searches for identity that were generated in class by the readings about Kafka's beetles, Joyce's odysseys and Borges's labyrinths. Hermann Hesse's *Steppenwolf* and Vargas Llosa's *La Ciudad y Los Perros.*

However, weekends were not for philosophizing. They were times to go to some party to listen to Elton John and imitate John Travolta in *Saturday Night Fever.* My friend Benjamín had a lot of rhythm, so I was jealous that all the girls wanted to dance with him. On my part, there wasn't much that I could do. Not even a horrendous pair of yellow, green and orange checkerboard pants—back then that seemed like the coolest thing—could help me much. Even today I dance to salsa and merengue music as if I were kicking a soccer ball, or worse yet, as if I were stepping on cockroaches. I never got into the dance thing. Fortunately at school I had other things to think about.

The worst, however, were the fathers, the Benedictine priests who used their position of authority and their supposed heavenly contacts to try and fill our heads, using blood, shouts, punishment and fear, with their reactionary ideas. Since I began school they had instilled in us a dreadful fear of the devil and hell. The school was located in the outskirts of Mexico City in an area that had not yet been developed and where clouds of swirling dirt were commonplace. We used to like to chase after them and run into the center of them. Naturally we wound up completely covered in dust, like breaded chickens. However, one day one of the nuns or priests, I don't remember exactly, decided to tell us that the devil was inside the clouds of dirt, and that was the last time we chased after them.

This irrational fear of the devil haunted me until my teenage years, when all of my worst nightmares were confirmed by the movie *The Exorcist*. The scene that showed the girl's face covered in sores and her head spinning 360 degrees still bothers me and gives me the chills.

The fear of *el chamuco* was very real; in fact, we were told that if we died without confessing our sins, we would burn in hell. Confession, however, was a terrifying and immoral way for the priests to control us, since the very priests who heard our confessions were the same ones who would punish us moments later. In other words, on Friday mornings we would confess our weekly transgressions to the priests, and shortly after (what a surprise!) entire groups of students would be looked at suspiciously. Secrets of the confessional? We always suspected that all of our secrets ended up in the ears of the school director and not because he was a mind reader.

For many years, however, the fear of the devil and hell was very real for me. That is why when I went to confession, I would store up sins in a kind of bank account so that if death were to catch me by surprise before the next confession, I would be protected by the extra payment of penance from the week before. I would confess that I had lied to the teacher, copied in class, hit my siblings—well, that was generally true—in order to have credit in my heaven bank. Of course later on, when I realized the sacramental manipulation the priests were using on us, I gave up religion and everything the priests represented.

For years I believed that the communion wafer we ate on Fridays and Sundays really became transformed into the body and blood of Jesus

Christ. One day, though, the wafer got stuck on the roof of my mouth, and I went to the bathroom to remove it without anyone knowing. It was so white, so ordinary, so like the bread I ate every day at home, that it bothered me that I had believed the priest's story for such a long time. That day their words ceased to influence me. As the wafer dissolved on my tongue, so with it went the faith that they had fruitlessly tried to instill in me.

The fraud, however, went beyond the spiritual realm. Every time someone would misbehave, forget his homework or arrive late to class, he ran the risk of being struck with a *neolaitazo* on the hands or rear end by the school prefect. The *neolite* was the leather sole of a shoe that burned on contact and left a red mark on the skin. In my journey through C.E.L., I received dozens, maybe even hundreds, of *neolaitazos,* and my hatred for the fathers grew with each one.

I was not, however, the one who was hit most. Classmates like Gerardo Solís, the Chino, Pavía, that is, the most restless and mischievous ones, received tons of *neolaitazos.* My brother Alejandro helped me to recall a brutal incident when a classmate was picked up by his sideburns and lifted up until his head hit the roof of the school bus several times. While I was not one of those who were hit most often, it left a mark on me nonetheless. I can only imagine the emotional scars that those disciplinary measures left on the students who were with me in the classrooms of the C.E.L. for more than a decade.

Father Rafael, a gigantic, bald, blue-eyed man, was threatening as he walked through the halls swinging to and fro like a monkey, with a *neolite* hanging from his pants pocket and some scissors to cut the hair, right there, of whoever looked too unkempt. Every time a student walked by him he would cover his rear end; it was not uncommon for Father Rafael to whip out the *neolite* or the scissors with the speed of a cowboy to hurry us to class. When we would complain about the force he used, the response was, "If you don't like the school, leave!"

Ironically, this was the very same teacher who taught us ethics—"And what are you going to do with your life?"—and who had sex education classes prohibited after the first day—"Boys get together with girls"—because all the students burst out laughing at the language of the teacher, who had obviously never had sex before. Father Rafael also perfected other methods of humiliation. Whoever had not learned his lesson after several *neolaitazos* was forced to kneel down in the middle of the schoolyard, in front of everyone, and then carry some heavy books, with his arms stretched out in the sign of the cross.

Father Hildebrand sang like an angel in the school choir, but he was uncommonly skilled at pulling sideburns. Once when a teacher could no longer control us, she called Father Hildebrand. "You see the storm and you don't drop to your knees," the priest cried out, at which a group of us knelt down right there in class. We thought it was very funny, but Hilde did not. By the end of the day I had no sideburns, a red rear end and a report for bad behavior sent to my house.

The cruelest of all, however, was Father Williams. He had blond hair cut in a military style, and he exuded hatred. I never could understand how such a depraved and heartless human being could become a priest. It always seemed to me that he let out all his frustrations and foul moods on us, the students. Besides viciously hitting us with the *neolite*, he was an expert in crushing morale and making you feel as big as an ant; it was his way of controlling us.

In November 1975, a group of us wrote a pamphlet protesting the way in which we were treated in the school; we called it *"Nosotros."* We were terrified of what the Catholic priests would do when they read it, but our indignation was greater than our fear. I wrote an article in it entitled, "Until Today We Were Silent," with sentences like "they have devoured our happiness," "fear is used as the basis for control" and "break your chains and take action." Rereading the text I realize that decades later, I have repeated many of the sentences and ideas I wrote when I was seventeen years old in different forms and about different subjects.

The discord with the disciplinary methods used was growing. On one occasion when after a great effort I passed the initial selection process for the Mexican track team in preparation for the Olympics, Father Williams did everything he could to prevent me from getting to practice on time. "Those Olympics are for supernatural people," Williams told me in his heavy American accent, "and you are no superman."

Father Williams's words did not affect me: rather I decided to change schools the first chance I had, and I did so in my last year of preparatory studies, after twelve years at the same school. Until that moment few things had given me such satisfaction as that declaration of independence. "I am leaving because of you," I told Williams. He was stunned; it was the first time he did not respond with a blow, a sarcastic smile or some punishment. The yoke had been broken. My hatred for the "good Catholic" Williams was so great that I often fantasized about grabbing hold of him and exacting revenge for everything he had done to me.

I have absolutely no doubt that those years affected the rest of my life. My problems with authority were quite clear, and my initial response to any rule set down by those in power—be it teachers, parents or the police—was outright rejection. Arguing with my father, coupled with my running battles with the priests at school, had begun to turn me into a rebel.

Probably the most important thing that happened to me during that period was my almost complete distancing from organized religion. My reasoning for this during my preteen years was very clear: if those priests who beat me were the representatives of God on earth, then I wanted nothing to do with the god that they represented. Without knowing it—since I was too young—I had become an existentialist. I would later learn during my college years that existentialism spelled out exactly what I felt: I had been thrown into this world with the absolute freedom to do as I pleased. But thinking this way caused me to have a typical "existential crisis," since I wasn't sure if there was life after death. But at least I was honest with myself.

Contrary to what our parents wanted us to believe, I realized that there was no such thing as destiny. I also realized that luck didn't exist, and that astrology and other esoteric media were charlatans' tools. In other words, my life was my own responsibility and no one else's. Furthermore, absolutely nobody could guarantee me anything after I died. Since then, I have held onto these beliefs, albeit with very slight modifications.

I believed that life had no reason, so I had to give it reason. Like all teenagers. I went through some difficult moments, during which I thought that my life lacked direction. Without the support of a religious belief system, I had to find another support mechanism. But instead of looking outward, I turned inward. I was overwhelmed by the doubts traditionally felt by young people, and which were enunciated so eloquently in Hermann Hesse's books: who am I? What's the purpose of my life? Why? How do we transcend our reality? I recall that I used to lie down on the living room rug, face down, listening to really loud music with the lights off and my hands on my head, trying to find answers to these questions that were so important to me. I continued doing this, until after several nights of anguish, I found two verbs that would be useful to me: "to be" and "to love." Does this sound tacky? Maybe it does, but it worked for me. I was certain that I had not been touched my any divine figure, so I thought that if I was honest and tried to love those around me, I could live a decent life. I then tried to practice what I preached. I still do.

My break with organized religion and the Catholic Church forced me to develop a very personal form of spirituality in which there was no room for saints, Virgin Marys, demons, popes or priests. I don't believe in miracles, apparitions or divine signs. Everything, or almost everything, has a much more earthly explanation. And my reading of Nietzsche only reinforced for me the importance of concentrating on the human instead of the divine. As the iconoclastic teenager that I was, I basically thought that if God really existed and there was life after death, God had to take into account the fact that I lived an honest life and that I didn't create make-believe worlds for myself. I enjoyed a different type of spirituality; it was more human, grubby, jumbled and full of uncertainties.

All this had turned me into an agnostic who wanted to be a believer. I have moments when I want to be certain that heaven exists, and that the people who I love will somehow one day be near me again, and that life doesn't end, it is transformed. I wish that I could be certain of that, but I can't. I feel terribly jealous of those who are convinced that indeed there is a heaven full of cherubim where I will be reunited with my father, my friend Félix and my grandfather Miguel. But then my doubts begin to surface again: How do they know that heaven exists? What proof do they have of its existence? I suppose that it's all matter of faith, a faith that I do not share. And if I ever had said faith, it was torn from me long ago.

Do I pray? Sometimes I do. When I found myself stuck in the crossfire during the war in El Salvador, or when I was flying in planes with mechanical problems in Venezuela and Saudi Arabia, I honestly prayed because I was very scared and I didn't know what else to do. I recall that as heaps of bullets fell all around me in El Salvador, I said an Our Father and a few Hail Marys. And yes, I know, these prayers made me feel better. This may all sound contradictory, or even hypocritical, but it is an honest desire to someday believe and have faith.

Although formerly Catholic, I have never felt guilty. I had my first sexual experiences without any feelings of guilt, and now, as a journalist, I feel at ease when I ask question about the Catholic Church that some might consider blasphemous. The Vatican's position on pedophilia and sexual abuse by priests terrifies me. I don't understand how the church still bans the use of condoms while AIDS is ravaging the African continent. I can't accept the logic of how Jesus Christ himself, by way of his actions, decided that women could not enter the priesthood. And as a journalist, I am very suspicious of the doctrine of papal infallibility, and of the papacy's refusal to give interviews or press conferences. I suppose that without the church, I live a freer, but more anguished life. Yet this is the price that I have been willing to pay.

I decided when I was very young that my spiritual life would never be tied to the church or any other religious institutions. From that environment of abuse and blows, however, I have to salvage the memory of Father Sergio Gaytan.

Father Sergio was the teacher responsible for discipline when I was in grammar school, before he requested a temporary leave from the Benedictine monastery, a leave that would later become permanent. I remember him, like in the movies, playing soccer in his long black cassock and then talking with us, with great interest, about our childhood worries. He never hit anyone. Rather, my friends Eduardo Fuentes, Mario Velázquez and I felt he was our protector from the rest of the priests who were convinced that lessons were learned through blows and fear.

When Father Sergio left the monastery, I lost track of him until June 22, 1988, when I received a letter, which I still have. It had been at least twenty years since I had last seen him. He had recognized me on TV, found the address of the program where I was working and written me a letter full of anecdotes and affection. Yes, he told me, he had left the priesthood but maintained his same ideals although now in the secular realm. A Fulbright scholarship had taken him to Columbia University in New York, and it was there he had seen me. The letter made me so happy, but it was a very difficult time in my personal life, so I did not respond immediately. Several months went by before I finally responded to the letter.

I was surprised that my letter was not answered immediately, but I figured that that I couldn't expect anything different after the long delay in my response. In fact, I wanted to know more about Sergio, and I wanted him to help me manage the hatred I still felt for the other priests at the school. It was a weight I wanted to get off my shoulders, and only he could help me.

A few weeks later I received a letter from New York from one of Sergio's fellow classmates. Sergio Gaytan had died. He was never able to read my letter. That experience was very painful for me. I cried over the death of a man who in his last moments had wanted to revive his memories and who had reached out to me. Unfortunately, I did not understand this at the time. Today I bear the weight of that extraordinary letter that Father Sergio—I don't know how to call him anything else—wrote me and to which I responded too late. In the end, Sergio left me one more great lesson: life is for today, death does not wait.

If my encounters with religious figures—with the exception of Father Sergio—were always troubled, my life as an athlete had its fair share of drama too. I entered the Centro Deportivo Olímpico Mexicano (C.D.O.M.) when I was about fourteen years old. I got in not exactly because I was a talented athlete, but rather because I managed to convince a member of the Mexican Olympic Committee that I wanted the chance to go to the Olympics. "I run very fast," I told him, "and at school I beat everyone." I persisted with such conviction that, without even knowing me, he picked up the telephone and told one of the trainers of the track and field team, "I am sending you a boy to try out." That boy was finally on the way to fulfilling his dream of going to the Olympics.

I started out with the high jump. At the time, everyone was jumping back first, like the American Dick Fosbury had done in the 1968 Olympic Games in Mexico City. I succeeded in jumping several centimeters above my head, but since I am so short, that wasn't even good enough for the Pan American games. But more important than learning how to jump, I learned how to control my nerves in stressful situations. I was very bothered by the fact that in competition I couldn't jump as well as I did in training; I would jump over the bar a few inches below what I did in training. But I always struggled to defeat that feeling of failure. Years later, as I sat in front of a television camera, I realized that I had really beat the fear of failure that I had felt as a high jumper.

My height and what then seemed like a slight injury to my back forced me to abandon the high jump and begin training for the four-hundred-meter hurdles. I competed with some success in several national championships, and my sights were set on joining the Mexican Olympic Team in 1976 or 1980. I trained hard after my classes for more than three years; and I'm sure that had I kept it up, I would have achieved my goal. What had at first seemed like a small spinal injury, however, became the end of my Olympic dream.

Medical specialists at the C.D.O.M. determined that my problem was a lumbar vertebra that was not completely closed. It was probably a condition that would correct itself in time, but at that moment, the injury prevented me from continuing to train. To do so would have required a dangerous operation fusing two vertebrae, the upper and lower ones, with the one that was half open. The risk of paralysis was very high. I was in no way going to undergo surgery, but I wanted to continue training at my own risk. But the Romanian coach refused. "You have spina bifida," he concluded. "You can't compete," and he sent me home.

That night, at home in the kitchen, I told my mother, and I began to cry like never before. My goal of going to the Olympics—which I had had since I was ten years old when I saw the Kenyan marathoners who were running in the 1968 Olympic Games in Mexico by my grandfather's house—evaporated like drops of sweat. So many years, so much hard work and so many plans, all in vain. That night something inside me broke.

If I learned something from that time, though, it was that running helped to relieve stress. Every time I was about to confront a difficult or complicated situation, I would put on those horrifying but extremely comfortable green Converse sneakers and go running. I soon discovered that my best ideas came to me as I was running, and nowadays it's not unusual for me to go jogging and come back with a new idea for a story, some vacation plans and an article, all perfectly written and organized in my head.

Besides running, I also learned other more important things at the C.D.O.M. It was there I met Ana Laura, the first girl I kissed. Actually, it was she, who was older and more experienced, who taught me how to do it on the corner of a noisy, well-traveled street. People stared, and buses ran right by us, but nothing broke my amazement or my concentration. Our relationship ended abruptly when she told me that she wanted to have a child with me. I was so frightened that I didn't even kiss her again. From that moment on I would be terrified by the possibility of having my career and freedom cut short by a pregnancy. I had always practiced safe sex, but after that experience, I never dared have sexual relations with a woman without first asking her if she used contraception or if I should. A self-imposed rule that, I believe, saved me many times.

When I traveled with a group of athletes to Oaxtepec for a national competition, I found out that almost as important as the races and the jumps, were the late-night escapes that were made in search of prostitutes. I never went with the group, and to avoid pressure—I was the youngest in the group—I would hide in the bathroom for an hour or two until they had left. The next day, with everyone preoccupied with the competition, no one said a word to me.

My short time as an elite athlete coincided with my sexual awakening. One of the most exciting moments of the day was the long shower after workouts. The men's and women's showers were separated by a metal door, but someone had come up with the idea to make a little hole in the door. Few times in my life have I stood under running water for such a long time, as I remained behind in the communal shower so I could watch the best female Mexican athletes through the hole in that door.

IN THE END, sports were not my future. In my daydreams, while I was a student, I would fantasize about being a rock star or a soccer player. I would be thrilled at the thought of playing in front of a packed stadium, hearing the crowd cheer for the team or roaring when we scored. Little by little, the written word—through an incipient diary—became my way of venting and a way to channel my frustrations. Music was not my forte. During my adolescence, I studied classical guitar for eight years. I wanted to play like the Beatles or the Monkees, and I asked my *papá* for a guitar. The problem was that the guitar came with an extraordinary teacher, Oscar, who in addition to teaching me to play the song "Michelle" by the Beatles, introduced me to Bach, Tárrega, Albéniz and Villa-Lobos.

I can't have been that bad, since I gave two recitals with a degree of difficulty quite respectable for a kid. In fact, my first television appearance was at the age of twelve in a guitar competition. As I grew up, however, the guitar did not allow me to express myself as I had wanted. Playing music without shouting out what was changing inside of me was very unsatisfactory. So, difficult as it was, I told Oscar that I was going to quit the guitar for a while, even though he knew that the decision was final. I know it was a hard blow since I was his most advanced student and he had great plans for me. I still have that very same guitar that I played as a boy.

With the guitar aside and my career as an athlete cut short, I entered the Latin American University completely confused. I chose the newest and most obscure career: communications. My father was right; deep down I didn't know what I was going to do with "that." I happened to join up with a great group of restless and fun students, however, who bounced with a singular joy from classes on Marxism and anthropology to others on advertising and statistics; from McLuhan to McDonald's, and semiotics to discotheques, and from functionalists to the partiers across from Tequesquitengo Lake where a buddy had a weekend house.

During that time I wrote a poem that I thought reflected the uncertainty and existential anguish of an adolescent in search of himself (just like in Hermann Hesse's books). The poem repeats the refrain, "at the age of twenty-one, I still don't know what I want to do" nine times, and it was a heartless, crude complaint about all the rules (family, religious, school and social) that were smothering me. At the same time, I was not at all sure about what I wanted to do with my life, but what I did know was that the Mexico that I was living in was suffocating me and becoming a dead-end road. I needed air, new ideas, a reason for being, and I was not finding that in Mexico.

Almost everything I am can be understood by looking at my childhood and adolescent experiences in that house in Mexico. In fact, I often act in marked opposition to the negative experiences I had back then. I flee from noise, broccoli and those who are solemn and stiff. I devour avocadoes and squeeze oranges for the juice the way my grandfather taught me. I react with violent indignation to authority figures. I slip like a fish out of social impositions, I try to jump higher than my head, I believe more in willpower than in faith and I never blame anyone for what happens to me. I live the life I chose. I don't believe in angels, horoscopes, tarot cards, shamans or magic.

We are made up of little pieces, and everything I know I learned in the house at 10 Piedras Negras Street.

THE FIRST OPPORTUNITY

A man is never equal to himself:
he mixes with the times, the spaces,
the moods of the day, and those fortuities
define him again.
A man is what he is, and also what he has yet to be.

—TOMÁS ELOY MARTÍNEZ (SANTA EVITA)

While I was attending university the Ramos family
fell on hard times. The Jesuits of the Latin American
University never understood that we did not have
enough money to pay my school fees or those of my
siblings. The scholarships for good grades that I received throughout much of my schooling stopped at
the university door. I had no choice, therefore, but to
look for a job.

There were days when I would get up at five in
the morning and take two buses and a subway to get
to class by seven. I would spend the entire morning
at the university, work out with the basketball team
at lunch, take a bus and a subway to get to work by
four in the afternoon, and get home at eight at night,
completely wiped out. By the time I returned home,
after having traveled around all of Mexico City by
public transportation—I lived in the north, the uni-

versity was in the south and my job was in the city center—I was half asleep, and I would have to do it all again the next day.

Money was always a matter that my papa handled privately, but it affected all of our lives. There were good times, like when the whole family went to Disneyland; we bragged about that in school for months. What I remember best, of course, are the things that we could not do when the lean years came along with my father's illness.

It was increasingly difficult for him to get a good job, and that was reflected in fewer vacations, not being able to buy the green and orange striped pants that were all the rage then, and sharing underwear with my brothers, the hardship my mama faced when it came to daily expenses, and in my having to go out a couple of times and sell nuts from my grandfather's ranch door to door, something that made me terribly ashamed. But thanks to that difficult situation, I learned to defeat my shyness and to deal with friendly and not-so-friendly gossip. The same way that I went up to total strangers (to offer them nuts), I would do decades later with presidents and high government officials.

From that point on, I think, I was very aware of the value of money and I began to save little by little in case of an emergency. I also treated the things that I liked with great care. For example, I had a yellow shirt that I loved, and since I didn't want to wear it out, I saved it for special occasions. Those occasions never arrived, I guess, because the day I wanted to wear it, it no longer fit; I had saved it so long that the shirt was now one or two sizes too small.

We lived right on the border of the middle class; sometimes, although not often, we were scratching at the top, and other times we were knocked back down toward the bottom. We were borderline middle class. In that sense, we were like millions of Mexican families fluctuating with every six-year crisis, the changes in government and the bad management of the ruling class. Those cycles, though, made it very clear to me what kind of life I did not want to repeat.

In the summertime and on some weekends I worked at Camp Lomas Pinas in Cuernavaca as a counselor and guide. Besides earning a few pesos, I had my first experience being completely independent as an adolescent.

It was at camp that I met an extraordinary Jesuit priest, Federico Zatarin, with whom I would openly discuss my existential doubts and with whom I learned, as he was director of the camp, my first leadership skills. Spiritually, Zatarin guided me through the turbulent waters of adolescence. He never imposed his beliefs or the dogmas of Catholicism on me. Conversation was his most convincing weapon. He was the first person to teach me about leadership when he made me director of a camp after two summers. I also discovered what Zatarin called "perfect moments." In other words, how to find the right moment, the ideal moment, to talk about important things, such as in front of a fireplace or before going to bed, as compared to discussing things in the middle of busy shopping center. That simple technique has been pivotal when I speak with my children or when dealing with work issues. I had learned how to create "perfect moments," but I still didn't have enough money for school.

Without enough money for the university tuition, I began to work at Viajes Horizonte, a travel agency owned by the parents of my friend Benjamín Beckhart. Mrs. Martha Beckhart, impeccably dressed, with a talent for management and the nicest black car of the year, was my boss and my lifesaver. Without her help—and she knew it—I would not have been able to continue studying at the university. It is quite possible that she did not need another employee in the agency, but she gave me the job out of kindness and, quite honestly, because I needed it. So I began to issue the agency's invoices and I learned to type extremely fast. (Years later that very skill would help me write news reports.)

More than spending four hours in front of a typewriter, however, what I most absorbed from that job experience was the pleasure of traveling. Mr. and Mrs. Beckhart traveled to all corners of the world, and I watched with great interest as customers came by to pick up their airplane tickets for Japan, Europe and Israel. Who had money to travel like that? I wondered, as I returned home at night on a noisy, rickety bus along Route 100 (Toreo-Satélite). Well, thanks to that job I was able to take my first trip to Spain, France and England and to continue studying at the university. In Paris, my friend Benjamín and I went to a bar in Pigalle where we met someone who we thought was just another beautiful Dutch woman. But in fact, she was a prostitute. Naively, we tried to talk her out of her life of prostitution over a couple of beers, and that then she leave with us. The whole thing finished badly when the bar owner noticed that we weren't drinking anything, and that although the prostitute may have been having a good time, she was wasting time. We ran out of the bar without paying. When I came back from Europe I knew that my future would not be in an office issuing invoices.

A career in communications would probably not be very useful in the future, but at that time it was giving me a very complete humanistic foundation and helping me plant my feet in the world. Existentialist thinkers had marked my philosophy on life since I was a young boy; we are thrown out into the world—according to Sartre and company—and everyone is responsible for his own life: that is our only certainty.

That agnostic, rebellious, slightly distressing vision that focused on the human being, not on heavenly matters, and that questioned the status quo, suited me. This, together with a good dose of Freud, Marx (imparted to me, ironically, by some of the Jesuit priest themselves) and the social work that put me in contact with some of the poorest Mexicans in Mexico City—barefoot children with worms in their stomachs, communities without drinkable water and shabby little houses with metal roofs full of holes—rounded off my intellectual and social formation. It was strange that in one of the most expensive universities in Mexico many students could have learned how to instigate a revolution. Few actually put the theory into practice, of course, but the seed for social nonconformity had been well planted.

I was not going to be one of those who go off to the mountains to change the world; there was so much to do in the city. Within the communications field, therefore, I decided to specialize in psychology. I would inevitably, I thought, end up as a psychoanalyst or a university professor. Journalism did not interest me then. "I don't like to chase after people," I told my friends who had already started to fall under the journalistic spell. "I prefer to make news, not cover it." It wouldn't be long before I would have to eat my words.

One morning in 1978, as I was walking down one of the halls at the university, a woman who said she worked for Televisa, the largest telecommunications company in Mexico, stopped me. Without even knowing me she asked, "Would you like to audition for a job at Televisa?" I didn't have to think long before I said yes; Televisa had a bad reputation for journalism, but after all, to get a job in radio or television would have much more to do with my career than continuing at the travel agency.

My enthusiasm over the possible change waned, however, when I arrived at Televisa for the audition and found hundreds of young people, just as excited about getting a job as I was. I recall having read a couple of texts in Spanish and then commenting on them in English and French. I was not particularly brilliant; in fact, my English was barely acceptable and my French was from a few classes I had taken. I thought that maybe being able to speak two other languages would give me a small advantage over the rest of the group, though, and so it was.

A few days later I received a phone call to report to work at XEW, the radio station with the longest tradition in the country, or as the famous slogan went, "the voice of Latin America from Mexico." In a practice typical of that time, an executive at Televisa presented me with a blank contract to sign. When I indicated that the salary was not stipulated in the contract, he merely responded by pointing to a line of the document: "If you want to work, sign here." I signed. The truth was that I didn't have a better option. Besides, this was my opening into the world of journalism.

My salary turned out to be quite a bit less than what I was making at the travel agency. I barely made enough to cover my school fees and bus fare, but I made up for that by making photocopies at work of the books I had to read at the university that I couldn't afford to buy. My wealthier friends would lend me their books in the afternoon, and I would return them the following morning. Despite the hard times, I was happy. "They are paying me to learn," I thought.

The XEW offices were located in a rundown area in the center of Mexico City, but the tradition of "W" was unequaled. I began my training there with a group of young people who had been chosen from the audition. There were only ten of us.

We began at the bottom, pulling information from the news wires, looking for facts and writing reports for other journalists. Little by little, however, we found out what the real objective was for our being hired. The news director of "W," a fellow named Armendáriz, wanted to have "the best voices in Mexico" on his radio programs, and he was hoping to find those voices in us. It now seems quite telling as well as troublesome that that radio station was looking for the best voices and not the best journalists, but back then I didn't even give it a second thought.

At that time, radio broadcasters and journalists used a very stiff style, with a projected voice and formal, distant language. The older broadcasters used to put a hollowed hand over one of their ears, making their words echo. While this helped them to hear what they were saying, it also developed into the terrible vice of not being able to talk on air without putting a hand over the ear.

I was not chosen to be one of the "best voices in Mexico," and I was given a job away from the microphone instead. Thanks to my voice not being approved by the news director, I was relegated to being the production assistant for a radio news program, the "Noticiero de América Latina," and it was there I received my first lessons in journalism.

My daily responsibilities consisted of getting stories from around the continent, and without intending to, I soon became a specialist in international subjects. This gave me a lot of freedom, since the national information was extremely restricted and regulated. In those days, a veteran reporter gave me some advice for surviving at the station: "The first thing you have to learn here, *muchachito*, is not to speak ill about the president or any of your colleagues."

This turned out to be difficult to do, because many of them received *chayotes*, or money from the government and its sources for tailoring the information to those interests who were paying them. I kept my mouth shut, though, and I concentrated on the international arena that no one paid any attention to, maybe because there nobody was paying "*chayotes*."

I had two great friends and allies at the "Noticiero de América Latina": Félix Sordo and José Manuel Gómez Padilla. With the patience and concern of true colleagues, they instilled in me a passion for journalism. I admired how they would read the news that I helped them prepare, and how they improvised with such ease whenever there was a problem on air. They would have animated discussions before and after every broadcast about the most obscure details of each story, and, more than anything, they enjoyed what they did enormously. Naturally, it wasn't long before I wanted to do just what they were doing.

By then Armendáriz's idea of hiring the best voices in the nation had been unofficially declared a failure, and he was fired. With this news I was able to think about a future with "W." Instead of the impossible Armendáriz, there was now a new news director who was much more open to other voices and other styles. Making the most of the circumstances, I suggested he let me do a news story or interview on air. He told me, nonchalantly, to do a trial interview and then show it to him. I left his office happy. *"Gol,"* I said, under my breath.

I immediately set out to conduct a telephone interview with the Mexican ambassador to Uruguay, where there was some type of international crisis occurring that, quite frankly, I now don't remember. I do remember, however, that the ambassador did not hesitate to take my call and speak with me. After all, I worked for "W," even though he didn't know it would be my first interview and my trial by fire.

I thought the interview went very well, but when the news director listened to it he looked concerned. "The interview is fine," he said, "but we can't put it on the air." Why not?" I asked him, suspecting that my future at the station was marked. "Because the interview is full of 'okays.' " In fact, I was so nervous during the interview with the ambassador that I replied "okay" to everything he said. "Okays" plagued the conversation.

Despite that first run-in with reality, the director gave me the "okay" to continue to do interviews and stories. I learned from my mistakes, and my next interview, with the director of the Palace of Fine Arts, aired with only one "okay." From that point on, I was given more airtime on the newscast and on other programs on "W" and on XEX, another Televisa radio station that broadcast news twenty-four hours a day. I covered the Cervantes Festival in Guanajuato—which although it was my first business trip, I remember well because I fell in love with a dancer from the American Ballet Theatre who paid no attention to me—and I explored new areas within radio. On Saturdays, for instance, I was assigned to work on the production of a radio serial on extraterrestrials. Fortunately, no one was worried about my voice.

At the same time I worked at the radio station, I was also finishing up my communications classes and beginning to write my thesis to graduate. I had no choice but to write on the two things that most intrigued me at that time: communication and women. With the grandiose, pretentious title, "The Woman as Communicator in Commercial Advertising on Mexican Television," in 535 interminable pages I explored the problem of the subordination of the female sex in Mexican media. Through my research I discovered the enigmatic figure Lilith, the first woman, according to mythology, to inhabit the earth but who was replaced by Eve for having rebelled against Adam. And I took as mine the criticism against the secondary role of women in modern society done by Simone de Beauvoir in her legendary book *The Second Sex*. More than an academic analysis, my university thesis turned out to be a frustrating exercise in writing and rewriting—in 1981 there were no personal computers—and a reflection of the enormous inequalities of a society in which I no longer felt comfortable.

My college classmates—especially José Luis Betancourt—and I were more preoccupied with learning how to live than with burying our heads in books. College for me became an internalized adventure where I tried to find answers for the most basic questions about life: "What are we doing here?" "What is our purpose for being here?" "Does this whole mess mean anything?" But three professors—Jorge González (who we called "Cepillín"), Alberto Almeida and Paco Prieto—pointed me in the right direction, so that I could find the answers for myself. Jorge opened my eyes to social responsibility with doses of Gramsci, Marx, Marcuse, Freire and trips to poor and rural communities. Alberto and Paco flung a few lifesavers at me (from the Frankfurt School and psychoanalysis, to Lacan, Erich Fromm, Erik Erikson and Ortega y Gasset), so that I wouldn't drown in my existentialist crises.

As if it were a work of fiction, all of this took place in a university whose campus collapsed in the earthquake of 1979. Surprisingly, no one was killed. Shortly after the tremor, a banner was placed over the rubble that read: "We are the university. Not the buildings." This may have been a moving statement, but we had nowhere to go to school. Until tin-roofed classrooms—which we christened "Chicken Coops"—were built on the site of the university, all of the students had to move to buildings generously lent to us by the National Polytechnic Institute.

When it rained, the noise inside the tin-roofed classroom was so loud that we couldn't continue with our classes. It was in one of those "Chicken Coops" that I took my first television media class. Since the earthquake we didn't have a studio in which to rehearse, so the professor in charge of the class took a piece of cardboard, and with a great deal of creativity, began to make a detailed drawing. A few minutes later, he proudly showed us his work. "This is what a television studio looks like," he announced. We didn't know whether to laugh or cry. That piece of cardboard with a drawing was the only television experience I had in college.

In pictures from those days I look as though I were wearing a uniform, dressed in a yellow sweater and bright green Converse sneakers. Those sneakers were my status symbol. Under the administration of Mexican Pres. José López Portillo, not everybody could get their hands on American sneakers. I was more attracted by the American lifestyle and American consumer products than the ideas that were beginning to be exported by President Reagan, which the Mexican press sometimes described as simplistic and reactionary, and sometimes as reformist and daring. The Cold War was in full swing. Nevertheless, the leftward turn—and clear distancing from Washington's policies—taken by the six-year-long administration of Luis Echeverría was being reversed by López Portillo. However, in those days my life was being shaped not by Mexico's foreign policy, but by the very personal decisions that would make my life what it is today.

I don't believe in destiny, nor do I believe in luck. I believe in being prepared to take advantage of opportunities that present themselves. I also believe that there is almost never a second chance.

On the afternoon of March 30, 1981, I was preparing the radio newscast when the news wires began to go crazy. There had been an assassination attempt on the president of the United States, Ronald Reagan, out-side the Washington Hotel, and his life was in jeopardy. As the hours passed, concern grew, and we had no one based in Washington. The directors at "W" knew that if Reagan died and they had no one to cover the story from Washington it would spell the end of their days in media.

The news director came charging out of his office like a whirlwind— no doubt thinking more about saving his own skin than about Reagan— and called together the entire team of journalists who were in the newsroom. "One of you is going to Washington," he shouted, and a murmur of approval ran through the room. At that time it was not customary to send someone abroad since transportation and communication were very expensive. This story, however, was one for which no expense would be spared. I never imagined, though, that I would be chosen to go to Washington; I was the youngest journalist in the group, and the one with the least experience.

"Who here speaks English?" the director asked. Only a handful of reporters raised their hands. "Whose passport and visa are in order?" To everyone's surprise. I was the only one whose hand was still up. I looked around and saw many annoyed faces, but the news director had no choice but to say, "Ramos, you're leaving for Washington right now."

The assassination attempt had occurred at 2:25 P.M. in Washington, and several hours had already passed by the time it was decided to send me. There were no afternoon flights scheduled from Mexico City to Washington D.C., so I caught a flight to Houston, where I would spend Monday night, and then continue on to Washington the next morning. I did it this way because I was afraid my bosses would change their minds and send someone else.

And so I received my first international assignment, even though there was no doubt I was the least experienced foreign correspondent covering that story. When I arrived in Washington on Tuesday morning, I didn't know where to go, how to arrange interviews or how to obtain the necessary credentials to allow me to attend the press conferences.

The newspapers were already reporting the arrest of a twenty-five-year-old, John Hinckley, who had used a .22 caliber pistol to not only try and kill the president but to get the attention of actress Jodie Foster, the star of the movie *Taxi Driver*. I was getting pressure from Mexico to send my first reports, and I didn't have the faintest idea how to set up interviews. What could I do?

The only thing I could think of was to go to a hotel and begin recording the interviews from the television. It was not the most professional thing to do, for sure, but it got me out of a jam. Later, when I had a little more time, I went to the hospital where Reagan had been admitted and I waited, along with hundreds of people, for the latest information. While I was there, reporting on the atmosphere after the assassination attempt, I noticed a woman who looked different from the others. I approached her and she turned out to be one of the nurses from the hospital who was treating Reagan. She did not want to speak, but I managed to get some good off-the-record information, and I saved my fragile reputation as a journalist in Mexico. My work, I admit, left much to be desired, but that was my first assignment abroad, and I had scraped by.

Even more important, however, was the impact that trip had on my short-term plans. Journalism, after all, was not bad. The idea of traveling anywhere in the world where news was being made is what I wanted to do. In radio, though, except in unusual circumstances, there was no money for travel. After a short while I was convinced that a move to television was inevitable if I truly wanted to be a reporter who would travel around the world. Television was where most of the company's resources were, and it clearly received much more attention from the executives.

Unbeknownst to my radio colleagues, I went to see the editor-in-chief of Televisa's newcast. I set to work writing an incomprehensible press release about the politics of oil, and in a couple of weeks I was working as a writer for Antena Cinco, one of the most well-known television news programs in the country. I left behind Félix, Juan Manuel and all the radio experiences that had introduced me to journalism. It was clear that I had to work in television if I wanted my career to move ahead.

In television, those who seemed to be in control of their careers were the anchors and reporters who were on air. This was easy to see. It was a time when a single name dominated television: Jacobo Zabludovsky, the commentator of the program "24 Hours." I never shared his style or his journalistic ethics, and later in my career, far from Mexico, I would have to confront him. Back then, on the Televisa news in the early eighties, however, whatever Zabludovsky said, went.

I never worked directly for him. Instead I worked for several months writing for a newscast for another channel—Antena 3—until the chance arose to become an investigator for "60 Minutes"—yes, the same name of the successful U.S. program that in Mexico was synonymous with tabloid journalism.

"Do anything to get what you want," our journalism professors at the university would say, "except work on '60 Minutes.' " I was aware of the awful journalistic reputation the program had, but I also understood that the best opportunity to become a television reporter could come from there; and that's exactly what happened.

Soon after beginning the job as investigator, I was given my first story, which was about violence in Mexican prisons. This led to a second, about the eruption of Chichonal in Chiapas. I was so eager to demonstrate that I could become a good reporter that I went as close to the volcano as possible, along with the cameraman and sound engineer, in a car with an automatic transmission. The rough dirt tracks and the ash stalled the engine. Naturally the car didn't get very far, and a group of locals who were fleeing the volcano's burning ash had to help us push it to the closest road. The insurance company declared the car a total loss.

We also found out two days later that shortly after the villagers had helped us, a powerful explosion caused by the accumulation of the volcano's heavy gases destroyed the very spot where the car had died. We were saved by a hair. The story nevertheless was well received by management and by my bosses. I was, I thought, on my way to becoming a recognized television journalist.

I had no idea at that time that the journalistic censorship practiced by Televisa and by most of the media in Mexico was going to be much more dangerous for my career than the eruption of Chichonal. My third television story was about Mexican psychology. The intention was to determine if there were characteristics typical of Mexican behavior.

For this I traveled to several cities around the country and interviewed experts in the fields of sociology and anthropology. I also included, however, two shrewd intellectuals, Carlos Monsivais and Elena Poniatowska, who, as to be expected, were very critical of the closed, authoritarian system of government that Mexicans had endured for decades. At that time, the Partido Revolucionario Institucional (PRI) had been in power more than fifty years, and it continued its abuses and electoral frauds, as cool as ever. It never occurred to me, though, that they would censor my story.

When I presented the script to the director of the program—a guy named Gonzalo who everyone called *"licenciado"* and who was more concerned about the fate of the América soccer team, which he also ran—he turned pale. "Those are not Televisa people," he said, furious, referring to Monsivais and Poniatowska. "No, they are not," I replied, "but they are two of the best writers Mexico has."

It was of no use, and the *licenciado* asked me to rewrite the script, which I did without using the contributions of the two intellectuals and maintaining the general idea of the story. The story talked frankly about the vertical authority that Mexicans had always experienced, from the Tlacopan Aztecs to the Spanish viceroy, culminating with the PRI presidents. In academic circles that kind of discussion was extremely common, but on television it never came up.

The *licenciado* flew into a rage again when he read the second version of the script. He took it away from me and gave it to "Kaliman," a loyal friend of his. "Rewrite it," he ordered. "Kaliman," as he was called because another one of his jobs was to write the texts for a comic strip hero by the same name, replied as meekly as always, "Yes, *licenciado.*"

Kaliman was the complete opposite of the comic strip character. He carried a gun, slept with what he referred to as "a pretty little whore" and destroyed the original script of my story, cutting out the interviews with those who were not "Televisa people." With the *licendiado*'s approval, I was given the script that had been rewritten by Kaliman and forced to record it. The original idea of the story had disappeared, and in its place there was a litany of praise for the PRI government and the natural beauty of the country. The Mexican Ministry of Tourism could have easily used that script as a promotional piece. It was not journalism.

I recorded the story one Friday night, with the producer's intention to begin editing on Monday, but I felt awful. I was giving in to censorship and violating one of the ethical principles of journalism. Many people at "60 Minutes" knew what was happening—Kaliman made sure of that—and if I gave in this time, I would have a well-earned reputation as a mediocre, censored journalist.

I couldn't sleep that Friday, and early Saturday morning I went to the offices of "60 Minutes," got the tape I had recorded using Kaliman's script and erased it. It was the right thing to do. It had taken a load off my mind, but I also knew I was about to be out of a job. So before they could fire me, I announced my resignation in a letter I distributed widely, from Mr. Emilio Azcárraga Milmo, the owner of Televisa, to every one of the *licenciado*'s bosses. I wanted it to be known exactly why I was leaving.

I submitted my letter of resignation, which I have saved as an important document in my career as a journalist, on June 28, 1982. It concluded with, ". . . what was asked of me goes against my honesty, principles and professionalism . . . having done it would also have been an assault on the most simple and clear idea of what journalism is: a search for truth."

When I got home after having resigned, I looked for my *mamá* and told her, "I burned my bridges." I was very young, but I knew what I had done.

Not long ago Eduardo, the producer of that story, confessed to me that that Friday night he had made several copies of my recording to protect himself in the event one of the tapes got ruined. In silent solidarity with my protest, however, he didn't tell anyone, not even the *licenciado*. Inside Televisa, there had always been a small, silent opposition to the practice of censorship that prevailed in much of the media. That resistance, though, almost never evolved into open conflict.

The Mexican press did not report my resignation, as I was an unknown, and in a matter of hours I had become an unemployed unknown with no chance of finding work in the media in Mexico. Who was going to want to hire someone who had accused Televisa of censorship? In the eyes of many, I had committed professional suicide, but on a personal level, rarely have I felt so satisfied. From this experience came my conviction never to submit to censorship, never.

I have gone over this incident time and time again in my mind. I have corroborated it with colleagues with whom I worked back then, and I am convinced that it was not about simply correcting the script of an aspiring journalist nor was it a personal tantrum. It was a classic case of censorship that was practiced at the time and that nowadays, given the freedom of the press that Mexican democracy enjoys, is difficult to understand. That's how I remember things.

There were two people at Televisa (Ricardo Rocha and Graciela Leal) who offered me a second chance with the company, challenging the policy of not being able to hire someone who had resigned. In fact, when the *licenciado* left his position, I returned to "60 Minutes" for a few months to work with Graciela Leal. Nevertheless, I no longer felt comfortable, and I decided to leave to try my luck in the United States or in Europe. "You're doing the right thing, *güerito,*" Graciela said to me. "If you want to grow, you'll have to leave Mexico."

The problem was how to leave. I had practically no money for a ticket, much less for supporting myself abroad. I thought the easiest thing would be to go with a scholarship to some university to get my master's, but the government agency in charge of granting scholarships—CONACyT—was a springboard for sending the children of politicians and those who were well connected abroad. The London School of Economics and Political Science in England accepted me, but they didn't award me any financial aid. My grandmother Raquel, the only one in the family who could possibly lend me a hand, became very quiet, and finally said, "I can't." (The rejection of my grandmother, more than indignant, made me promise never to let anyone in my family go through what I was going through.)

I considered heading north as an undocumented immigrant, but if I wanted to work in the American media, which was my plan, it would have been impossible without legal documents. I was finally accepted to a program specializing in television and journalism at the University of California, Los Angeles, and in just a few weeks my life changed.

I sold a red *bochito* that I had, a broken-down but beloved Volkswagen, my first car, withdrew the savings that I had accumulated over more than two decades from the *domingos* my grandparents would give me, said a sad farewell to my girlfriend of eight years, and said good-bye to my family.

When I had enough money for the trip in Mexican pesos, something happened that almost botched all my plans. At the end of his term in office in 1982, Mexican Pres. José López Portillo nationalized the banks, causing a terrible devaluation of the peso and temporarily preventing the withdrawal of funds. When I got home that night, I found my mother crying. "You aren't going to be able to leave, *m'hijo,*" she said. "You can't take money out of the banks." I looked at her without saying a word, then I went to my room and from the back of my underwear drawer—my secret hiding place—I pulled out an envelope. I went back to my mama, showed her the envelope and said with a big smile, "Don't worry, yesterday morning I took all of my money out of the bank and changed it into dollars."

Many years later I would find out that my siblings, especially Eduardo, felt as if I had abandoned them without any explanation. It was a while before even I understood exactly why I had left. It would be an unfair oversimplification to say that I went to the United States because of the censorship I experienced in Mexico. It was certainly an important factor in my decision, but it wasn't the only one. What I am certain of is that, more than going to the United States, I left Mexico; that is, there were more things that drove me from Mexico than things that attracted me to the North. If an opportunity had come up in France, England or somewhere else, I would have gone there just the same.

Mexico in the early eighties was suffocating me. If I had remained in Mexico, I would probably have been a poor, censored, frustrated journalist, or maybe a psychologist or university professor speaking out eternally and pathetically against those who censored me. Politically, the system of the PRI disgusted me, which is why I never voted in an election. The military inspired a complete lack of confidence in me—the massacre of 1968 was still taboo in the media. And Mexican society was burdened with very traditional values that would have been difficult for me to defy without being ostracized. Pressure to follow in the footsteps of my parents and grandparents, meaning get married, set up a home, have children, work for someone else, suffer economic hardship and make up for it on the weekends, was subtle but always there. I wanted a different life, more independent and free, less structured, open to the world.

That is why I left, Eduardo.

I bought a ticket with an open return. "In a year or two, at the latest, I'll be back," I told family and friends. I spent Christmas and New Year's at home, and on the afternoon of January 2, 1983, I boarded a Mexicana flight that would take me to Los Angeles.

TWO | THE AMERICAN EXPERIENCE

FREE IN LOS ANGELES

don't remain motionless
on the side of the road
don't contain the joy
don't love reluctantly
don't hold back now
or ever
don't hold back.

—MARIO BENEDETTI

I arrived in Los Angeles in the evening, and when I claimed my baggage I felt an incredible sense of freedom. I was able to carry everything that I owned with my two hands, absolutely everything: my suitcase, my briefcase and my guitar. Nothing tied me to the past. Light on baggage, as the Serrat song went, I drew the line with what I wanted to leave behind, and I began a new life, from scratch. It was the freedom of one who can leave everything behind and start over again somewhere else.

Now Mamá tells me that she used to cry when she looked at one of the pictures of me in the house in Mexico; she did so until an indigenous woman who helped her with the cleaning said to her with great wisdom, "How nice that you cry for him alive and not dead." I was, in fact, more alive than ever.

I spent the first two weeks sleeping in the living room of my friend Shawnesee Colaw's Westwood apartment, which she shared with two other UCLA students. It was there I had my first lessons in music and double entendres in English. I had fun with Shawnesee and her roommates, trying to repeat sentences and rude remarks that my poor English had never heard. I pronounced the B and the V exactly the same, just like in Spanish, the R on my lips sounded crude and my vocabulary was that of a grammar school student.

When Shawnesee, whom I had met years before in my country, introduced me to her girlfriends and told them I was from Mexico, their response surprised me: "But you don't look Mexican." I don't really know what they were expecting. What was it? A mariachi with sombrero, guitar and mustache? A gardener with his nails full of dirt? A criminal with a gold tooth?

It was obvious that these nice girls had no idea that Mexico had been conquered by the Spanish and that many Mexicans and Latin Americans have light features from racial mixing with Europeans, like my green eyes and chestnut-brown hair; likewise, my olive skin and almost complete lack of hair on the chin and chest give away my indigenous roots. An explanation of that sort, however, seemed a bit abrupt for someone extending such a warm welcome.

In my two decades in the United States, however, I have received the same response hundreds of times when I am introduced to someone. "But you don't look Mexican." Without knowing it, that sunny January in 1983, I was confronting the tendency that generations of Americans have of stereotyping minorities in order to explain in some way the inevitable process of racial mixing that is occurring in the United States. I now understand better that in the eyes of these blonde, white girls it was important to emphasize what we had in common—eye color, for example—and not what differentiated us, which seemed threatening.

At the same time, I had to make an effort to get to know the symbols and reference points of American culture. For some time I began conversations by saying, "In Mexico . . ." trying to link the present to the past and my host nation with my homeland. Still, I quickly sought immersion in the American experience.

Once I arrived in Los Angeles, my pathetic budget allowed for only a radio and a television with a hand-sized screen. With these machines, I could increase my poor English vocabulary and I could also monitor the Spanish-language news, which I wanted to work for someday. I remember that the greatest luxury I gave myself at that time was a pair of Timberland Topsiders, like the ones that the students at UCLA wore, and which I bought so that I could look like them. Moreover, wearing shoes without socks, silly as it may sound, was another way of liberating myself from my country's norms.

In those days, Toto's song "Africa" was really hot:

> I bless the rains down in Africa,
> Gonna take some time to do the things that we had

Some of these verses—notwithstanding their lack of poetic worth—bring back to mind images of bright sunshine and lungs full of freedom.

The environment in Los Angeles at that time, in the early eighties, was much more permissive with respect to sex and drugs than I ever could have imagined. AIDS had not yet become an epidemic, marijuana and cocaine flowed freely throughout discos and student gatherings, and I was ready, with my eyes wide open, so as not to miss any experience. I wasn't the only one.

During what promised to be a boring weekend, I went to a nude beach in San Diego with my friend and former classmate from the Latin American University, Paco Guarneros. It was a new experience for both of us. We took off our clothes and began to walk, just like everyone else, pretending not to look directly at the girls. "It's rude," we were warned, "and it will give you away as novices." The experiment of trying to go unnoticed failed when we stopped to take a break, and a very curvaceous Californian girl undressed in front of our eyes. We both noticed that something below our stomachs was beginning to move and we quickly lay facedown, hiding our excitement in the towels on the sand. A short time later, we got dressed and returned to Los Angeles, defeated voyeurs, laughing all the way back.

On another occasion, I returned to San Diego with Paco in a van to go out with two girls we had met. With no money but a lot of imagination, the four of us spent that cold night in the van, making it squeak until the sun came up.

I met a group of good friends in California who were always up for a good time and a better conversation. From that time I still maintain a close friendship with Willy Lizarraga, a Peruvian writer who dated an American girl, and who, just like me, learned how to daydream in California. Although the years have passed, when I see Willy or when we talk by phone, in just a couple of words we are able to catch up.

Before I left Mexico, I thought I knew the United States; after all, we were bombarded with the television programs, fashionable clothing and gastronomic trends—namely pizza and hamburgers—from the North. The world changed first in the United States, and then it filtered slowly south across the border. Of course, sharing three thousand kilometers of border and a history of conflict, in which Mexico lost half its territory to the United States in 1848, naturally fostered the perception among many Mexicans of a common although clearly unequal course. I was not immune to the cultural bombardment from the North or its excesses, but I did not really know the United States.

When I arrived in Los Angeles, California, in 1983, Ronald Reagan was a popular president: his ideas—simple yet striking—were transforming the country. The notion that tax cuts would make the money of the rich cascade down unto the poor—trickle-down economics—was still taken very seriously, and some of my college classmates had only one objective: to make a lot of money and become multimillionaires before the age of thirty. The way I saw it, Reagan's public persona had an important symbolic value: it was the attempt against his life that took me out of Mexico for the first time as a correspondent. Furthermore, I was arriving in his state of California, where he had been an actor and governor, at a time marked by Reagan's ambitious policies, among them, of course, the so-called "Star Wars" program, and constant verbal exchanges with the leaders of the Soviet Union. In Los Angeles I could feel the winds of change, although I did not agree with Reagan's simplistic and dangerous ideas.

WHEN I WAS A BOY my paternal grandparents, Gilberto and Raquel, took me by car from Mexico City to Laredo, Texas. My grandfather was terrified of airplanes. What I most remember from that trip was the incredible variety of clothing and toys we found in, of all places, a pharmacy where my grandparents liked to go. The other experience that I associate with my arrival in the United States was a trip I took to Pittsburgh to visit my great friend, Benjamín Beckhart, who was studying at Wharton in the early eighties. It was the middle of winter, and naturally I was not prepared with warm clothing, nor was I prepared to see salt on the sidewalks that was used in order to prevent the snow from accumulating. I naively picked up a grain of salt from the sidewalk and put it in my mouth; it just about disintegrated my tongue.

My perception of the United States was formed watching the television series "Combat," a trip to Disneyland in which I was surprised by how white and fat so many Americans were, purchases at a pharmacy in El Paso, school lessons about how the traitor Gen. Santa Anna sold part of Mexico to the gringos for a million pesos, the anti-imperialist dogmas that I took in ravenously at the university, a grain of salt that almost destroyed my mouth, my amazement at the urine detectors in pools—a luxury out of the reach of most people I knew—and the illusion of living in a nation that looked forward without being dragged down by the past. I arrived in Los Angeles with all this baggage, yet with the innocent idealism of an adventurous dreamer.

After two weeks at Shawnesee's apartment, I began to look for a permanent place to live. The laughter that my unintelligible accent in English caused ran the risk of becoming an annoyance. But I didn't have enough money to rent an apartment on my own; in fact, I didn't even have enough money to share one with someone. So I ended up at the home of an older Mexican, Jorge, who lived in the library with his nephew and who illegally rented out the rest of the rooms to international students for five dollars a night.

The house, which we called the Pink House, because of its color, was in the elegant Westwood neighborhood and just one block from UCLA. It was a dump, but it was fun. Jorge had inherited it from a family member, and he had compulsively accumulated books, papers, furniture and many other things. It reminded me of the dark house in "The Addams Family," which I used to watch on TV when I was young.

The house had not been painted in years, and it was stuffy. We were able to use the refrigerator but not the kitchen, thus forcing us to buy small burners so we could cook in our closets. Jorge never caught us, but sometimes he would burst into our rooms unannounced with the intention of catching us at work red-handed.

My first roommate was Charles, from the Ashanti tribe in Ghana. He used to prepare a strange concoction in the closet using tomatoes, and for hours he would listen to the voice of his wife on cassettes that he had brought from Africa. Charles wrote to his wife almost every day; this was how he placated his homesickness. One afternoon he received a package in the mail. Inside were all the letters he had written in the last six months.

Desperate, he went to the bank to withdraw some money to call his wife by phone, a luxury he could not afford more than once or twice a year. From the other end of the phone, his crying wife explained to Charles that the mail trucks in the country had run out of spare tires and the government of Ghana had no money for new ones. Consequently, entire communities had not received their mail. I don't know what made me sadder, Charles's shocking misfortune or the unmistakable smell of tomato that permeated my clothing when he would cook in the closet.

Charles's story hit home with all of us who lived at the Pink House— there were usually anywhere from six to ten students in the house—so we developed a system that would allow Charles to call home and the rest of us to call our homelands, too. Jorge had installed a public coin-operated telephone inside the house, as we were not permitted to use his. We attached a thin thread to a twenty-five-cent coin that we could pull in and out of the telephone slot. The telephone would record the in and out of the coin as if it were a new coin each time, and for weeks we spoke to Ghana, Mexico, Pakistan, Iran, Brazil . . . At some point the telephone company detected that something was up with that phone, and they installed a padlock on it. That was the end of our free phone calls.

I went from the tomato-infused room of Charles to the obsessively clean room of Emil, an Iranian. He would scrub the bathtub with a toothbrush, but just like the rest of us, he would also cook in the closet so as not to starve to death. His dishes were more normal, mostly pasta. My specialty was a dish of rice and noodles Spanish style. I would buy a box of Rice-a-Roni at the supermarket, boil some water and then pour the contents in.

For months I ate rice and noodles in a closet. Sometimes when I got bored of the same thing, I would prepare spaghetti with meat sauce. The red-hot burner would glow in the darkness of the closet while the spaghetti was cooking, and then, in the same pot, I would cook the meat with a little butter. That was a luxury and a delicacy for me. Sometimes when Jorge would allow us to sit at the kitchen table, I would make an enormous green salad, and that would fill me up. In desperate times, when my hunger was uncontrollable, I would turn to entire loaves of white bread. That was my diet as a student.

Kuas, my girlfriend from Mexico, came to visit me in Los Angeles a couple of times, and on those occasions Emil preferred to go to his rich cousin's house for a few days rather than endure the hardship of seeing me wake up every morning with her just a few meters from his bed. In Iran, he told me, that kind of behavior would have landed me in jail in the best of circumstances.

Hashmi, a religious Pakistani, tried a more direct approach to avoid that kind of moral conflict in the Pink House. "You have to marry her," he would say to me. You must marry her, he insisted. Hashmi married his wife in a Muslim ceremony the same day he met her. It was not love at first sight; it was a marriage arranged by their parents.

I can't forget Hashmi's description of the moment he first laid eyes on her. The parents sat them down, side by side—neither was even seventeen—and they placed a mirror in front of them. In this way, they could both steal glances and avoid the embarrassment of looking each other straight in the eye. After the ice had been broken and they had talked for a few minutes, she disappeared and Hashmi went off with the men to celebrate his marriage. He would join his wife that night at his parents' house. Hashmi's mother would emerge happily the next morning, showing family members and strangers alike the bloodstained sheet from her daughter-in-law, who had been a virgin until the previous night.

I didn't marry Kuas, as Hashmi had suggested, but we did go to Hawaii to see the Kilauea volcano, just as she had always wanted to do. My money was running out, I had paid for the UCLA extension courses in advance, to be sure that by the end of the year I would have a certificate in television and journalism. Unfortunately, a car accident in a friend's car took much of the meager savings I had left. The accident was my fault. As soon as the light changed, I made a left without noticing that a fast-moving motorcycle was coming straight at me from the other side of the street. For a few seconds I thought about fleeing the scene, since I had been in Los Angeles for just a few days and I didn't want to have problems with the police. In retrospect, I think this quite a normal response, even if acting upon my initial instinct would've been disastrous. But finally, two blocks down, I stopped, since I thought the man on the motorcycle was dead and I couldn't have that on my conscious. I returned to the scene of the accident, shaking all over, and I took a deep breath when I saw that the motorcyclist was standing next to a heap of scrap metal. He was fine, but the motorcycle wasn't.

Of course I had no insurance and I had to pay in cash. I did some quick calculations and realized that the money I had left would only last six more months. So I would have to get a job, soon. I withdrew my savings and we left for Hawaii. There, on the black-sand beaches of the Big Island, I would figure out what to do.

I squandered the little I had left on that trip to Hawaii, which forced me to look for a job. I told a Brazilian with whom I lived at the Pink House that I needed a job, and he told me that they needed another waiter in the restaurant where he was working. I had an interview with the owner of Chez Louise, a small European-style restaurant in Beverly Hills, and I was hired on the spot. My salary was fifteen dollars a day plus a meal. It goes without saying that the most important part was the meal, the only one I had all day. The money was barely enough to pay the rent and my school expenses, but at least I was able to eat once a day until I was about to burst.

I was a terrible waiter. It's the hardest job I have ever had. I didn't know how to open wine bottles, and I became very nervous when trying to explain the menu to customers. My primitive English did not allow any linguistic flexibility, and when I was asked, "How is the meat prepared?" I was limited to responding, "It's good, very good." My job as a waiter did not last more than two or three months. One morning I learned that someone had stolen money from the cash register and the owner, Louise, threatened to call the police. I let a couple of days go by and then I quit. The last thing I needed during my first few months in the United States was problems with the police.

Louise suspected that one of my roommates at the Pink House, the fun-loving Brazilian who spent his nights at discotheques, was responsible. And she was right. One morning, when Louise was at the bank, I caught the Brazilian taking money out of the cash register. He even offered me some money to keep quiet. I didn't take the bribe, but I knew that there would be trouble anyway. The restaurant made so little money that a few missing dollars would immediately be noticed. So I decided to quit. I wasn't going to be nor could I afford to become the scapegoat. Anyway, I knew that my Brazilian roommate would be capable of accusing me of the robbery in order to get out of trouble. That last day I gorged myself with lasagna and then quit with the excuse that I had too much schoolwork.

The day I left the restaurant I went home to the Pink House, opened my checkbook and, as I recall, realized I had only $127. The situation was so serious that I discussed with my housemates, half in jest, the best technique for preventing holes in one's socks. (Never wear them two days in a row and change them from one foot to the other.) In other words, I didn't even have money to buy new socks. I had to find another job, and fast. "No," I thought, "I can't go back to Mexico yet." The mere idea of returning to Mexico as a failure terrified me. Then, the phone rang.

It was my friend Marco Antonio Mendoza, a former classmate from the Latin American University. He invited me out for sushi, which I had never tried before. "Are you sure a piece of raw fish over vinegar rice tastes better than *taquitos al pastor*?" After listening to my financial woes he offered me a job.

Marco's family owned the Fiesta Theater, located in a poor Latino neighborhood in central Los Angeles. In the evening they showed movies, but during the day the theater was used as an office for exchanging pesos and dollars and for sending money to Mexico. The Mendozas needed someone they could trust to run the day business, and I wound up learning firsthand how Mexicans in the United States support millions of families in Mexico. (Remittances are the third greatest source of income in Mexico, after oil and tourism. Unofficial estimates at the beginning of the century suggest that Mexicans were sending more than eight billion dollars a year back home.)

I also learned other things. It was not unusual for there to be shootouts at night outside the Fiesta Theater or on Pico Boulevard. The neighborhood was full of little markets that sold typical Mexican foods and offices of second-rate lawyers who promised to resolve the immigration status of the undocumented for a few dollars. When I compared my situation to many of my fellow countrymen's, there was not the slightest doubt that I was one of the fortunate ones.

Part of my fortune consisted in having access to the Mendozas' gigantic white car and a huge motorcycle that I would never have been able to pick up were it to fall on the ground. I was finally mobile. Even more important, however, I was able to snack on the chocolate and popcorn they sold at the movies. This saved me at least one meal a day.

At that time my friends Benito Martínez and María Amparo Escandón had just arrived in Los Angeles to try their luck. They wanted to open a travel agency with Marco, and for weeks they slept in the office at the Fiesta Theater beneath a roof that was crumbling because of the humidity and fought with the mice at night over the supply of candy and popcorn.

Years later, they would have their own advertising agency, Benito would become a talkative but brilliant artist and María Amparo would become a well-known novelist. Her first novel, *Santitos* or *Esmeralda's Box of Saints,* was a worldwide success. During those months in late 1983, however, Benito and María Amparo were my faithful and fun companions on the tough adventure of finding one's way as an immigrant in Los Angeles.

After Benito and María Amparo, José Luis Betancourt and his wife, Angélica, came to Los Angeles. José Luis had been my classmate at the university, but the years we spent in California united us more than ever. My friends became my adoptive family. I ended up at José Luis and Angélica's house on every important occasion; they never left me alone for a birthday, we discovered the city's trendy restaurants together, and the greatest parties were always with them. José Luis, *"el pelonchón,"* is still one of my best friends.

At these parties, we listened to Spanish-language music for nostalgia's sake, to recall what we left behind. Nevertheless, the music that we heard outside of these parties was sung in English. Jane Dalea, a friend from UCLA who I had started to date, took me to a Supertramp concert in exchange for my company at a more than four-hour-long marathon: that's how long hyperpatriotic Bruce Springsteen's concerts used to be. Jane eventually left me for an Australian cab driver, and no matter how well intentioned our later attempts for reconciliation were, they never worked. But I still have great memories of her. She took care of me, and at the same time, she freed me from a series of prejudices that I had carried from Mexico. We used to laugh a lot together.

As a matter of fact, when I listen to music from the eighties on the radio—as well as when I smell certain odors—I am transported back to a time when the world began to open for me. I was experiencing a unique feeling of freedom. Barriers were falling all around me. In the presence of Jane's astonished eyes and her laissez-faire attitude, Madonna and Cindy Lauper's yelling, Dan Fogelberg's softness and the catchy and fun tune from Men at Work that asked: ". . . do you come from the land down under, love," the social limitations that I had come to accept in Mexico City had begun to melt away, one by one.

AMONG MY MANY DOCUMENTS, before leaving Mexico I had saved a small paper with the name Pete Moraga. The "60 Minutes" reporter Armando Guzmán had given it to me. "He's the director of Canal 34 in Los Angeles," Armando told me. "Call him, he's a good guy."

Once my financial situation was partially resolved—I was working at the Fiesta Theater in the mornings and studying in the afternoons—I sought out Pete Moraga. Pete was indeed a good guy. He gave me an appointment without even knowing me. We got along well, but he had no job to offer me. We agreed to keep in touch, and we did. When I was about to graduate from the program at UCLA, I went to see Pete again, in the old, creaky studios of KMEX on Melrose Place, and to my surprise he had a job for me. "Look," he said, "you're going to be reporter on a trial basis for three months; if it works out, you'll stay, if not, you'll have to leave."

I did my first story on January 2, 1984. I remember it perfectly because it was the day after the Rose Parade. With Pete's direction and the patience of cameraman Eduardo Kashkovski and sound engineer Mario Jurado, "Homeboy" came together. My professional reference points were from Mexico, and I had to get rid of them one by one. I did not know the differences between a county and a city, and for me the idea of interviewing a sheriff was something out of an old Western movie. My English had improved somewhat, but I still hesitated to ask questions at press conferences.

Three months finally passed, and no one said anything to me. I thought they were going to let me go, and I went home depressed. The next morning I went to Pete's office and asked him what had happened and why I wasn't going to be hired. Pete burst out laughing. "You're hired," he said, "now get to work."

My new job gave me two great opportunities: first, to leave behind my typical diet of Rice-a-Roni, lettuce and bread—when I got my first paycheck I thought it was a small fortune: around twenty-eight thousand dollars a year—and second, to cover the Olympic Games that were going to be held in Los Angeles in 1984. My teenage frustration of not being able to be on the Mexican Olympic team was eased a bit once I had a front-row seat at the Olympics. I was the most inexperienced reporter at Canal 34, and there were days when I had to prepare two, even three stories. During that time the growing Hispanic community in Los Angeles did not have much media of their own. Besides, politicians who didn't even speak Spanish represented it. *"Yo soy* bilingual," a redheaded Angeleno council-man stated proudly. The truth was that there were not even press releases in Spanish or bilingual press agents. No one seemed to care. There *were* many Latinos, but their political power was almost nonexistent. Even Hispanic politicians spoke Spanish poorly, and few black or white leaders made an effort to have spokespeople who could convey their orders and messages to the Latino community in their own language.

Canal 34 was a wonderful school. Once I was chosen to narrate, live, a parade, and of course I accepted. The parade was on a weekend, and I thought I had done a decent job. However, when I got to the office on Monday, the general manager's secretary called me in to scold me. "You used the word *precisamente* throughout the entire parade," she said. "I was so tired of hearing you say that word I had to turn the television off." I re-viewed the tape and it was true. I was so nervous during my first live broadcast that I used the word *precisamente* as a crutch to give me more time to think of what I was going to say next. It was dreadful. I must have said the word *precisamente* hundreds of times during that two-hour broad-cast. When I went to see my boss, Pete Moraga, he just said, "The parade, *precisamente."* I promised never to use that word on air again, and I began to clean my language of all the crutches and vices.

Little by little I adapted to my new reality. I left the Pink House for a small apartment, I bought an old orange Fiat and I turned in my jeans and sneakers for two stylish sport coats that I alternated with the ties that my grandfather Miguel had worn. In the morning I would iron only the front part of one of my three dress shirts, and I would leave to make my way across the city. I traveled a great distance around the city because "Home-boy" had been a gang member, and I was afraid to go through areas of the city that were controlled by other gangs.

While I wrestled with language problems in a city that was increasingly multicultural, I also wanted to develop my own journalistic style, and I did so using as a comparison the stiff, official style that prevailed on Mexican television. "Television is the most artificial medium that exists," said Paco Crow, an old sea dog of television. "Therefore, being natural in front of the cameras is the most effective way to communicate. Television is about projecting life, just as it is. The stiff reporter is a dead man in this business." The advice of Paco, whom I met at Canal 34, is something I still remember.

Nothing that I learned during my time in Los Angeles, however, would prepare me for covering the earthquake that destroyed sections of Mexico City on Thursday, September 19, 1985. At 7:19 A.M., a tremor registering 8.1 on the Richter scale shook the Mexican capital. I learned of the earthquake when I got to the office. The images, taken directly from Mexican television, were devastating. Telephone communication was cut off. Things looked terrible, and I had no way of knowing if my family had survived the catastrophe.

Once again, just like with the assassination attempt against Reagan, I was the only reporter available with a passport ready to travel to cover the earthquake. Canal 34 used its influence to get a cameraman, a producer and me on a plane leaving for Mexico City. And so, on the night of the earthquake, I returned to my country amid circumstances very different from when I left.

THE FIRST THING I DID was find a public phone and call home. To my astonishment, the call went through and my mother answered. My parents and siblings were fine. I sighed with relief and prepared to work through the night so I could send my first report the following morning. I stood for several hours outside a school where students were supposedly trapped beneath the debris. At daybreak you could no longer hear noises, and the rescue workers and desperate parents began to admit defeat.

The government of Pres. Miguel de la Madrid took days to ask for international assistance, and this delay probably cost the lives of many who could have been saved by more experienced teams. The city was in chaos. The government lost its ability to lead, and the citizens, without waiting for help from the state, took the initiative in the rescue effort. That bad experience with the government eventually formed part of the movement that ousted the PRI in the 2000 presidential elections.

After sending my report via satellite to Los Angeles, I went to the hotel and called my friend Félix Sordo. I was expecting to hear his voice, but his mother answered instead, and what she told me left me numb. Félix had not turned up, and they feared he was buried beneath the rubble at Televisa, the television station where I too had worked and that had been completely destroyed. Rumors were flying among journalists: that Félix had been spotted at the hospital, that rescue workers had taken him to the Red Cross, that he was fine and had gone home. It was all untrue.

The afternoon of Friday, September 20, 1985, one day after the earthquake, I was getting ready to go to my house and then go out in search of Félix when I felt the ground move under me. My room was on the thirty-sixth floor of a hotel on Paseo de la Reforma, and the building began to sway. It was swaying so much that at one point I thought it would hit the hotel across the street. It was an aftershock. It was not as strong as the first quake—7.6 on the Richter scale—but it was still strong. Never in my life have I gone down the stairs of a hotel so fast. The lights had gone out and you could hear shouting everywhere. I managed to see the frightened cameraman who was with me pushing people—women, old people, it didn't matter whom—so he could get down the stairs.

After a few hours on the street, they checked the hotel for possible structural defects, and when they found none I was able to go back to my room. I got my things and left for my house. That night I had no intention of sleeping on the thirty-sixth floor of a hotel.

When I got home, I told my parents about Félix; they offered to go with me to look for him. First we went to the Military Hospital, on the edge of the city, where I was able to slip by security and search all the floors with those who had been injured in the earthquake. It was a devastating sight. There were long rows of beds with the wounded gathered in the hallways, as there were not enough rooms. I saw people with missing limbs, broken limbs, blank stares and bandaged heads. There were no cries of pain, but there was a plaintive murmur of *ays* and of names of lost family members floating in the air. *"Patricia, Juanita, m'hijito Pedro . . ."*

Nothing, however, could stop me. I went from bed to bed, making sure that none of the wounded who were asleep, under anesthesia or had lost consciousness were Félix. He wasn't there. I went to other hospitals and it was the same story. Félix was definitely not among the wounded, and I began to brace myself for the worst. The same boy, just one year younger than me, who had revealed to me the magic of journalism and who had helped me write my resignation letter to Televisa, who I would see every time I returned to Mexico City, who made me laugh with his ironic sense of humor, and who behind his journalistic seriousness hid an innate desire to protect his widowed mother, his sister, José Manuel and me . . . was not there anymore.

I had to go back to Los Angeles. While Canal 34 was very interested in the tragedy in Mexico as a news item, it did not have the money to keep its reporters there two or three more days. I kept working at my usual pace: two or three stories a day, press conferences, interviews on the street. My mind, however, remained on Félix.

Was it possible that he had been trapped and was just waiting to be rescued? Félix was such a resourceful person that I wanted to believe he was invincible. He always found a way to keep going, nothing got in his way. "If anyone can survive an earthquake," I thought, "it's Félix." Besides, the constant reports of incredible rescues — including those of some newborn babies who survived beneath the rubble of a hospital for several days after the earthquake — kept my hope alive.

One night, however, I received the call from Mexico that I had dreaded. It was my mother. "They found Félix," she told me. Then there was a long pause. I didn't even have to ask her if they had found him alive. The way she said his name was enough to know that one of my best friends was gone.

Félix lived life in a hurry. "I don't have much time," he used to say, and he wasn't referring to all the things he had to do that day. His words had a much more profound meaning. "I can't wait for the news anchors to die so that I can move up," he insisted. He kept pushing his professional career upward. Now I understand that his typical comment, "I don't have much time," was a kind of premonition, as if he always suspected he would die young.

The morning of the earthquake, Félix was working at the Televisa studios where he presented the news. He, like me, had recently jumped from radio to television, and that sealed his fate. They found his body among the debris at the station, just a few feet from his desk. I have never stopped thinking that if I had stayed in Mexico, I might have been in that same place, next to him, at the moment the earthquake struck. Since we had known each other, we had always worked as a team, and I doubt very much that new stage of his professional life would have been an exception.

I was saved. Leaving Mexico had saved me.

I did not mourn for Félix, just as he would not have mourned for me. It was not his style. Félix had always been wonderfully irreverent. On the other hand, I thought, the best way to remember him was to do my job well, and that is just what I set out to do.

The year that I began at Canal 34, in addition to my reporting work, I was offered the spot on a morning news program next to Felipe *"El Tibio"* Muñoz. It was an extraordinary opportunity, not just because I would become an anchor for the first time, but also because I could work alongside *El Tibio*, who had won an Olympic medal in swimming in 1968, beating an American and a Russian. *El Tibio* was a true sports hero in Mexico, but neither he nor I had the faintest idea how to do the news.

The program was called "Primera Edición" or "First Edition." However, it should have been called "Primerizos" or "First Timers" because it was the first time that Felipe and I were trying to read from a TelePrompTer and receiving instructions in our ear through the IFB device. We were a disaster on air. We didn't know how to change cameras, and we were only able to read a few stories without making a mistake. As a gimmick to distract attention from our frequent mistakes, Felipe and I would have coffee on the air, and we would read the morning newspapers out loud. Among our colleagues, the morning news was known jokingly as "El Cafecito."

Much to our surprise, the executives at Canal 34 did not cancel the morning news program. When Felipe and I would ask how we were doing, everyone would say, "You are very natural." No one said we were good, only that we were "very natural." In fact, at seven thirty in the morning, almost no one subjected himself or herself to the torture of watching us, not even our bosses.

Once, in order to prove the theory that no one was watching us, I invited my friend Benito Martinez to show his paintings and sculptures on the program. This would normally have required advance approval, but I never requested it. Benito was on the air for a while promoting an exhibit of his work. No one ever said anything to me because no one was watching the program.

The conviction that none of the KMEX executives were watching us gave us great peace of mind and tranquility while on air. We no longer made mistakes at every turn, and the TelePrompTer became less difficult to read; Felipe and I were getting better.

One of those mornings when we thought no one was watching, two executives from the Spanish International Network (SIN), which is now Univision, were watching. René Anselmo, the president of the network, and Rosita Perú, programming director, had just arrived from New York and were suffering from jet lag. At 7:30 A.M. Los Angeles time, they were wide awake and so they put on the morning news.

Rosita called René's room—as she would later tell me—and told him, "Put on Canal 34 and tell me what you think about the Mexican guy." They were looking for someone to do a new national morning program, and they had their eyes on me.

Rosita sent for me that morning, and she told me that I was very natural on the news—bad sign, I thought—and she asked me if I would consider going to Miami to do a program called "Mundo Latino." It had been months since I had had any contact with Gustavo Godoy, the news director at the network, and despite his promises, he had never called me to be a national correspondent for the SIN news.

Being in Miami would make it easier to jump over to the *Noticiero*— which had earned a good journalistic reputation covering the war in Central America and which was really where I wanted to work—and I said yes to Rosita. The morning program itself did not really excite me, but it was definitely a good career move. Rosita, however, did not want to finalize anything that morning, and I understood why; she barely knew me.

That same day at lunchtime, I went to a Hungarian restaurant that was across the street from René Anselmo's television studios. He was having lunch with the managing director of Canal 34, Danny Villanueva. Without even introducing himself, Anselmo asked me point blank: Do you want to live in Miami? "Yes" was the short reply. I never spoke with him again in my life. When Anselmo died many years later. I recalled nostalgically how that eccentric television executive who had a grand piano outside his office changed my professional career with one single question.

Two weeks later, in January 1985, I was unpacking my things in an elegant hotel in Coconut Grove, Miami.

THE FIGHT FOR THE NEWS

Good journalism doesn't have to be boring.

—WALTER ISAACSON, PRESIDENT OF CNN

Before she turned fifteen, my daughter, Paoli, asked me: "Papá, have you noticed how the little things can change your life?" I hadn't expected this observation from my daughter. She really surprised me. Paola is very perceptive, and with those words, she scratched the surface of my heart and of her own history. It was then and there that I had to tell her about her mother and me.

I met Gina Montaner during a sushi dinner in Coconut Grove in 1986. From that moment on we began to spend a lot of time together, creating a bond that would exist—through Paola—for the rest of our lives.

My personal life as a bachelor was going very well, thank you. I had just moved to Miami from Los Angeles, and I had no absolutely no intention of becoming emotionally involved with or committed to anyone. Freedom had penetrated my being while I was in California. At long last the inhibitions that I felt during my adolescence in Mexico City had disappeared. The world was opening before my eyes. I had a new and prestigious job, some money to spend and a whole new city to get to know.

But one almost never picks the moment to fall in love. Shortly after arriving in Miami, I fell in love in a marvelous and unexpected way. Gina was a producer at "Mundo Latino," the television show that I had just begun hosting in Miami. After having lived for a long time in Madrid, Gina had decided to leave Europe to seek new challenges—both personal and professional—in America.

The unusual circumstances of our early relationship—she was coming out of a relationship and both of us felt like interlopers in Miami— surely hurt some and bothered others. My untraditional courtship with Gina, a Cuban journalist, and our quick decision to live together elicited criticism in some Miami circles. I understand why.

I perfectly recall when I first met her parents, Carlos Alberto and Linda. We even had difficulty explaining our decisions to them. In reality, there wasn't much to explain. We were in love and we wanted to stay that way. In practice, the intensity of our first few weeks swept away the negativity, rejections and criticisms that surrounded us. Two months after starting our relationship, Gina was pregnant with our daughter, Paola: the bond between us will now never be severed. Back then I could have never imagined that fifteen years later, on a quiet afternoon in a boiling Miami, I would be telling my daughter the delicious and interesting prologue to her life.

Our coworkers would tell us, with smiles of complicity on their faces: "This is like a soap opera." For a short while, that's what it seemed to be from the outside. We shared an extraordinary emotional bond and we forgot about the rest of the world for a time.

While I was getting used to my new and intense life in a relationship, and while we awaited Paola's birth, the Cuban exile radio commentators in Miami were attacking me. They didn't do this because of the scandal that my personal life may have caused (and that we managed to keep secret from the local media's gossip mill), but because I was Mexican.

For some people, it was an insult that a Mexican journalist was hosting a national television program based in Miami (as "Mundo Latino" was) while the Mexican government maintained wonderful relations with the Cuban dictatorship. It was difficult to make them understand that my ideology had nothing to do with Mexican foreign policy. On one occasion, when the microphones were opened to the radio audience on one of those programs, a man told me. "Look, Ramos, for me you are a Mexican before a journalist, and that's why I'm not going to believe anything you say."

It was in that hostile environment that I began "Mundo Latino" along with Lucy Pereda in 1986. The Cubans represented a small part of the morning program's national audience, but it was very uncomfortable to listen to their personal attacks on Miami radio about matters over which I had no control or responsibility. Following the advice of Joaquín Blaya, then general manager of Canal 23 in Miami, I stopped listening to them and I listened to other stations while in my car. Problem resolved.

The morning program put me to the test in unimaginable ways. With very limited resources, we had to know a little bit about everything and to be able to improvise constantly. Sometimes we would discuss news, other times we would cook with a guest or I would dance salsa with a rumba instructor. Even though that was not what I really wanted to be doing, it gave me the experience and confidence I needed to survive on a live television program.

In that year, 1986, the most important news item for Latino immigrants in the United States was the amnesty that legalized the immigration status of more than three million undocumented aliens, and which also imposed fines on employers who hired workers who were in the United States illegally. Naively, it was thought that this would solve the problem of illegal immigration. But the plan had two fundamental flaws. First of all, it did not take into account the fact that the flow of undocumented aliens to the north has more to do with the supply and demand of jobs in the United States, than it has to do with law. In other words, it is an economic problem. Second, without a migration accord between Mexico and the United States, the border will remain out of control, resulting in the tragic deaths of those courageous enough to journey toward life in a new land.

Fifteen years after the amnesty, there are now more than eight million undocumented aliens in the United States. It was a Republican—Ronald Reagan—who signed the immigration amnesty in 1986. It is interesting to note that at the turn of a new century, it would be another Republican—George W. Bush—who would have to answer the call for an amnesty or the implementation of a massive program of normalization of immigration. The issue of undocumented immigration is, of course, far from being solved.

I WAS WORKING for a national television program, but the station did not have the glamour or the money that viewers might imagine. One of the cameramen, Aldo, cut my hair under a tree for five dollars. Aldo would sit me down on an overturned pail in the garden next to the studio, and, to the rhythm of *snip snap*, he would tell me hilarious stories of his days as a dancer in Cuba. The other cameramen, Felipe, Frank and Turk, were witnesses to these haircuts. We thought it was funny knowing that a national television anchor had his hair cut under a tree.

I was always ready to deal with any technical or editorial problem that might arise during the program, but I never suspected that after only a few months of hosting "Mundo Latino," the company would experience a huge crisis. The Noticiero SIN, which would later become Noticiero Univision, had been involved in a national and international dispute for years. It is undoubtedly the most influential news program in the Hispanic community in the United States, and the fight to control it involved both coasts of the country, Mexicans, Americans and Cuban Americans, several nations and different business interest groups. Part of that battle to dominate the most influential and prestigious news program of the network was among executives, journalists and professionals from Mexico and the United States.

Confirming rumors of several weeks, on Friday, September 5, 1986, commentator Jacobo Zabludovsky announced that he was leaving the news program "24 Horas" in Mexico to work for SIN in Miami. "I am closing one chapter to begin another," Zabludovsky said as he said goodbye after more than fifteen years on the program.

"It can't be," I thought when I heard the news. "I fled the kind of journalism that Televisa was doing in Mexico, and now Zabludovsky—the main representative of that kind of journalism—is coming to the exact place where I am in the United States." Had all the professional trappings come back to me in the form of Jacobo?

At first the morning program would not be affected by Zabludovsky's arrival. My colleagues at Noticiero SIN, however, were worried. There wasn't the slightest doubt that Televisa had played a fundamental role in the censorship that the Mexican political system had imposed for decades, and it was more than documented, both inside and outside of Mexico, that Zabludovsky's news reports manipulated the news to favor the PRI. Proof of this was in the awkward silences from Televisa every time there was electoral fraud and when Mexican presidents passed power, one to another.

Adding more fuel to the fire, just a few days after Zabludovsky's announcement, the new president of Televisa, Miguel Alemán, publicly justified the strong alliance between the company and the Mexican government. "We have a boss who is president of the Republic." Alemán said. "For me he is the captain of the ship and I have to support the president." [1]

Nevertheless, the journalists at Noticiero SIN did not want that captain. The first time Zabludovsky came to the tiny studios in Miami, he arrived by limousine. First mistake. The second was to deny that his news program was an instrument of the government. In short, the SIN reporters did not believe Zabludovsky, along with millions of Mexicans, and they threatened to resign if he were in charge of the news department. For almost two months the SIN reporters, headed by director Gustavo Godoy, defied Zabludovsky's efforts to take control. It was an open battle in which it became clear that Zabludovsky was not welcome in the United States.

Two examples: 1) The Mexican magazine *Proceso* interviewed Tomás Regalado, director of radio station WQBA in Miami, who said he had received hundreds of complaints from listeners and that "the presence of

---

[1] Claudio Capuzano, "Nuevo Orden Periodístico," *Periódico Noticias del Mundo,* September 30, 1986].

Zabludovsky jeopardizes the objectivity and independence of the news, because of his servility toward the governing party in Mexico." 2) The *Miami Herald* (8/25/86) published an editorial by Guillermo Martínez that said, "For Americans of all origin, the idea of using a newscast as a propaganda vehicle for a foreign government is repugnant . . . That is precisely what all this is about."

In order to prove that it was not only the Cuban Americans who opposed the presence of the Mexican commentator, in his article Martínez quoted the Mexican American editorialist from the *Los Angeles Times*, Frank del Olmo: "[Televisa's] pompous anchorman, Jacobo Zabludovsky, is as famous in Mexico as Walter Cronkite is in this country, with a big difference: Hardly anyone gives credence to what Zabludovsky says. That is because Zabludovsky and his Televisa bosses such as Emilio Azcárraga are notoriously close to Mexico's political leaders and the increasingly corrupt system that they control. Fairly or not, Mexicans regard any news item broadcast on [the program] '24 Horas' as the version of events that the Mexican government wants to get across. U.S. Latinos share that cynicism."

EMILIO AZCÁRRAGA, the owner of Televisa, had a very obvious progovernment bias.[2] If he hadn't, he would have lost the rights to his radio and television stations. That kind of favoritism, however, was frowned upon outside of Mexico, especially on newscasts.

The headline of an article written by Lourdes Meluzá in the *Miami Herald* on Friday, October 31, 1986, read: "Mass resignations from Noticiero SIN. Crisis over the appointment of journalist Jacobo Zabludovsky." The article reported the resignation of the news director, Gustavo Godoy, and of at least fourteen other producers, reporters and technicians. "From the very first day we refused to compromise our jour-

---

[2] Journalist Teresa Lourdes wrote the following about Emilio Azcárraga Milmo on January 15, 1988, from Querétaro, México: "We are with the PRI, we have always been with the PRI, we don't believe in any other way. As a member of our party, I will do everything possible to see that our candidate prevails."

nalistic integrity and we resigned out of principle, in the name of freedom of the press," said José Díaz Balart, who was the temporary anchor. "They thought they could come to the United States and pull off a coup," said correspondent Ricardo Brown.

That was also a very difficult time for me. Of course I was opposed to the journalistic practices of Televisa and Zabludovsky; that was one of the reasons I left Mexico. However, I did not feel like part of Godoy's team either. Gustavo Godoy had created the best Spanish-language newscast on American television with distinguished journalists such as Ricardo Brown, Pedro Sevsec, Carlos Botifol, Armando Guzmán, Guillermo Descalzi and Teresa Rodríguez. The success of the newscast was based on its being a program of high technical quality, with the same journalistic values that the three large American networks upheld and with an angle that emphasized news about Hispanics and Latin America. Never before had the Latino community had a first-rate newscast like the one Godoy created with such limited resources and an extraordinary and optimistic group of journalists.

Hours after his resignation. Godoy invited me to his apartment in Miami and he offered me a job as correspondent in Madrid for a new newscast that he planned to launch in order to compete with SIN.[3] The offer was tempting because Gina wanted to return to Spain, but I decided not to accept. I had always wanted to be a correspondent for Noticiero SIN. In fact, when I was living in Los Angeles, I had had several conversations in which it was mentioned that I would soon be hired by the newscast. Nevertheless, the hopes I had were never fulfilled, and now the offer had come too late.

Jaime Dávila, executive vice president of SIN, had offered me the job as the new anchor of the Noticiero. The ghost of Zabludovsky, however,

---

[3] Steve Beale, "More Changes at SIN," *Hispanic Business*, January 1987. "Gustavo Godoy, the veteran newsman who built Noticiero SIN into a nationally respected network newscast, has left SIN to launch his own national Spanish-language news show, bringing a sizable chunk of his former staff with him . . . Mr. Godoy's new venture [will be] called the Hispanic Broadcasting Network."

was still present, so I added an indispensable condition for accepting the offer: that no one, not Zabludovsky or Televisa, would become involved in the editorial content of the newscast. Dávila accepted.

Finally, the executives at Televisa decided to back down and send Zabludovsky back to Mexico, abandoning their plans to launch a twenty-four-hour newscast (called E.C.O.) from Miami. The morning of November 3, 1986, *The New York Times,* quoting a SIN source, said, ". . . Mr. Zabludovsky would probably not come to the United States to take up the new post after all." Dávila cited "personal reasons" for Zabludovsky's withdrawal.

With this, the threat of journalistic control over the Noticiero SIN by Televisa and Zabludovsky disappeared, but now there was no experienced team to do the newscast. Godoy had taken with him some of the best producers and correspondents, and they had no intention of returning after Zabludovsky's withdrawal.

At 6:30 P.M. on November 3, 1986, I became the anchor of the Noticiero SIN. At twenty-eight years old, I was one of the youngest national anchormen in the history of American television. Teresa Rodríguez, coanchor of the newscast back in the days of Godoy, decided to stay with the station, and she was my salvation.

Teresa was not only a great friend and coworker, but she guided me, step by step, through the technological labyrinth of a national newscast. I remember vividly her impeccable red nails on my script, underlining the words as I read them, just in case I got lost reading the TelePrompTer—something that happened frequently.

It was clear that I was an erratic newsreader and that I had never interviewed a president, but it was also the only viable alternative SIN had at that time of crisis. Nevertheless, I was well aware that I would not last long in the job if I didn't improve. I had a baby face and zero credibility.

There were even doubts among those working on the newscast that someone with such little experience deserved to be one of its anchors. One of these doubters was reporter Guillermo Descalzi, who because of his seniority and journalistic reputation should have gotten the job. During Pope John Paul II's visit to Miami in early 1987, Descalzi did not let me utter a single word during a brief live broadcast that we were supposedly doing together. I quickly transformed that embarrassing experience into a lesson. Never again would I allow anyone to silence me on camera. Silence is a mortal sin on television.

We have never discussed this incident, but I think that Descalzi didn't let me speak on that occasion on purpose. I'm sure that it was his way of complaining to our bosses and letting them know that they had made a mistake when they chose me as the news anchor and not him. Descalzi never made my life easy. But I never gave up. This conflict forced me to work harder, to try to be better than him and to do exhaustive interviews. Without a doubt, Guillermo Descalzi was one of the most daring and feared journalists of his time. I remember how the Central American presidents would ask with dread in their voices: "Did Descalzi come?" Years later, Descalzi was dogged by personal problems—he even wrote a book explaining how he descended into the world of illegal drugs—and eventually went to work for our rival network, Telemundo.

That was a very complicated period for the U.S. involvement in Latin America. The American president, Ronald Reagan, was obsessed with stopping Communist expansionism in the region, so he aligned himself with some of the repressive and reactionary elements in Central America. That is why he decided to ally himself with the Salvadoran military in the struggle against the Farabundo Martí National Liberation Front (FMLN), although it was renowned for its human rights violations. And in Nicaragua, the American government openly promoted the case of the *Contras*—even when it meant that it had to break its own laws—in its struggle to overthrow the leadership of the Sandinista revolution. The Sandinistas were successful in putting an end to the Somoza dynasty, but once they came to power, they began to implement authoritarian policies—such as the obligatory draft—and to hold elections that were marred by clearly undemocratic methods. Billions of dollars flowed from the vaults of the U.S. Treasury with little supervision into the hands of the Nicaraguan Contras, and of Salvadoran, Guatemalan and Honduran military figures tied to the fight against the guerrillas. The region had become polarized, so journalists had to make a daily effort not to take sides and to try to explain, in the simplest of terms, a very complicated and dangerous situation. At that same time I became the anchor of the most watched Spanish-language newscast in the United States, which also happens to have a great deal of influence in the region where the conflict was taking place: Central America. It was an enormous challenge, and the pressures on me were constant.

A FEW WEEKS AFTER having being named anchor for Noticiero SIN, I conducted my first presidential interviews, interviewing the presidents of Guatemala and Honduras, and Sylvana Foa, an Italian journalist who would go on to work for the United Nations, was named news director. Later I would learn to read the TelePrompTer more naturally, without the help of Teresa's red nails.

During that turbulent time, my daughter, Paola, was born. Rather than further complicating my life, this event gave my life meaning. I set my priorities; she, not the newscast, was the most important thing in my life.

Fatherhood suited me just fine. I found myself to be much more loving and affectionate than I ever thought that I could be. The whirlwind of emotions that preceded Paoli's birth disappeared the moment that I first held her. Neither my parents nor Gina's had arrived in Miami on time, since the delivery came a few days early. Therefore, Gina and I spent the whole night together and alone until Paola decided to be born as the sun rose on January 20, 1987. When they took her out of the delivery room, swaddled in a white blanket, I didn't know how to carry her. Nevertheless, I took her from the nurse and held her close to my body. She wasn't crying. She was at peace, and so was I.

Of course, that didn't mean that Paola slept much. I clearly recall being so tired those first weeks after her birth that when I dreamt, I would see myself sleeping. I dreamt about sleeping. And while I was awake, I only thought of Paola and the life that awaited her. I didn't think about the news.

There's a picture that was taken a few weeks after her birth that shows Paola resting on my shoulder. The two of us look exhausted. But the bond that already exists between us is beyond question. And in spite of distance and so many separations, we have been able to maintain that very bond. After Paoli's birth, my personal life was experiencing, at long last, calm moments. Better yet, a very short calm moment.

I had barely begun to feel at home in my new job when there was another change. Televisa may not have been able to impose Zabludovsky in the news department, but it still controlled the future of the network. In 1987, it changed the company name to Univision, and in summer it shut down—perhaps out of revenge for the Zabludovsky situation—its operations in Miami and decided to move the newscast to California.

The official argument, at least, made sense: we should be producing the newscast on the West Coast, where more of our viewers—Mexicans and Mexican Americans—lived. Teresa decided to stay in Miami, and I began to do the Noticiero Univision with the Uruguayan Andrea Kutyas. After just a few months of broadcasting the newscast from the Raleigh studios in Los Angeles, we moved to the heavenly city of Laguna Nigel, north of San Diego. It was a beautiful, peaceful, very expensive city that had very few Latinos. What's more, because of the three-hour time difference with the East Coast, by four in the afternoon we would have finished the newscast, and the news team would often meet by the pool, at the beach or to sip a margarita and watch the sun sink into the ocean. The executives at Univision never thought they were sending us on an early retirement, but that is what it was. Covering Central and South America from Laguna Nigel was a true odyssey of constant traveling, airplane changes and hours lost in airports. Laguna Nigel was indeed beautiful, but it was one of the worst places in the world from which to broadcast the news.

A few months after moving to Laguna Nigel, Guillermo Martínez, an experienced journalist from the *Miami Herald*, was named news director. Thanks to him, we developed a competitive style in the search for news, and we were brought up to date on the ethical practices and codes of conduct of the main journalistic institutions in the country. I learned a lot from Guillermo, who always had a refined sense of smell for what is news, and who never hesitated to use the few resources we had to cover international crises. Martínez resorted to financial juggling to make sure we were witnesses to every important news story, regardless of budgetary limitations. That, of course, led to many confrontations between him and the other executives at the network. Despite the pressure, however, he never felt that a war—like the one in the Balkans, for example—was not "relevant" to the Hispanic audience in the United States. He was first, and always, a journalist.

It wasn't long before Martínez named María Elena Salinas to join me as coanchor of the newscast, replacing Andrea Kutyas. Our goal was to produce a newscast that was as good as or better than our English rivals.

We never dreamt that the growth of the Latino market—due to the high birth rate among Hispanics and constant immigration from Latin America—would be so considerable. Our growth was so significant that in some cities we had higher ratings for our newscast than did the ABC, CBS and NBC networks. While English-language newscasts were losing their viewing public—due to increased competition from cable—our newscast continued to grow, and has since then remained at number one.

For the last fifteen years we have competed against Spanish-language newscasts produced by HBC, CNN, NBC, Telenoticias and Telemundo, but we have never lost the ratings war. Furthermore, it is surprising that we were able to significantly erode the television audience of English-language newscasts in cities with large Hispanic populations. But since they could choose to get their news in Spanish or English, even bilingual people began to opt for us. All of this was happening in spite of the fact that we were producing the newscast from Laguna Nigel.

The move to California was a futile last resort by Televisa. A federal judge had ruled that Televisa, a Mexican company, had violated American law by having more than 25 percent control in a television network in the United States.[4] So the arrangement that René Anselmo had initiated with

[4] Matt Moffett and Johnnie Roberts, "Mexican Media Empire, Grupo Televisa, Casts an Eye on U.S. Market," *The Wall Street Journal:* "In the 1980's [Azcárraga] had a major stake in what is now Univision. But he sold to Hallmark Cards Inc . . . to end a bitter and prolonged controversy over whether he was in violation of U.S. laws that limit foreign ownership of U.S. broadcast outlets."

Emilio Azcárraga in 1961 — broadcasting from San Antonio with Televisa programming in Spanish — was thwarted. Azcárraga was forced to sell all his television stations in the United States and after a long and complicated process, on November 19, 1987, the sale to Hallmark Cards was official.

The decision was another blow to the expansionist plans of the Mexican magnate who, years before, had tried unsuccessfully to launch his twenty-four-hour newscast from the United States. Nevertheless, for the Mexicans at Televisa, the sale of Univision to Hallmark would not be an *adios* but rather an *hasta luego*.

As soon as Hallmark executives had taken over, there was talk of returning Noticiero Univision to Miami. That was part of an undeclared war between Cubans and Mexicans for control of the most influential Spanish-language newscast in the United States. Ironically, it was a visionary Chilean executive, Joaquín Blaya, who wound up in control of Univision.

Blaya not only positioned Univision as a large American television network, but he also invested millions of dollars in producing programs made in the United States that reflected the cultural diversity of the country. Under his leadership, Univision earned international renown, modern facilities were built in Miami, and in 1991 the newscast was moved back from California. Televisa, however, was still on the lookout.

Despite successful ratings, Hallmark had not been able to get Univision out of financial difficulties, and Hallmark, without Blaya's knowledge, decided to sell the network to businessman Jerrold Perenchio: Televisa of Mexico and Venevisión of Venezuela would join as minority partners.[5]

"Joaquín Blaya, acting president of Univision Holdings was in his Miami office Wednesday morning, April 8 [1992], when Hallmark Cards CEO Irv Hockaday walked in," reported *Hispanic Business* in its May 1992

---

[5] According to an article in the *Miami Herald* in May 1988 ("Shake-up in Spanish TV"), Univision had lost $257 million between 1987 and 1990, and Hallmark was losing money with the sale of the Univision network and its stations.

edition. ". . . this visit stunned Mr. Blaya. Mr. Hockaday got right down to business. Hallmark, he said, was selling the company that Mr. Blaya heads, the nation's largest Spanish television network and station group."

The news, of course, did not go over well with Blaya. "I am deeply disappointed by the secret way in which Hallmark handled that transaction," Blaya said in a statement picked up by the *Miami Herald*. "They have shown a complete lack of respect for the group of professionals at Univision who have worked tirelessly in order to change the face of Spanish television in this country."[6]

No one was surprised when Blaya resigned on May 22, 1992. Ray Rodríguez, committing himself to maintaining Univision's leadership in Spanish television, was named president of the company. "This is an important opportunity to continue producing Spanish-language television programming that meets the needs and interests of U.S. Hispanics," said Joaquín Blaya, president and chief executive officer of Telemundo Group, Inc.[7]

Blaya's departure questioned Univision's commitment to produce programs aimed specifically at Hispanics, and it suggested that soap operas and news and entertainment programs produced in Mexico and Venezuela could replace such programming. My greatest concern, however, was the bad reputation that both Televisa and Venevisión had with respect to journalistic objectivity.

No one had to tell me about the practice of censorship and self-censorship at Televisa in Mexico; I had experienced them. Venevisión was subject to incidents of strong governmental pressure to modify its information in accordance with the regime in power.[8] In other words, I didn't

---

[6] Beatriz Parga, "Soplan Vientos de Cambio en TV Hispana," the *Miami Herald*, April 11, 1992.

[7] Telemundo, PRNewswire, May 26, 1992.

[8] The *Miami Herald* published an article entitled "Perez Refutes Declaration of the SIP (Sociedad Interamericana de Prensa) about Obstacles to a Free Press," which said the following: "The SIP condemned the treatment given to the Venezuelan press and identified this country as one of the most alarming examples of steps against freedom of expression in America."

want the same restrictions on freedom of expression that journalists had in Mexico and Venezuela to be imported to Univision with the sale by Hallmark to Perenchio, Televisa and Venevisión. First we had to deal with Zabludovsky, I thought, and now this.

I remember as if it were yesterday a meeting called by Jerry Perenchio at the Univision studios in Miami to clear up any doubts with respect to the purchase of the company. Jaime Dávila, of Televisa, and Gustavo Cisneros, of Venevisión, accompanied him. Hundreds of employees were present. I armed myself with courage, raised my hand and asked the question that many of my fellow journalists had on the tip of their tongues. "We all know that both Televisa and Venevisión practice censorship of the press in their respective countries," I said as an introduction. Then, addressing Perenchio, I asked, "Can you assure us that that will not occur here in the United States?" Before Perenchio, Dávila or Cisneros could respond, there was loud applause in the studio. It was from my coworkers, and it was obvious that I was not the only one concerned about this. When Perenchio eventually responded, he said, "Here there will be complete freedom of the press, and if you ever have any problems, call me."

Today I can say with complete satisfaction that none of the owners of Univision or the president of the network, Ray Rodríguez, has ever imposed a news story on us or called us to prevent some kind of information from airing on the newscast. Perenchio kept his word, and I never had to call him to complain. Both Rodríguez and Perenchio showed that a highly profitable business, as Univision is now, can operate without violating the strict code of ethics that should govern all journalists.

For those who have not lived in Latin America—and who don't know about the attacks on the press, the ridiculously low salaries of reporters, the threats of drug traffickers, politicians, the military and businessmen, the fear of publishing controversial information that might harm the owners of the various media that pay for the schooling of your children, the self-imposed censorship by the bosses in order to keep their jobs, the extreme difficulty in being an ethical and just journalist—these concerns might seem unfounded. To cite one example, the United States guarantees freedom of expression in the first amendment to the Constitution.

Criticisms similar to those that are constantly made in more developed nations, however (of presidents, congressmen, businessmen and the military) have cost the lives of many Latin American journalists.

It was truly a nightmare for me to imagine that the same vices and restrictions on freedom of expression that drove me from Mexico could have followed me to the United States. Fortunately, in the end this was not the case.

During all this time as the anchor for the Univision newscasts I have tried to remain sensible with large doses of realism and good humor. This has saved me. I have seen so many people come and go through the same position that I now hold that I have no doubt that sooner or later, I too will go and someone will replace me. The interesting thing is that many of my colleagues—both English and Spanish-speaking—behave as though they were immortal and all-powerful. And some of them are not even reporters: they only know how to read the TelePrompTer well. Television fame has a very, very short lifespan. I believe in the "three week" theory: after three weeks off the air, the television audience will begin to forget even the most renowned reporter, without causing a major drop in the ratings. One day too, I will be a face, obscured by time, alive only in memory.

MARÍA ELENA SALINAS

María Elena Salinas joined the Noticiero Univision team in the spring of 1988, and since then I have seen her almost every day. I have known María Elena longer than my wife, and I have spent more time with her than with my siblings. Together we have experienced some of the most important historical events of recent years, moved from city to city several times, traveled around the American continent and, last, we have occupied the same office for more than a decade. That is patience . . . on her part, clearly.

We know each other so well that with just a look or by the way she enters the office, I can already tell what kind of mood she's in. On the air, we don't need to say much; with just a pause or a couple of words, we know whose turn it is to read the next story, who is going to do the interviews and whose job it is to send the program to a commercial break. I am sure she knows all my suits, shirts and ties by heart. She knows when I wear the same thing over again, which combinations look good on me and which ones look like they came straight from a mental hospital. She recently gave me a couple of ties, and I got the hint: I went through my closet and, sure enough, it was time to update my wardrobe with the colors and styles of the day.

We have been on the air together for so long that many people think we are married. "Where's María Elena?" I am often asked when I am traveling. "At home," I usually respond. Her own, of course. I have grown tired of explaining to people that just because we work together eight, nine or ten hours a day does not mean we live together, even though sometimes it seems like it.

Like all couples, we go through stages. Sometimes we talk a lot and see each other at parties and gatherings outside of work. Other times we keep our distance and get caught up in our own routines. Because we have shared the same office for such a long time, just by the tone of voice on the telephone we know if the call is personal or work related, and one comment is enough to suspect that something is wrong. What is surprising, though, is that we have had an extraordinary work relationship for a decade and a half: we have never raised our voices or had a serious argument.

Naturally we have our differences. We are both very competitive; that, I believe, is the only way to survive in this business. We are both set in our ways and our ideas—I won't use the word *stubborn*. On several occasions we have both wanted the same interview, the same trip or the same story, but eventually the matter is resolved and we return to our routine of covering wars, airplane crashes, military crises, coup d'états . . . you know, a normal day's work.

If I could describe María Elena with just one word, I would say she is a "*luchadora*," a fighter. She was born in Los Angeles and is the daughter of Mexican immigrants. As a little girl she had to learn how to help the family and to work in order to get by. Even today she continues to be the economic and emotional pillar for her family. She was the youngest girl, but her sisters know that she is really "*la grande*." She has compensated for not being able to continue her schooling with her effort, dedication and passion for detail. I know few people who fight so hard to make sure that a fact or figure in a story is correct.

When I see her—leaving the beauty salon, dressed in expensive clothing, decorating her house so elegantly or driving in her pretty blue convertible—I can't help but think of that little blonde girl who had to fight so hard to get what she has and who has made her parents so proud to see what she has accomplished. I am not surprised, therefore, that in schools and universities she is called a role model for young Latinas.

There is nothing that María Elena thinks she can't do, and that is the secret to her success. And I admire that. She is persistent like few, and I cannot recall many interviews or stories she has gone after that she hasn't gotten. When something gets into her head . . . watch out! In her childhood and adolescence as well as her professional career, she has proven that wanting to is being able to.

I recently heard her talking about soccer with Julia, one of her daughters. She said, "Don't let anyone push you around, get the ball and run, run and run until you get to the goal." María Elena did exactly that in her life; she didn't let anyone push her around, and she ran and ran until she achieved her goals.

She is also aware that she was called upon to grow up in a man's world, and that getting ahead for her has been more difficult because she is a woman. Sometimes she complains about machismo, but instead of acting passively, she resists like a boxer and keeps fighting until she gets what she thinks is fair. She gets her revenge by earning more than almost any man. Truthfully, I wouldn't want her as an enemy, and when she is angry, those of us on the Noticiero know not to get too close. Just in case . . .

I believe that the most difficult challenge for María Elena has not been finding a way out of the economic problems of her youth or becoming a reporter or being considered one of the most influential Latina broadcasters in the United States. The main challenge for María Elena has been finding balance in her life.

María Elena is someone who wants it all: professional success, financial stability, family, friends and to make a contribution to society. It is very difficult, however, to be a journalist, mother, wife and heroine in just twenty-four hours a day, and that is exactly what my friend tries to do: find moments to write articles for the Internet and commentaries for the radio, prepare stories and interviews for TV . . . and be a mother, work out, cook and organize parties and get-togethers.

Still, María Elena is not a superwoman, but she is the closest thing to it that I know.

LIVING WITH AN ACCENT

If we forget what we are, what we experienced, on
what map would we be?

—CARLOS SAURA (TANGO)

Ethnicity seems to be destiny in the politics of the
third century (of the American democracy).

—HAROLD EVANS (THE AMERICAN CENTURY)

I might not look like a Mexican to some people, but I
definitely sounded like one. The hours and days
spent studying English in Mexico had prepared me
very little for my arrival in the United States, beginning with the simple fact that the letters in English
are not pronounced they way they sound. The O
sounds like an A, and the E like an I. My Rs in Spanish are strong, coarse sounding; in English the R is a
murmur. The Ñ does not exist. Never before had I
had to differentiate between the B and the V, and now
I had to make a conscious effort to separate my lips in
order to say simple words like *vacation, Venus* or *veg-
etable.*

With all these new rules in my head, I got tongue-
tied; I definitely sounded like a Mexican. My job as a
waiter when I first arrived in Los Angeles was tor-

ture. How can you explain with a *chilango* accent and the vocabulary of a grammar school student that the fish is prepared in a garlic sauce with a light touch of cilantro and parsley? How can you describe without laughing that the *penne* is prepared *al dente* in an *arrabbiata* sauce when everything that comes out of your mouth sounds like a play on words?

If I had a hard time trying to explain things in English, the Americans had—and still have—serious problems just pronouncing my name. Saying *Jorge* in English is almost a tongue twister. In Spanish both the J and the G in Jorge are soft. The R is hard, unmistakable. In English, however, there are some people who put too much stress on the J, as if they were saying John, or they emphasize the G like in Gary.

Pronouncing the letter R is an insurmountable obstacle for many Americans; you run the risk of being spit on as the inflexible English-speaking tongue tries to roll. The O in Jorge is not a problem, but the final E ends up sounding like the squeaking noise of a mouse. The first three letters of my name sound the same as those of *horse* in English; the G is soft, and the final E is like the e in jet. In other words, saying *Jorge* in English is a linguistic impossibility for most Americans I know. That's why when it's not important, I change Jorge to George. So, for many people I was simply George.

Once I had resolved the pronunciation of my first name—Jorge for some, George for others—I had to make other adjustments. My full name is Jorge Gilberto Ramos Avalos. Everyone in Mexico and the rest of Latin America has at least two names and two last names. When I opened a bank account or signed up for a course in journalism and television at UCLA, my name caused a lot of confusion. Not only was it unpronounceable but also to the American mind it didn't make sense; it was too long. There was too much of it.

In the United States you automatically lose the mother's last name. I think this is a real shame. Machismo in the United States is subtler than in the southern part of the continent. The best example of this is how women in the United States adopt the last name of their husbands, discarding their own, and do not include their last name in their children's name. It's as if they didn't exist; a child's name in the United States hides the mother, and I didn't want to hide mine.

"Don't get rid of Avalos," my maternal grandfather, Miguel, said to me when I learned of the U.S. custom of cutting off the mother's last name. So for a long time I insisted on being called Jorge Ramos Avalos. I never liked my second name, Gilberto, much—it carries with it the authoritarian tradition of my paternal grandfather and of my father—and I dropped it without a problem. Soon after, I began to receive mail addressed to Jorge R. Avalos.

In honor of my grandfather Miguel, I tried to keep my full name, and I engaged in various quixotic battles explaining to an endless number of officials and bureaucrats the Mexican custom of having two last names. Nobody cared. The letters kept coming addressed to Jorge R. Avalos. In the end, I gave in and opted for the most practical solution: I gave up one first name (Gilberto) and one last name (Avalos) and became Jorge Ramos, plain and simple, or George Ramos, at your service. I'm sorry, *abuelo* Miguel.

THE FIRST TIME I INTERVIEWED George W. Bush in late 1999, we had an interesting conversation. I told the then governor of Texas that his name in English is very similar to my name in Spanish: George is Jorge, and Bush resembles Ramos. The anecdote resulted in the now president recognizing me in the sea of journalists, and that always helps at a press conference or when requesting an interview.

Since my arrival in the United States, however, it was clear that I would never be mistaken for an American—even though to many I didn't seem Mexican either—and that I wouldn't speak English like an American. Besides, I didn't want to. My accent will always give me away as a foreigner, and that's what I am in the United States—it's a truth I would never want to hide.

My accent carries with it origin, history and direction. It says who I am and it shouts out where I'm from. The accent is like a fingerprint: unique and nontransferable. The accent carries with it "the wound of the earth," using an expression of writer Carlos Fuentes, and its scar can be disguised or covered up, but it can never be erased.

As a student in Los Angeles, I had the opportunity to regularly visit a television station with a group of other students from UCLA. There I had the chance to approach the news director. Openly, naively, I asked him if he thought that someone with my accent in English would have a chance to be a reporter at his station. "No," was his curt reply.

That was the reality. In those days there was a radio journalist by the name of Michael Jackson, who became known for his British accent. In Los Angeles there were millions of Mexicans and only a handful of British. His accent was accepted, nine was not.

When I moved to Miami I toyed with the idea of working in the English-language media. The budgets for broadcasting news in Spanish were ridiculously low compared to those of the large networks, and I thought that, at the very least, I should explore my options. Never mind my experience as a journalist, it was obvious that the main obstacle I would face would be my accent in English. So I decided to study with an accent reduction specialist to help me with my foray into the mainstream.

The very first time the specialist heard me she looked concerned. "You're never going to be able to speak English without an accent," she said. The long hours spent reading aloud were in vain. After the second class, the teacher declared me a lost cause, and I gave up any hope of crossing over into the English market.

I really learned English at the age of twenty-four, when I arrived in the United States. Although I don't have any problems communicating, it's obvious that it's not my maternal language. Quite honestly, the confirmation that I would never speak English without an accent made me more secure in my job. I would never have to fight with Peter Jennings, Tom Brokaw, Dan Rather or Ted Koppel for an interview with the president of the United States. I would never fight with Barbara Walters or Sam Donaldson for a story. In this way I convinced myself that my future was in Spanish-language media, and I was intent on doing the best I could. "They might do a good job in English," I thought, "but I'll try to do an even better job in Spanish."

In the end, I wound up competing with the same journalists I just mentioned, but not at the same company. When Spanish-language media began to win viewers and listeners away from the English-language stations in the late 1990s in cities with high percentages of Latinos, the competition between radio and television stations increased, regardless of the language in which they broadcast.

Nevertheless, both inside and outside of my profession, my accent has set me apart, and it has caused me to be treated differently on more than a few occasions. It is no longer a question of blatant discrimination, like the signs in public parks in Colorado and various other parts of America in the not-so-recent past, that prohibited the entrance of dogs and Mexicans. Now it is a more subtle discrimination. It is not being waited on in a restaurant with the same haste and attention as the rest of the customers, the rude impatience of someone who says they can't understand you, being received with the question, "Where are you from?" before "Hello," or being laughed at when you say you weren't born in the United States. One of my mantras is this: the best things about the United States are its opportunities; the worst thing is the racism.

There are more and more people like me in the United States. The border with Mexico is porous; every day an average of one thousand people cross the border illegally. This is not going to stop with immigration agreements or with increased surveillance. It is basically an economic problem; as long as there are not enough jobs in Mexico and job opportunities in the United States, the border will continue to be a sieve.

Many Americans became angry when Mexican president Vicente Fox said that one of his long-term plans was to open the border between both countries. He merely wanted to recognize and legalize what was already common practice. Anyone who has spent one night in Tijuana or at the Rio Grande in Texas, watching the game of cat and mouse played by agents of the U.S. Border Patrol and Mexican immigrants, can state with conviction that the border is more legal than real.

I SPEAK A SPANISH that is *madreado,* or beaten up; that is, a Spanish that has been molded by my mother and beaten up by my homeland. I speak an

English that is *madreadísima*, which can often barely be understood. I get along just fine in both, though, just barely.

My accent gives me away, exposes me, tells my history in a fraction of a second and puts the other person on alert. My accent, however, is also my flag. In just a few words it says who I am and where I come from.

The first news director with whom I worked in the United States, Pete Moraga, trained me to lose my strong Mexico City accent. The unique singsong of someone from Mexico City is unmistakable. Pete attempted to mold my speech so that my *chilango* accent would not turn off a large part of Canal 34's audience in Los Angeles, which was Mexican but not from the capital. In Mexico there has always been tension between the capital and the provinces. For centuries, political, economic, religious and cultural power has been concentrated in the capital, and with this, came arrogance. That's why those from the capital have a bad reputation.

At first it was hard to alter my accent in Spanish, but I soon learned that accents are basically created by elongating or shortening vowels and emphasizing or deemphasizing syllables. So, I attempted to say *"información"* and not "iiinfoormaciooon," *"fútbol"* and not "fuuutbool." Pete's suggestions worked well, so well that even today I speak a kind of neutral Spanish that few can identify with Mexico City. Some who hear me on the newscast have thought I was Peruvian, Colombian, Ecuadoran, Bolivian and even Cuban.

The irony is that I never lost my accent in English but I neutralized my accent in Spanish. If you add to this the enormous number of Spanglish words used typically by Latinos living in the United States, including myself, the final effect is truly unique and unmistakable. It is my accent.

For some time, I tried not to give speeches at colleges or at public events in order to avoid committing gaffes in English. Obviously, this distanced me from American society and confined me to the Hispanic world. As a matter of fact, when my daughter, Paoli, accompanied me to public events, she would correct my pronunciation on the way home. "That's not how you say it," she would tell me in good humor. Finally, I realized that I had an almost irreparable accent, that I didn't have to apologize for having learned English too late in life, and that my accent, far from being an obstacle, could become my letter of introduction. I may still feel different, but I am at peace with the way I speak.

My accent reveals that I am from somewhere else, like more than thirty million people in the United States. Sometimes I am caught by surprise when I walk past a building, seeing a group of gardeners at work, or when I am in a restaurant being served by a waiter, and inevitably think that I too had to begin, like them, at the bottom. There are times when it saddens me when they recognize me—"look, there goes they guy from the television," and they see I am well dressed and have a nice car, because I don't want them to think that I have forgotten where I came from, for I, too, am an immigrant. My journey from Mexico to the United States has defined me more than most things in life.

"Can you imagine if you had stayed in Mexico?" Paola asked me recently. "Have you thought about how small things can later have an enormous impact on the future?" How wonderful to be able to talk with your own daughter like that!

I went from being Mexican to being Latino, or Hispanic. Even though the word *Latino* is used more in California and *Hispanic* is used more in the East, I use Latino and Hispanic indiscriminately. It is also a generational issue; Latino is more frequently used among the young. What matters is that I stopped being a resident of Mexico and became an immigrant. In other words, I left stability behind for change.

For years I also refused to identify myself to others as Latino or Hispanic. None of my friends identify themselves that way. When I ask them, "What are you?" they reply, "Peruvian," "Argentine," "Colombian," "Honduran," but almost never "Latino" or "Hispanic." The term *hispano* or Hispanic was an invention of the Census Bureau in order to group together citizens and residents of the United States who had come from Latin America, and in order to differentiate us from other white groups the category of non-Hispanic whites was created. Despite these kinds of definitions, however, Hispanics are not a monolithic group.

While Mexicans and Central Americans talk endlessly about immigration laws and getting amnesty or permanent residency, Cubans are obsessed with Castro's dictatorship and Puerto Ricans with the lack of political definition they have with respect to the United States. In the same way, American citizens of Latino origin—regardless of what country they come from—are more concerned about improving levels of education and access to good jobs than about immigration matters, Castro or the future of the island of Vieques.

From this perspective, someone might conclude that there are more things that divide us than unite us. Besides, there is no national leader who unites the different Latino communities as, say, Jesse Jackson does for African American communities. Nevertheless, the Spanish language, our Latin American and Iberian origin, and certain traditional values like the importance of family and Catholicism unite Hispanics. While these characteristics are a question of degree and not absolute concepts, the reality is that Latino immigration to the United States is different from other waves of immigration that have come to this country, like the Irish, the Italians and the eastern Europeans.

Neither the Italians nor the Polish or the Germans had national radio and television stations in the United States, nor did their languages wind up invading every corner of the nation. On the other hand, Hispanics have maintained the Spanish language contrary to all predictions. Far from disappearing, the Spanish language is stronger than ever in the United States.

This can be explained in part by the proximity of our countries of origin. Geographically, it makes more sense to cross the border from Tijuana to San Diego than to get on a boat and set sail from Sicily to New York. It's not the same to go and visit your family members in Venice or Warsaw as it is to go to Veracruz. It is easier to maintain family unity if the family member lives in Michoacán as opposed to Milan. Besides, new technology has made communication by telephone much cheaper. Calling San Salvador costs much less today than it did to call the Vatican fifty years ago, and the Internet allows us to stay in constant contact, at a reasonable cost regardless of where we live. That did not occur with the waves of European immigration in the last century. The melting pot dried up.

"It is the first time in history that immigrants have not had to pass through the process of the melting pot, which implies the adaptation of their customs with those of the English-speaking population so they can be recognized as Americans," said Peruvian writer Mario Vargas Llosa. "Hispanics have not had to lose their language or their culture in order to assimilate: on the contrary, many have defended that culture."

Spanish has also become a symbol of social identification for Hispanics. Spanish is not only spoken in most Latino homes in the United States but it is also the sign of belonging to a group. Even those Hispanics who don't speak Spanish well greet each other with *"hola"* and say good-bye with an *"adiós,"* and they throw a word or two of Spanish into their conversations. Even when we are upset we shout our bilingual, bicultural and binational circumstance into the air. "This fucking *perrrra* won't let me sleep," said a close acquaintance who prefers to remain anonymous (for obvious reasons) when her dog's internal clock wakes her up with loud barking at two-thirty in the morning.

These hybrid expressions of bilingualism and biculturalism are so important to us that even U.S. politicians interested in the Latino vote have learned a few phrases in Spanish by heart. The most obvious and pathetic case of this came from vice president and former presidential candidate Al Gore, who in order to appeal to Latino voters in the campaign repeated phrases like *"sí se puede," "claro que sí," "p'alante, siempre p'alante,"* and *"comunidad boricua."* To be fair, Bush did the same, yet perhaps with a better degree of comprehension.

Spanish is spoken more and more in the United States. It has resisted all efforts to legally prohibit it, as well as the inevitable linguistic integration and the pressures of living in a country where English is the dominant language. Contrary to what happened with Italian or Polish, Spanish—because of the high birth rate among Latinas and immigration from south of the border—is proliferating in the United States even though not in its pure form and, at times, to the horror of members of the Royal Academy of the Spanish Language.

The United States is not a white country; it is a mixed, multiethnic, multicultural nation. One of the tendencies that has predominated because of this racial mixing is the Hispanicization or Latinization of the United States. We are not talking here about just the refusal of the Span-

ish language to die in Yankee territory, but of the enormous cultural influence of U.S. Hispanics.

In the United States, more tortillas and salsa are sold than bagels and
ketchup. Spanish-language media casts a shadow over those that broadcast
in English, politicians with last names like Hernández and Sánchez are replacing Dornan and Smith, and there is a real cultural invasion in music,
art and literature. It is a cultural reconquest. And it has a name in Spanish:
la reconquista. The same territories that Mexico lost in the mid-nineteenth
century are beginning to play an important role in this process of recon-
quering culturally what Mexicans lost geographically and politically.

The same racial and ethnic integration that the United States is experiencing is found inside the Hispanic community, and that integration has
touched me personally. It is unlikely that I would be defined only as Mexican, and I'm not American despite having lived in this country for almost
two decades. I identify much more with the natives of Oaxaca and Chiapas
than I do with residents of Wisconsin or the Dakotas. Their history is one
I do not share. I am not simply a Mexican; I am a Mexican in the United
States, period.

These combinations are also found on the family level. My wife, Lisa,
was born in San Juan to Cuban parents. When she travels to Latin America for business she is considered American. In Puerto Rico, however, she
is Cuban, and in Miami she is Puerto Rican. For her not only her origin
but also the place where she happens to be defines her.

My son, Nicolás, was born in Miami and could be defined as Mexican-
Puerto Rican-Cuban-American. My daughter, Paola, who was also born
in south Florida and has spent much of her childhood and adolescence in
Spain, would be Spanish-Cuban-Mexican-American. In short, my children are new Americans.

This is part of my daily world. I have spent much of my career reporting on Latin America (because most of those who watch the newscast
come from there) and speaking about Latinos (because, after all, that's
what I am). As a Latino journalist, however, I have a responsibility, along
with many others, that I never expected.

When Hispanic journalists emphasize matters that tend to be forgotten by other media but that form an integral part of our lives, we become the voice of those who have no voice. When we report on racism and discrimination against Latinos, for example, when those who speak Spanish are attacked, when immigrants are hunted down like animals on the Arizona border, and when anti-Latino proposals like Proposition 187 in California arise, we are giving a voice to those who have none. We aren't taking sides, but when we speak of people who are generally overlooked in the English media, like Latinos or undocumented immigrants, Hispanic journalists are presenting to the rest of the world a view that is unfamiliar to millions, and we do so with an accent and a familiarity that cannot easily be replicated by others.

My accent carries with it the history of the Ramos and Avalos families. My grandparents are no longer living. My grandmother Raquel died not long ago, and the five Ramos Avalos children have been left hanging. Now whom do we ask about our past?

My siblings say that I was the favorite of my grandfather Gilberto, Raquel's husband. Could be. Every Sunday he gave me a few coins, always one or two more than he gave my siblings or cousins. Thanks to that privileged relationship with my grandfather, though, I got to know, firsthand, my father's aunt and uncle who lived in Ramos Arizpe, Coahuila, just a few hours from the U.S. border. I never acquired the accent of my family from the north, but the conversations we used to have at the dinner table after a meal of *cabrito*—in which my grandfather would dish out the eyes, cheeks, tongue and brain of the animal as if they were the most exquisite delicacies—have stayed with me forever. I'm sure I repeat at certain times expressions and idioms that I heard for the first time seated in front of those revolting *tacos de cabrito*.

My grandfather Miguel was a wonderful conversationalist. Every Thursday he would come to the house on Piedras Negras Street to eat with us, and during the long table talk, he would not only tell us how the Second World War was won, but grandfather Miguel would also tell us about the excesses of the Roman Empire and the dictatorship of Porfirio Díaz in Mexico. Later, when we went to eat at his house—almost every Saturday—I would notice where he got his topics of conversation: from loads of books that were piled up on his nightstand (as they are now on mine). Sometimes we would arrive before midday and we would catch him in pajamas, reading in bed, with the curtains blocking the sun, and with the aid of a lamp that gave just enough light to be able to read two paragraphs at a time, and that rested on his prominent belly. The half-filled chamber pot that was hidden under his bed proved that not even the need to urinate could interrupt my grandfather's reading.

Miguel, my mother's father, was born along with the new century, in 1900. Through his unhurried conversation I felt the emotion of a boy who sees electric light for the first time. During the christening of his sister Blanca in 1910, his father—my great-grandfather Gregorio Avalos—managed to have electricity brought to the small mining town of Taxco, thanks to contacts he had in the federal government. I also remember, as if I had been there, when my grandfather Miguel slept in the bed of Empress Carlota in Chapultepec Castle in Mexico City. His father, Gregorio, was the building superintendent, and I guess that one of the benefits of his job was to take advantage, even if just for a night, of the luxury of an empress's bed. I'm sure that my vocabulary is punctuated with words and accents from my grandfather Miguel's extraordinary stories.

I never met my grandmother Consuelo. She died when my mother was still a girl. The memories she left, though, were so vivid and her death so sudden, that my mother made her into a real presence in our house. I can almost hear her contagious laughter, smell the delicious dishes she would prepare (and whose recipes are still prepared in my house in Miami) and enjoy the parties she organized with such flair. Her expressions and words are now also mine, as are the odors associated with her, thanks to the bridges built by my mother. My house smells like her newly-starched blouses, her shrimp stew and the face creams that she would put on her extremely legendary white skin, which I was never able to see.

My mother is a wonderful storyteller, and all of her stories are true. She calls them "true stories." These are family stories that have passed down from generation to generation, and that she has taken upon herself to keep alive. Without these "true stories," I never would've known how my father burned his delicate feet in the middle of their honeymoon (and which caused the cancellation of a long-planned skiing trip), nor about my aunts bickering with one another as each tried to appear right next to my grandfather Miguel in pictures, nor would I know anything about the asthma attacks that left me green and pale whenever we visited my uncle José's house in Valle de Bravo. These true stories have given us a sense of family history, and probably, in my own way, I have tried to keep this same tradition alive, a tradition that my mother has continued, word by word.

The expressions of my grandparents and my father, my mother's stories, the endless dinner conversations at my grandfather Miguel's house, the absent presence of Consuelo, in other words, my past and my point of reference, are reflected today in my accent. I may never manage to speak English without an accent, but I don't care. My accent represents the footsteps and the scars; I walk happily, and I carry my baggage with me.

NEWS OF THE RECONQUEST: THE FUTURE OF SPANISH-LANGUAGE MEDIA IN THE UNITED STATES

In the autumn of 2000, in the midst of the election campaign in the United States, I received a phone call from the political analyst Sergio Bendixen. "A journalist from the *Wall Street Journal* is looking for a television presenter who is well known to Hispanics but unknown to those who do not speak Spanish," he said, "and I immediately thought of you." This struck me as funny, but it was completely true.

Spanish-language journalists in the United States live in a world that is parallel to the rest of the country. We dream in Spanish, speak in Spanish at work, write in Spanish and inform an audience that prefers to hear the news in Spanish. Most of the United States, of course, does not understand us; moreover, many people do not even know we exist.

The "Christopher Columbus syndrome" is the name given to the cyclical practice of "discovering" Hispanics every time there is a national election in the United States, and then almost completely forgetting about us. I am now used to this. Before the November 7, 2000, elections, I appeared on CNN, ABC, NBC and Fox News, and in I don't know how many newspapers and magazines to talk about the importance of the Hispanic vote. And how important it proved to be! It was clear in the mind of George W. Bush—and he told me so in an interview on January 19, 2001—that thanks to the Latino vote, and the Cuban American vote in Florida in particular, he succeeded in getting to the White House.[9]

The United States is not a white country; it is a multiethnic and multicultural nation. In less than sixty years it will be a nation composed solely of minorities. The fluid process of racial and ethnic mixing is very evident in states like California—where non-Hispanic whites are no longer a majority—and in the 100 largest cities in the country—where blacks, Hispanics, Asians and members of other minorities make up on average more than 50% of the population. Non-Hispanic whites moved to the suburbs.

When I began to work in television in the United States in 1984, the debate was over whether there was a future for Spanish-language media. Many analysts believed, mistakenly, that Hispanics would integrate into the melting pot of American society just as the Irish, Polish and Italians had done before. This did not happen.

Spanish-language media is more alive today than ever, and the audience continues to grow. First, because eighteen of every one hundred births in the United States are to Hispanic women. Second, legal and undocumented immigration guarantees hundreds of thousands of new television viewers, radio listeners and readers in Spanish every year. Third, the close proximity to our countries of origin in Latin America, lower airfares, and technological advances, like the Internet and cell phones keep us in contact with our families and our roots, delaying the inevitable process of cultural integration. And last, even though the Latino community is not a homogenous bloc, speaking Spanish is a symbol of identity and pride

---

[9] David Avon, "El Voto Latino," *Foreign Affairs en Español,* Spring 2001. "[The matter of] Elián was very much related to the Cuban-American vote in Florida . . . The percentage of Latino votes rose 40% from those previously registered in 1996, reaching close to 7 million votes, 7% of the national total . . . Even though Latinos are still a political minority, this number of votes was more than ten times greater than the national margin that separated Al Gore and George W. Bush."

among all groups of Mexicans, Cubans, Puerto Ricans, and Central and South Americans.

This last point is important. Nine of every ten Hispanics speak Spanish at home. An article written by Dorothy Sharp in the May 8, 2001, edition of *USA Today* bore a title that recognized the inevitable: *"Si Usted No Habla Español Puede Quedarse Rezagado"* (If You Don't Speak Spanish You Might be Left Behind). The article revealed, ". . . speaking Spanish is becoming more of a necessity than a choice in many parts of the country." The same article points out that more people in the world speak Spanish as their first language—332 million people—compared to 322 million who speak English. (Mandarin, spoken by 885 million Chinese, is the most widely spoken maternal language in the world.)

It is also important to note that there are more and more Hispanics watching Spanish-language television. An article published in *Hispanic Trends* in August 2000 concluded that 45 percent of Latino voters preferred to listen to the news in Spanish. Ten years ago, the percentage of Latino voters who watched Spanish-language television was less than 25 percent.[10]

"It would have been unimaginable a dozen years ago: The top-rated television station in a major American city broadcasts in Spanish, Miami's WLTV, owned by the Los Angeles–based Univision network, finished first in the February ratings 'sweeps' beating out six English-language stations."[11] The phenomenon repeated itself over and over again, in Miami as well as other cities. In Los Angeles, the Univision affiliate KMEX put up billboards a few years ago in the major cities of the country that read: "L.A.'s #1 News Hour in Spanish."

Few Americans know that the fifth largest television network in the United States (after ABC, CBS, NBC and Fox) is Univision, a Spanish-language network. Many are also surprised to find out that our Spanish-

---

[10] *Hispanic Trends,* August 2000. "Forty-five percent of Latino registered voters are tuning in to Univision and Telemundo, while 49 percent watch national news on English-language stations . . . Ten years ago, the percentage of Hispanic electorate that got its news from Spanish-language television was less than 25 percent."

[11] The *Washington Post,* April 27, 1998.

language newscast has an audience that is ten times greater than the CNN program at the same time,[12] that more young people watch Univision than MTV, and that more women prefer our network to Lifetime (according to surveys by Univision).

It is not unusual, therefore, that a survey in *Hispanic* magazine in the year 2000 chose three people who worked for Univision—Henry Cisneros, Cristina Saralegui and me—for its list of the most influential new Hispanics in the United States.[13] Perhaps we are influential, but the real problem lies in transforming the power of numbers into political and economic power. It is a question of empowerment.

We are many in number, but we lack power; power in politics, in the English-language media and in the ability to secure a larger percentage of the national advertising budgets for radio and television programs and for advertisements in Spanish-language newspapers.

The census indicated that in 2000, there were 35,305,818 Latinos, slightly more than the number of African Americans, which was 34,658,190. Nevertheless, despite making up more than 12 percent of the population, Hispanics had only 19 representatives in Congress in 2001, which is equal to only 4 percent of the seats. Blacks, on the other hand, had 39 representatives in Congress. (In that same year, there was not one American governor or senator who was black or Hispanic.)

On the local level, the lack of political power is obvious. At the beginning of the century, 46 percent of the 3,700,000 inhabitants of Los Angeles were Latino, but they made up only slightly more than 20 percent of the voters in the election in which Antonio Villaraigosa could have become the first Hispanic mayor since 1872.

---

[12] The *Wall Street Journal,* Page 1, October 3, 2000. "When [Ramos] and co-anchor María Elena Salinas deliver the 6:30 evening newscast, they reach an average audience of 1,057,000 viewers in the 18-to-49 age group that advertisers prize. This is almost 10 times the audience of CNN's 'Moneyline Newshour' in the same time slot, according to Nielsen Media Research."

[13] *Hispanic Magazine,* "The Most Influential Latinos 2000" 1) Edward James Olmos 2) Henry Cisneros 3) Jorge Ramos 4) Gloria Molina 5) Ricardo Montalbán 6) Gloria Estefan 7) Bill Richardson 8) Luis Gutierrez 9) Cristina Saralegui 10) Lincoln Díaz Balart.

The Hispanics' lack of political power finds its match in English-language television programs. Only 2 percent of fictional characters on American TV are Latino. In the world of television news, things are even worse. Hispanic correspondents presented only 1.3 percent of news reported on English-language newscasts in 2000.[14]

The disparity between the population figures and the lack of political power for Hispanics and the absence of Latinos on English-language television is also reflected in the dollars spent by large companies on Spanish-language media; newspapers, magazines and radio and television stations would jump for joy if they could collect even 2 or 3 percent of the national advertising budget.[15] (In 2001, it was estimated that U.S. companies spent only $2.1 billion on advertising in Spanish.)[16]

One example in New York illustrates this disparity well. In 1997, the Univision affiliate, WXTV—Channel 41, which broadcasts in Spanish—wound up in a virtual tie in ratings for the year with WWOR, Channel 9, which broadcasts in English. However, the Spanish-language station took in only $27 million that year while the English-language station took in $155 million, almost six times more. Why did this occur if both stations had the same number of viewers? Well, according to a report in *Crain's New York Business*, "the discrepancy between ratings and revenues is a clear illustration of the latent prejudice of advertisers and their

---

[14] James Poniewozik, "What's Wrong with this Picture?" *Time*, May 28, 2001. "According to the 2000 Census, Hispanic Americans number 35 million, or 12.5% of the population, a nearly 58% jump since 1990. But on TV? A report by the advocacy group Children Now found that in prime time, the number of Hispanic characters dropped since last season from 3% to 2%. (Blacks make up 17%, the study found, Asian Americans 3% and Native Americans 0.2%; they are 12.3%, 3.6% and 0.9% of the population.) In all of prime time, Hispanics account for only 47 out of 2,251 characters. As for nonfiction TV, the Center for Media and Public Affairs found that Latino correspondents reported only 1.3% of all network evening-news stories in 2000."

[15] The *Miami Herald*, May 21, 2001. "Although Hispanics represent almost 13% of the U.S. population, only 1.5% of a company's advertising budget goes toward the Spanish-language Latino market, said James McNamura, president of Telemundo . . . The percentage is very poor in proportion to the English-language networks."

[16] The *Miami Herald*, May 21, 2000.

ad agencies, coupled with ignorance of the growing buying power of minority communities."[17]

In fact, the buying power of Hispanics in the United States—$387 billion in 1998—is greater than that of Argentina, Colombia, Chile, Peru and Venezuela.[18] In 2010, the economic purchasing power could surpass $1 trillion, but for many this is an invisible power.

Why? It is not because the programming is of poor quality. It is true that a high percentage of Spanish programming comes from outside the country, but in the late twentieth century, Univision produced more than 50 percent of its content in the United States. Shows like *Cristina* and *Sábado Gigante* can compete with any programs of their kind in any language.

The Noticiero Univision—on which I have worked since 1986 and which, since November 1993, has been under the direction of Alina Faleón as vice president of news—received an unusual number of acknowledgments for programs in Spanish. In 1996, it won the Edward R. Murrow Award (Radio and Television News Directors Association) for the best newscast, and in 1999 it won two Emmy Awards.[19] I received Columbia University's Maria Moors Cabot Award in 2001. This was such an important event that my mother was there, on her birthday, braving the possibility of another terrorist attack. This was the first time that she saw me receive a prize at a public event. It was a way of letting her know that has son was doing well.

Our newscasts tend to reflect the cultural diversity of the United States better, and they include many more international stories than

---

[17] Valerie Block and Matthew Goldstein, "Ad Bias Lingers in NY," *Crain's New York Business*, August 3–9, 1998.

[18] Hispanic Consumer Market Growth to 2010. DRI/McGraw-Hill, 1998. (Univision) A Market with Real Purchasing Power.

[19] National Academy of Television Arts and Sciences, September 1999. Two Emmy awards for outstanding instant coverage of a news story: "Tragedy in Central America," and outstanding instant coverage of a news story in a regularly scheduled newscast, "Hurricane Mitch."

English-language newscasts.[20] We report on Hispanics, immigrants, and Latin Americans like no other network. When we say we present the world in twenty-two minutes, it is more than just a slogan.

Journalists who work for English-language newscasts grumble that year after year they are losing more viewers, while journalists who work in Spanish consistently increase their television audience. The reason for this goes beyond demographics. For example, at the beginning of 2002 it was normal to see extensive coverage on the English-language newscasts about the conflict in the Middle East; Israelis and Palestinians were killing one another and there seemed to be no other alternative than war. This seemed to be the only conflict in the world. And yet, at the time there was a war going on in Colombia that English-language newscasts usually did not dedicate even one minute in coverage to. The number of those killed in Colombia often surpassed the number of dead in Israel and the Palestinian territories. Why did the American networks, such as ABC, CBS, NBC, Fox and CNN take the decision to cover the conflict in the Middle East but basically forget about the one in Colombia? Which newscast would a Latin American interested in the war in Colombia watch, ABC or Univision? The journalists who air their newscasts in English whine about their declining television audience, and one wonders why. The answer is simple.

In spite of this, both English- and Spanish-language newscasts share the same dilemma of reporting the news in a balanced and impartial manner. Of course, we all have our prejudices and ideological beliefs (although not all journalists admit it). For example, it's well known that I have always defended undocumented aliens, and that I spent years fighting the Institutional Revolutionary Party (PRI) of Mexico. At Noticiero Univision we

---

[20] America Rodríguez, *Made in the USA: The Production of the Noticiero Univision* (College of Communication, University of Texas, August 1994). "The largest difference between the two networks (ABC and Univision) is found in those sound bites categorized 'Latino': just over one percent of ABC sources (6 out of 466) were U.S. Latinos; 35 percent of Univision sound bites were of U.S. Latinos"; (page 26) "Nearly half, 45 percent, of each Noticiero Univision is about Latin America while just under two percent of ABC's World News Tonight with Peter Jennings is taken up with news of Latin America, an enormous disparity in story selection, and the most direct evidence of the distinct world views of these two U.S. television networks." (page 43)

have established a system that stops these prejudices from seeping into the newscast. For instance, and in one specific case, one of the newscast's executive producers, Rafael Tejero, would edit the stories that I wrote about Mexico, and he would edit those that I wrote about Cuba. So with journalists from Cuba, Mexico, Chile, Colombia, Venezuela, Peru and the United States—among other nationalities that can be found at Noticiero Univision—we try to counter the obvious: that every journalist has his or her personal opinion. As the number of our viewers increases, so does our credibility before the public. Our salaries, however, have not seen the same increase.

Although we are competing head-on with Rather, Jennings and Brokaw in the most important markets of the United States, our salaries are still far from the multimillions of dollars that those anchors make. Furthermore, neither our budgets nor our working conditions are comparable to those enjoyed by English-language anchors. No one is in charge of my mail nor does anyone answer my e-mails. I read every one of the dozens of letters that I receive every year from prisoners assuring me that they are innocent and pleading with me to help them get out of jail. I don't have a secretary, or an assistant, or a chauffeur or bodyguards when I go out to cover a war. Not having any of these perks prevents the fleeting fame of television from going to my head. Or so I tell myself every time I see my paycheck.

These enormous differences should gradually change as the Spanish-language networks convince advertisers that Hispanic consumers react positively when they get their news in their native language.

On a couple of occasions I've thought of working for English-language television, but inevitably two questions always come to my mind. Are the American networks ready to accept someone with an accent like mine? We know that accents like Henry Kissinger's and those of many Australians and British are acceptable, but would the accent of a Mexican immigrant be acceptable too? In early 2002, during the book tour for my first book in English, I was happy to receive several invitations from NBC, Fox, PBS and CNN, among others, to hear what I had to say about Latinos and immigrants. In these situations, my accent didn't hurt, since it went well with the topic at hand. But would it be the same if I reported the news on

Israel, changes in Social Security or if I covered political conventions? I don't know.

The second question concerns the professional conditions I've grown accustomed to. Although I am absolutely sure that I would make a lot more money, I'm not sure that I would want to constantly have to fight with the big stars of the English-language networks in order to get an interview with the president of the United States or with the most newsworthy person of the moment. Right now, just by being a representative of Latino immigrants and working at the number-one network in Spanish, access to the most influential people in the United States and throughout the Western Hemisphere is guaranteed. Furthermore, I'm lucky to be able to cover the area of the world that most interests me—Latin America—and to be able to help the immigrant segment of the population with accurate information. In my case, working in Spanish has its advantages.

Spanish-language television in the United States, which first appeared in 1961,[21] has a future that is guaranteed in the decades ahead.[22] As soon as

---

[21] Geoffrey Fox, *Hispanic Nation: The Image Machine* (New York: Birch Lane Press, Carol Publishing Group, 1996). "The first Spanish-speakers in the United States able to watch television in their own language at home were in San Antonio, where a non-Hispanic entrepreneur, René Anselmo, started transmitting in Spanish on KWEX-TV in 1961. Soon other cities were connected by satellite to Anselmo's Spanish International Network, or SIN . . . By 1976, SIN had a network of 11 'markets,' as media people call their audiences: New York, Miami, San Antonio, Corpus Christi, Los Angeles, San Francisco, Fresno, Hartford, Sacramento, Albuquerque and Phoenix. In 1987 it changed its name to Univision. The network has had a succession of owners but has continued to grow, now with over 500 affiliates and reaching over 90 percent of Hispanic households in the United States."

[22] Univision, July 12, 2001. Press release, Univision Communications Inc. (NYSE: UVN), the leading Spanish-language television broadcast company in the United States, reaches 93 percent of U.S. Hispanic households through its 18 owned and operated stations, 33 broadcast affiliates and 1.109 cable affiliates nationwide. The company's operations include UNIVISION Television Network, the most-watched Spanish-language television network in the U.S.; UNIVISION Television Group, which owns and operates 12 full-power and 7 low-power television stations, including full-power stations in 11 of the top 15 U.S. Hispanic markets; UNIVISION Online, the company's new Internet portal and ISP venture; and Galavision, the country's leading Spanish-language cable network. UNIVISION is headquartered in Los Angeles, with network operations in Miami and television stations and sales offices in major cities throughout the United States.

it manages to solve the puzzling disparity between ratings and revenue, it could threaten markets that have historically been dominated by English-language media. Its political influence—based on captive audiences of those who have recently arrived from south of the border and on the importance of Spanish to the cultural identity of the Hispanic—is more than proven.

If not, just ask George W. Bush.

ONCE UPON A TIME in California, at the beginning of the 1980s, it was almost impossible to find a politician who spoke or wanted to speak Spanish. When I worked at the Univision affiliate in Los Angeles, KMEX, our orders were to conduct the interview in Spanish if possible. When we would arrive for an interview with some member of the city council or the board of supervisors, we always asked them if they spoke Spanish or if they had a spokesperson who did. Most of the times, the answer was a resounding no. But on some occasions, while we were setting up for the interview in English, the interviewee would say to me, "I don't speak Spanish, but my driver does," or, "My daughter's baby-sitter speaks Spanish, and my daughter's learning it now."

Have things changed! Nowadays it is very difficult to get elected in certain districts in California, Florida, Texas, Illinois and New York without speaking Spanish. In the last twenty years I have noticed a substantial change: not only has the resistance to speaking Spanish disappeared, people are now proud to be able to say some words in the language of Cervantes, Borges and Fuentes. Almost all of the politicians that I used to interview who didn't speak Spanish have vanished, replaced by Hispanic politicians. In the case of some Hispanic politicians, their vocabulary may be poor, but the voters have no doubt about their backgrounds. And that generates votes. In some cases, Anglo and African American politicians are dusting off their high school Spanish textbooks.

In reality, the issue is not whether a politician speaks Spanish or not; it has to do with a politician showing interest in the Hispanic community. The identity of Hispanics is tied to their countries of origin and language. George W. Bush is the first American president to speak Spanish, or better yet, who thinks he speaks Spanish. An advisor to Spanish Prime Minister José María Aznar confided in me that Bush's Spanish is "a disaster." In a brief talk with Spanish journalists in the White House, Bush confused *"hombro"* ("shoulder") for *"hambre"* ("hunger"), while he invited them for an informal *lunch* (instead of *"almuerzo"*).

I have spoken with Bush several times and I have to pay close attention to what he wants to say. I have no doubt that he understood most of the questions that I asked him in Spanish. But of course, I asked them very slowly. Regardless of how he speaks Spanish, Bush's efforts to speak the language, no matter how grammatically incorrect or how terrible his pronunciation, had a huge political effect.

This directly affects the validity of Spanish-language media. If the mayor of a city didn't consider us worthy enough to speak to us, imagine the trouble that we had trying to get to speak to a governor or a president of the United States? We were always the last ones to speak with a politician, and we were never given more than five or ten minutes for an interview. And if we got an interview, it would usually take place after the politician asked his or her press secretary: "What's Spanish International Network? Is it a Mexican network?"

All began to change during the administration of George Bush. This coincided with the demographic explosion of Latinos in the United States and a notable increase in the number of immigrants coming from south of the border. And no doubt, the president's Texas sensibilities helped too.

In that period, every time that we entered the White House, it was a big deal. I would say to my colleagues: "Could you imagine, I'm going to interview the most powerful man in the world." I kept the picture that I later received from the White House in 1990 showing me interviewing Bush as a symbol that at last, the Spanish-language media were being taken seriously in this country.

The interesting thing about this is that at the beginning, we were the ones who exhaustively searched for presidential candidates in order to interview them. If we were lucky, they answered our phone call. But most times, they were calling us back to say no to an interview. Before they hung up, you could perfectly hear a campaign advisor say: "What the hell is

Univision?" Sometimes, the press secretaries didn't even get on the phone. Instead they would have their secretaries give us the bad news. But now the press secretaries go out looking for us.

With the exception of Bob Dole—who never wanted to give us an interview because he didn't understand the impact that the Spanish-language media would have on his campaign—all the other candidates in the last three presidential elections have asked us to interview them. But it wasn't until the last presidential campaign between George W. Bush and Al Gore that we really felt important and influential. The candidates not only made an effort to say, or mangle, some sentences in Spanish, they also wanted to make it known that they were knowledgeable and concerned about Latin American issues. For example, Gore and Bush knew that during each interview we were going to ask them about Mexico, Cuba, Puerto Rico and immigration issues. These were obligatory topics. And they were always ready to respond. Rarely did they dare stray from the memorized answers nor did they venture into making complicated analyses. It was clear that it was easier for them to talk about Israel than about Colombia. However, as a journalist, I was grateful for their willingness to be interviewed. After all, what a presidential candidate has to say about Colombia would certainly be reported on Noticiero Univision, although I'm not sure if the candidate's opinions on Israel, South Africa or the Middle East would.

I have had the chance to interview the last three American presidents, and I am still amazed by that wonderful lack of formality demonstrated by politicians in this country. In Latin America, many politicians tend to have airs of grandeur and they take on an aggressive demeanor in order to let others know that they are powerful. That is not the case here. I knew for certain that I was in the presence of men who had the destiny of millions in their hands. Nevertheless, they treated me nicely; they were even friendly.

But two things have also caught my attention during my interviews with American presidents. One of them is the huge amount of makeup that is applied to cover the bags under their eyes. On television they look rested and relaxed, but in person that type of makeup looks like a thick, impenetrable white paste. The other thing that has caught my attention is the way that once the interview begins, the candidates disconnect from the world around them, and take great care to measure every one of their words. That extraordinary ability to concentrate can be frequently found among Latin American and European leaders as well, although I must admit that I have been in the presence of several Latin American presidents who, in obviously pathetic behavior, think about other things while speaking in front of the cameras.

I never managed to leave such an impact on either George Bush or Bill Clinton that they would recall who I was in the following interview or press conference. Every time that I greeted them—months or years later—it was as if it were the first time. But that is not the case with the current president, George W. Bush. I even think he knows me by my first name. His familiarity with Hispanic culture in general gave him the job he has today.

George W. Bush is the president of the United States because he speaks a little Spanish and he supported the Cuban Americans in the case of Elián González, the six-year-old Cuban boat child who was forcibly sent back to Cuba by the Clinton administration. At least that was the argument that prevailed among many Latinos in south Florida when Bush was declared the winner in the presidential elections in a five-four decision of the Supreme Court on Tuesday, December 12, 2000, at 10 P.M. I think they were right.

Bush's slight advantage over Al Gore in Florida can clearly be attributed to the Cuban exile community. Most Latinos in the United States voted for Gore in the elections on November 7, 2000, but not the Cubans. Thanks to this, Bush carried Florida's twenty-five electoral votes, and with them, the presidency. That is the argument.

No presidential candidate in the history of the United States had ever made such an effort to speak Spanish as George W. Bush did. In the two interviews I had with Bush prior to the election, the governor of Texas and Republican candidate for president always made an effort to communicate in Spanish.

Sometimes his sentences contained serious grammatical mistakes, others combined English and Spanish, and when he found himself in a tight spot, he immediately reverted to English. His words in Spanish, however, were always enough to fill the limited space we had on the newscasts and magazine shows.

While editing those interviews we always tried to set aside his responses in English and make the most of his replies in Spanish. Therefore, the television viewer could get the impression that Bush spoke more Spanish than he really did. Were we in the Spanish media, then, the ones who involuntarily pushed Bush toward the presidency?

In the weeks prior to the election, I was interviewed on several English-language television programs. In a way that now sounds almost prophetic, I insisted that if the vote on November 7 was very close, the Hispanic vote in Florida would be the determining factor in choosing the next president. That is exactly what happened.

One of every two Latinos listens to Spanish-language news in the United States, and there are cities like Los Angeles, New York, Chicago, Houston and especially Miami where the percentage is much higher. So millions of Hispanics decided who to vote for in the 2000 elections based on what they saw on Spanish-language television. The question of just how much influence we, the journalists who report in Spanish in the United States, had in making Latinos in Florida vote for Bush still makes my head spin.

It is true that Bush made an effort to communicate with Latino voters in their own language, publicly opposed Elián's forceful return to Cuba and showed a particular sensitivity with respect to immigrants and Latinos. After all, these were not new issues for him; as governor of Texas, he was very aware of the problems caused by undocumented immigration and of what motivates someone to leave everything behind in Mexico and head North; what's more, his nieces and nephews, the children of his brother, Jeb, and Jeb's Mexican wife, Columba, are Latinos.

On one occasion during the presidential campaign, I told Bush that his nephew George P. Bush—who was helping out a great deal with the campaign—had been called a wetback and a tar baby. In Spanish he told me that the matter of racial discrimination in the United States, and in this case against a member of his own family, was *"una lástima,"* a shame. Then, he agreed with me that if something like that could occur to a Bush, what would you expect would happen to a González, a Rodríguez or a Torres.

This kind of directness and these responses with concrete references to Hispanics were absent from Gore's campaign. Gore did not speak Spanish, even though he could repeat certain phrases by heart: *"sí se puede," "p'alante, siempre p'alante," "comunidad boricua"* ("Yes we can," "Forward, always forward," "Puerto Rican Community.") Because of this his interviews had to be translated from English into Spanish, and some of the emotion and meaning is always lost in translation for television.

In a very simplistic first impression, Gore looked much stiffer than Bush. In the only interview I had with him as presidential candidate, I reminded him that in 1998 he had sung a rap song in Spanish, hoping that he would at least repeat a few lines of it on camera. Gore didn't even laugh. He opened his mouth, as if trying to laugh, and continued talking about other things.

If we add to this Gore's ambivalent position on the Elián case—and the complete identification the Cuban American community made between Gore and Clinton after the boy was snatched away from his family in Miami and turned over to his father—I haven't the slightest doubt that, at least among Hispanics in Florida, Bush was presented by the Spanish-language media as a more humane and charismatic candidate. Those votes that Gore lost in Miami for not speaking Spanish and for his attitude in the Elián case probably cost him the presidency.

When I spoke with Bush in Guanajuato, Mexico, on February 16, 2001, during his first television interview as president, I asked him if he had any problems of legitimacy in the White House. "No," he replied without hesitation, and we discussed the matter of the Hispanic vote that had sent him to Washington.

"Did you win the election because of the Cuban vote in Florida?" I asked him.

"Yes, I think they had a lot to do with it. And I'm most proud and very thankful and very grateful for the strong support I received *de los cubanos en el estado de Florida. Y por eso no voy a olvidarlos"* (from the Cubans in the State of Florida. And that's why I won't forget them).

George W. Bush, and his father, George Bush, are the kind of people who make you feel very comfortable in their presence. They repeat your name, look you in the eye and ask about your family. That is to say, they are decent, well-educated people, and it's hard to imagine them committing an act of violence. However, George W. Bush, as governor of Texas, authorized dozens of executions of criminals on death row, and his father headed an international coalition in the Persian Gulf War.

Ironically, the same enemies George Bush had—Saddam Hussein and Fidel Castro—are also enemies of George W. Bush, and their strategies with both countries are very similar. The same day that he visited the president of Mexico, Vicente Fox, at his ranch in Guanajuato, George W. ordered an air strike against Iraq. "Our mission is to make the world more peaceful. Our mission is to make a clear statement to Saddam Hussein that he shall not develop weapons of mass destruction," Bush said.

As for Cuba, Bush reaffirmed the same policy as his father. "I believe that lifting the embargo would be a mistake because it would empower Fidel Castro, and until Fidel Castro is willing to have free elections and welcome freedom, I think it's in the best interest of the United States to maintain this policy." This statement could have been made by either of the two Bushes. The father's influence on his son in foreign affairs was undeniable.

The contrast between courtesy and violence in the two Bushes has always intrigued me. For example, in the case of George W. Bush it is hard to reconcile that the same person who so kindly took a photograph with my daughter on a train during the electoral campaign in California, who choked on ice when he spoke and then roared with laughter, and who shouts "Hey, big man!" when he sees me, is the same person who started the war against terrorism in Afghanistan, who ordered an air strike against Iraq and who authorized the execution of dozens of convicts who had been sentenced to death in Texas.

That is the dilemma of all U.S. presidents. However, it's very difficult, as a journalist, to be able to read a person who is gentle on a personal level, and yet aggressive on a political one.

Both Bushes are bound by something else. George W. Bush is trying to avoid what for him would be a (political) tragedy foretold. These days, he is trying to fight off his father's ghosts. What concerns him is not how successful or not he will be with his War on Terrorism, but rather that he might share his father's political fate. George Bush won the Persian Gulf War, but he lost reelection because of economic problems. His political foes would say, "It's the economy, stupid." George W. Bush is now in a similar situation. He won the war in Afghanistan, but the recession and the rise in unemployment could derail or postpone any economic recovery before the presidential elections of 2004. And that ghost terrifies his advisors more than Osama bin Laden. And if this weren't enough, Saddam Hussein is still on the loose. It's now up to George W. to finish the job that his father didn't.

I MET GEORGE BUSH at the White House on November 29, 1990, shortly before he declared war on Iraq. We spoke about the possibility of sending American troops to Kuwait to put an end to Saddam Hussein's invasion. Bush entered the room where the interview would take place calmly, but he looked worn out. I couldn't help but look into his eyes, or rather, beneath his eyes, where he had white makeup to conceal the bags. His makeup artist, a magician in the tricks of television, knew that the white would not reflect on camera, so the bags under his eyes from long days and nights without sleep would not show.

"Is there going to be a war?" I immediately asked Bush. His response was that he still hoped to find a peaceful solution. However, by the tone of his response, it seemed that the decision to attack had been made.

"He must get out of Kuwait," Bush said. "And I think up to now, we have failed to make Saddam Hussein understand how the world feels . . . The world will prevail . . . Saddam Hussein must get this message: the rape, the plunder, the pillage of a small, neighboring nation will not stand."

A few weeks after the interview with Bush, the international coalition began an incessant air and naval attack against Iraqi military positions. After a quick and unexpected ground offensive, Bush ordered a cease-fire the morning of February 28, 1991. Iraqi troops in Kuwait had been defeated, but Saddam Hussein would remain in power, only to become a headache for George W. Bush ten years later. My interaction with another American president was a different experience all together.

I was never able to question Bill Clinton about Monica Lewinsky. I met him on four separate occasions, but the last was on October 16, 1997, a few months before the sex scandal in the Oval Office broke. The truly extraordinary thing about Clinton is his ability to divide and isolate the most important matters in his life in such a way that one does not affect the other. Psychologists call this the ability to compartmentalize. Clinton is a master.

For example, during my last encounter with Clinton—a continental teleconference transmitted from Buenos Aires, Argentina, during his South American tour—as well as in an interview at the White House with other members of the Spanish-language media, Clinton showed no indication he was facing a personal or political crisis. In fact, three days after our interview in Washington on May 5, 1996, Clinton saw Monica Lewinsky at a reception at the Saxophone Club, and they had already been involved intimately for six months. Clinton, as always, looked confident, alert and optimistic during the interview.

How did Clinton hide what was most troubling him? How did he learn to be such a good liar?

Clinton, for starters, is a master of public relations. He shakes hands, looks you in the eye, asks your name and then repeats it even though it may be difficult to pronounce. Few could resist hearing their name in the mouth of the president of the United States. If he wants to show you that he is grateful or happy to see you, he puts both hands over your hand or he squeezes your arm, near the biceps, with his left hand. I have seen him do this dozens of times. Something about this ritual struck me. Despite having seen him on four separate occasions—once as a candidate and three times as president—his manner was always distant and professional, like when you meet someone for the first time. His staff, of course, would tell him before the interview how many times he had met you. My presence obviously never made much of an impression on him.

Bill Clinton was a good student of Latin America, but I get the feeling he was never very interested in the region. It was clear from the start that his strength would be in domestic and not international politics.

I spoke with him for the first time at the Democratic Convention in New York on July 16, 1992, and his responses with respect to Mexico, Cuba and Puerto Rico—and even his pronunciation of these nations— were very hesitant. Later, as time passed, his responses ceased to be mere vague remarks and became more specific. Of course he had a lot to do with the passage of the Free Trade Agreement between Mexico, the United States and Canada, and in the enormous financial recovery of the Mexican economy in 1995, but he didn't travel south of the border until his second term as president.

Clinton, as president, was a sponge: he learned quickly and bounced back from crises. He took risks and he won. His relationship with Gennifer Flowers did not cost him the Democratic nomination for president, nor did his nine intimate encounters with Monica Lewinsky force him from the White House. One must wonder, though, what Bill Clinton was thinking when he risked so much for so little. He was an eternal adolescent. It's difficult to understand how someone so obsessed with his place in history could have oral sex in the Oval Office with a twenty-one-year-old intern. In the collection of anecdotes from the Clinton years, the economic boom experienced during his presidency will be pushed into the background.

GEORGE W. BUSH had just finished lunch. He had removed his tie long before. One of the members of the Mexican delegation offered him a cigar, which the president of the United States accepted discreetly. He looked around, as if to make sure no cameras were rolling, and he lit it. He took two deep puffs and gently exhaled the smoke. It did not look as if he disliked it, nor did it look like the first time he had smoked a good cigar.

I observed all of this from the living room of Mexican president Vicente Fox's ranch in San Cristóbal, Guanajuato, site of the first official meeting between the two presidents. I was waiting, along with a television crew from Univision, to interview Bush as soon as he had finished lunch.

The morning of February 16, 2000, had been particularly stressful for Bush. Not only had he traveled from Washington to Guanajuato on his first trip abroad as president, but just hours earlier he had ordered an air strike against Iraq. Bombs on the one hand, embraces on the other. Despite the tension, however, Bush seemed happy and relaxed.

Whatever he would say that day would become world news. Bush, of course, could have chosen one of the major English-language television networks like ABC, CBS, NBC, Fox or CNN to make his statements. He decided to grant his first television interview as president of the United States, however, to the Spanish-language network Univision, and I was chosen to interview him.

The decision to offer that interview to a Spanish-language network was not gratuitous. Bush knew that with us he could show off his incipient control of Spanish, and that the conversation would be broadcast not only in the United States but also in thirteen countries in Latin America. No English-language network could have offered him such wide coverage in the region. Nor am I sure that they would have focused the conversation—as we did—on international affairs.

It was also a matter of personal importance to me. "Not bad at all," I thought, "that this Mexican immigrant got Bush's first television interview as president, and, what's more, on such a newsworthy day." It was, without a doubt, a journalistic privilege. Any of my colleagues, whether from the English or Spanish media, would have wanted to be there.

Bush stabbed out the cigar, got up from the table and entered the living room, putting an end to my reflections. As soon as he recognized me—I had already interviewed him twice during the presidential campaign—he raised his right hand and let out his characteristic greeting, "How are you doing, big man?"

There I was, standing opposite one of the men who would change the world. An extraordinary privilege, without a doubt. But now, more than ever, it is the politician who benefits from being interviewed in Spanish.

WITHOUT ACCESS to the most powerful people in the world—like Clinton and Bush—it is very hard to do a good job as a journalist. That's why it was important to break down the resistance that existed at the White House and in both parties, Democrat and Republican, to giving access to the Spanish-language media. Of course access benefits the Spanish media, but it also benefits the politicians. I cannot imagine any candidate nowadays who thinks that he or she can win without the Hispanic vote, and you can reach the Hispanic vote through the Spanish-language media.

For the first time in the history of the United States, in March 2002, the two candidates for the Democratic nomination in the Texas governor's race—Tony Sánchez and Dan Morales—debated mostly in Spanish. The debate was broadcasts by the San Antonio affiliate of Univision, and it caused a great controversy. Isn't English the principal language of the United States? Why do you need to speak Spanish? The reality is that in a state like Texas, where one in three people are Hispanics who speak Spanish, it was absolutely necessary to debate in a language other than English. That Spanish-language debate was a political necessity. In the end, the candidate who spoke better Spanish won the election: Tony Sánchez. (Of course, the millions he spent on his campaign didn't hurt.)

But there's another lesson in that debate. My friend Sergio Muñoz, a member of the editorial board of the *Los Angeles Times,* wrote in an article: "In (Texas) there are nine Spanish television stations and 126 Spanish radio stations. This is the reality today in the state of Texas, and whoever doesn't recognize it, cannot hope to lead its future." This debate was a reflection of the other debate that is informally taking place throughout the nation.

THE MOVEMENT to make English the only official language of the United States has extended to several states. But in my opinion, "English only" and movements like it are, in the best of cases, nostalgic visions of a country that no longer exists. And in the worst cases, it seems like just plain ignorance, especially in a country where ever increasingly, more and more languages are spoken.

The attack on the Spanish language manifests itself on more than one level. It is visible in the effort to make English the official language, and the abolition of bilingual education and affirmative action programs. Furthermore, we often hear of cases where workers are fired for speaking Spanish, or of bosses who prohibit their underlings from speaking any language but English.

I can't take those people very seriously. The reality is that although there are negative consequences to their actions, they are very short-lived. Regardless of what they accomplish with their retrograde legal maneuvers, reality is much more powerful. More and more people in this country speak Spanish. As a matter of fact, in states like Texas, California and Florida, Spanish is the de facto secondary language.

There are people who believe that speaking Spanish will divide the country. I don't think this is so. If millions of people speak Spanish, it simply means that the United States is finally the multiethnic and multicultural country it has always claimed to be. I am fortunate to be able to read Shakespeare and Hemingway in English, and Cervantes and Fuentes in Spanish. What binds the United States together in not language. The most defining factor of American society has two elements: tolerance toward diversity and acceptance of immigrants. Although sometimes you still are forced to repeat the obvious: everyone in this country—with the exception of Native Americans—is an immigrant or the descendant of one.

What surprises many academics is that Latino immigrants have not totally assimilated into the prevailing linguistic environment, as the Italians, Germans and Poles previously did. On the contrary, they have preserved their mother tongue. That doesn't mean that Latinos have not entered the mainstream in other areas, such as in business and politics. The majority of Latinos that I know are bilingual, and various academic studies— including one from the University of Southern California—show that Hispanic immigrants are making more money, getting better educations and learning English quickly.

Yet we are different in one way from other groups. The majority of Latinos speak Spanish at home, and we continue to have strong ties to our countries of origin. Sometimes these ties are strictly emotional, especially in families where everyone has immigrated to the United States. In my house, we speak Spanish. Period. Paola and Nicolás only speak Spanish to me, and the phone bills for calls to Mexico, Puerto Rico and Spain are huge. But that's the type of life that we have chosen to live. Far from disappearing, these tendencies continue to grow due to the high birth rate in Hispanic families, and the enormous flow of legal and undocumented aliens who enter the United States every year.

For someone such as I, who was told in the early eighties that Spanish would practically disappear in the United States, this is a rare moment. Around thirty million people now speak Spanish in this country, and if the demographic trends hold, there may be anywhere between ninety and one hundred million Spanish speakers in fifty years in the United States. This would make it the number-two Spanish-speaking nation, second only to Mexico, and greatly surpassing Spain, Argentina and Colombia.

This reaffirms my conviction that America's survival depends on the quality of the links that hold very different groups together. I agree with the Mexican poet Octavio Paz when he says that this is the United States's true challenge.

During the tour for my first book in English, *The Other Face of America*, I had three debates with the ultraconservative former presidential candidate Pat Buchanan, who's convinced that Latino immigrants are invading the United States, and that they are destroying Western civilization and American culture. But now I understand that deep down inside, Buchanan and people like him are afraid of me and immigrants like me. Their world—white, exclusivist and domineering—is disappearing and making way for my world: mestizo, inclusive and full of external influences.

THIS IS WHY NO ONE should be surprised that Univision has created a third Spanish-language network called Telefutura, and that NBC has decided to pay more than $2 billion for Telemundo. This hasn't happened because they are well-intentioned angelic figures. Not at all. These are businesspeople who want to make money. As a leading executive at NBC told me, we are riding a *"Café* Wave" that is washing over the American media. And whoever doesn't get on board now will miss, in the near future, his chance to get his piece of the media pie. For the moment it seems that becoming more Latin, and consequently more "Hispanicized," is an unprecedented phenomenon that can't be stopped.

When we face this reality, we realize that the efforts made by those who want to make English the official language of the United States are laughable and absurd. We already have two de facto official languages: English and Spanish. No legal maneuvering can stop the *"Café* Wave." I don't also see a Balkanization or divisions arising, as some say. Neither Texas nor California has independence movements. The loyalties of millions of Hispanics are squarely behind the United States, especially after the events of September 11, 2001, and there's no reason why two languages cannot be spoken simultaneously in one country, as is the case in several European countries. The growth of Spanish in the United States is a result of an open and dynamically changing society.

I have been involved in the Spanish-language media in the United States for so long that I should be perfectly used to seeing how one by one, newscasts and radio shows in English are losing viewer- and listenership. But I have to admit that I am still a bit surprised when I check the ratings every morning and I realize that for newscasts, on any given day with no breaking news, more people watch Univision than CNN, MSNBC and Fox together.

For someone such as I, who was told to lose his Spanish accent if he wanted to work as a journalist on American television, this is divine justice. I don't need to stop speaking Spanish, and at the same time, I can compete against the best television networks in the world and enjoy the benefits of one of the most free societies that has ever existed. I have the best of both worlds.

I BELIEVE THAT the principal challenge to the contemporary journalist is staying in contact with a world that changes in astonishing ways without losing credibility.

The Mexican philosopher José Vasconcelos wrote in 1925 that, "the ulterior goal of History [is] to attain the fusion of peoples and cultures." [23] One can agree with this opinion even when the Vasconcelian idea of a cosmic race ("made with the treasure of all previous ones") has been cast aside later on, even by him.

What Vasconcelos was quite clear on, however, was that the future of humanity would be marked by the fusion and synthesis of cultures. The cultures that have fought to maintain their purity tend to commit the greatest excesses and tend to be characterized by violence, racism and discrimination. On the other hand, when a nation accepts its "multi" condition, the potential is great for that nation to invigorate ingenuity through tolerance and humanity.

The fall of the Berlin Wall in 1989 turned out to be an extraordinary analogy in a world that left behind the bipolar system of the cold war in order to enter a new era of globalization. What marks this era is the fall of traditional limits and barriers—commercial, political and cultural—and the tendency to see world problems like poverty, environmental pollution and racism, in a global way. This vision also has its disadvantages, but like it or not, it is the vision that prevails.

Never before in the history of the world have there been so many immigrants—150 million—so much tourism and so many international business agreements. Never before have communications and new technology—in telephone communications, aeronautics and digital computation—brought us so close to one another. The barriers have fallen in such a way that the well-known phrase of Marshall McLuhan that the world is a "global village" is now commonplace.

We live in a time of diversity, racial mixing and globalization. No population can survive without being able to coexist with others. Likewise, no language can survive without being subject to external influences, not even a language as strong as Spanish. Today there is no nation or language that can set its borders or pretend to live in a vacuum. The journalist who works in Spanish, then, finds himself, or rather, is immersed in a world

---

[23] José Vasconcelos, *La Raza Cósmica. The Cosmic Race.* (Baltimore, Md.: The Johns Hopkins University Press. Bilingual Edition, 1997).

where change is constant and where cultural, linguistic and racial diversity is the norm.

Globalization naturally has its equivalent in journalism. Just as democracy has spread worldwide and the opening of markets is an international phenomenon, journalists are also seeing many barriers disappear. With each barrier or border that disappears, two or more worlds converge. That is what is new to modern journalism: convergences and mixtures.

There used to be a clear differentiation between national and international news. Not anymore. Before, journalists worked for a single medium. Not anymore. Before, journalism was clearly separated from entertainment and from the concerns over profits in the media. Not anymore. Before, one language was enough to report the news. Not anymore. Spanish has no choice but to adapt to these convergences. English does too. The mixture, fusions, the fall of walls and barriers, necessitates enormous attention and openness to make sure that the language we use is effective and communicative.

Journalists of this new era of convergences must adapt in order to succeed. That is, however, not only a challenge professionally, but one that may raise the bar for how humans treat each other.

THREE | GOING GLOBAL

WAR AND LOVE

I do not feel, nor will I ever feel,
like a cold recorder of what I hear and see.
In every professional experience I leave a piece
of my soul.

—ORIANA FALLACI (INTERVIEW WITH HISTORY)

The most powerful and important moments of my personal life have always coincided with wars. In my personal experience, love, pain and war have almost always been tied to one another. It may have something to do with the intensity that love and war both have. Yet one builds and the other destroys. Or maybe wars make me so vulnerable that my feelings begin to flow (before, during and after the war) more than they do otherwise.

Before leaving to cover a war, I always call my mother and siblings, one by one, to let them know that I am leaving. But I try not to sound as though I were saying good-bye. I have never covered a war fearing that I would never return. Of course, when I call them, I don't tell them anything about my predeparture routine, such as careful reading my life insurance policies and will, and the inevitable call to the bank to make sure that there's enough money in the account just in case of an emergency. But of all the phone calls that I make, the most difficult one is to my brother Gerardo. He and I have a very close relationship full of emotions, but very short on words. Even before I tell him that I'm off to cover a war, I can tell by his voice that he knows, and that a couple of tears are already rolling down his cheeks. He always tells me: "Póte, be really careful. Remember that you have a family waiting for you." And then we hang up right away so that we don't burst into tears. The first thing that I do when I return to American soil is call Gerardo. Of all my siblings, he is probably the most sensitive, and the one who hides his feelings the most. Perhaps that's the way we Ramos Avalos are.

It's true. I do tend to repress my feelings. This is not only due to some personality disorder caused by my profession—I am convinced that no one hired me to cry in public or to give my wise opinions on a televised newscast—since I've always repressed my feelings. People tend to use the same traits that are useful over and over, so being able to suppress my feelings has worked for me when I have set a professional goal for myself. Unfortunately, we can't turn the "feelings switch" on and off. So on many occasions, when I've tried my best to feel at ease, impulsive and glad, it just hasn't worked. Sometimes I would like to dance, jump and have fun without regard to what those around me might think. But I must confess, it would be very hard for me to do. I'm not the type that loosens up easily. I am usually in control of things. Rarely do I lose my grasp of the situation at hand.

Perhaps the intense fear that I feel when I have to go off to cover a war puts me in touch with my emotions, opening doors and windows that I usually keep under lock and key. Perhaps I think that the danger in a war zone is like that shot of adrenaline that one feels when really in love. Perhaps I'm a little crazy to think that in a war I can discover the best in others and me. But the truth is that in the four wars that I have covered—two of them after making strictly personal decisions—I have felt more alert and alive than ever. Maybe I've been expecting—like a soldier returning from war—to finally come home and never leave again.

For example, in Afghanistan, I felt the greatest fear of death ever. It seemed to me that a couple of more days there would be deadly for me.

In Macedonia, fear and uncertainty made way for other burning feelings. In the days surrounding my coverage of the war in Kosovo, I got in touch with my feelings of true love, understanding and human solidarity, all of which felt totally new to me, and I fear that I may never feel again. This saddens me greatly. Sometimes I even think that the war in Kosovo brought out something in me I will never catch a glimpse of. Emotionally, I touched the sky.

After the Persian Gulf War, I met my wife, Lisa, in circumstances that seemed like a scene right out of a movie. Before going to off to cover a battle in El Salvador, Paoli's mother, Gina, and I had decided to separate. The four conflicts that I have covered—Afghanistan, Kosovo, the Persian Gulf and El Salvador—have not only been professional challenges, they have been really personal ones as well.

Before going to cover my first war in El Salvador, my home life was collapsing. During the previous Christmas, Gina and I had decided to separate. I asked her to wait until I returned from El Salvador before she left with our daughter, Paoli, for Madrid. And she did.

From the beginning of our relationship, Gina and I had our problems. Geography was the first one. Gina wanted to return to live in Madrid, while I had my life in California. After living in Miami for a while, Univision's newscast moved to Los Angeles, and from there, to Laguna Nigel. I felt more comfortable in California than in Florida. California was more familiar to me; I understood it better. But for Gina, the panoramic mountain views and the laid-back California lifestyle only made her more nostalgic for the crowded and intense city life that she was missing out on in Spain.

Apart from the geographical differences, there were the emotional gaps. It hurt when we realized we didn't want the same things from life, and we started to plan things separately. Finally, during a very somber Christmas in Mexico, we realized that we should put an end to us as a couple. After two years of fruitless efforts, we had no other alternative but to separate. We cried a lot. And I mean a lot.

Now the question was what to do with Paola. I couldn't even think of living without my daughter. Nevertheless, it would have been inconceivable that she could have stayed with me in California instead of leaving with her mother for Spain. I had no other solution but to travel often to Spain and to communicate with her, the most I could, through the mail and by telephone. Like old friends who are resigned to their fate, Gina and I planned the details of her departure upon my return from El Salvador.

EL SALVADOR: MY FIRST WAR

El Salvador, March 1989. "I don't want to die. I don't want to die. It's too soon to die," I kept thinking. Bullets were flying close, and I didn't know if the metal roof we were hiding under was going to withstand the machine-gun fire from the helicopters. It wasn't seven in the morning, and I was scrambling to save my life.

If we hadn't found a shack on the roadside we'd be done for. I was terribly scared. I wasn't sure when the firing would stop. I was so scared, I pressed my body as flat against the wall as I could. My head, my shoulders, my butt, my calves, the heels of my feet, everything was flush against the wall. I wasn't even sure if the thin walls would stop the incoming bullets. We stormed through the door of the house without knocking, and the *señora* who lived there was still in bed.

I felt like we were going to leave there like colanders. I began to laugh. I didn't know why I was laughing. The wall probably won't stop a thing. I hoped the army realized that the guerrillas they were after had gone the other way. The bullets hitting the metal roof made a terrifying sound.

"Where did Sandra and Gilberto go?" I asked.

"I don't know. When the shooting started they took off running, and I haven't seen them since."

Poor Sandrita. What a bang I gave her head. When we heard the first shots we both threw ourselves on the floor of the van, and I smacked her head. I thought she was dead because she wasn't moving. I really thought a bullet had hit her. Then, when she began to move, I was relieved to see there was no blood on her face. But there was no time for apologies. We were still being fired upon, and if we didn't get out of the van they would make mincemeat out of us. I was too scared to move. My legs wouldn't budge.

This is what I remember of a Sunday morning in March 1989 in El

Salvador. The foul language that came out, with no censorship or social control. After all, in a time of crisis like that, I was hardly worried about what I said. There I was, with Sandra Thomas, the Mexican producer, and Gilberto Hume, the Peruvian cameraman, covering the presidential elections.

We reached the neighborhood of San Ramón on the outskirts of San Salvador, and while the driver was driving down a dirt road, the *rat-a-tat* of machine-gun fire caught us by surprise. Gilberto instinctively grabbed his camera, told the driver to stop, opened the door and took off running in the direction of the gunfire.

"Where are you going?" I shouted after Gilberto. "You're crazy!"

Shouting was no use. I don't think Gilberto heard me. That absurd feeling of invulnerability that some journalists feel when they put a camera on their shoulder has always intrigued me. Many cameramen whom I know, however, say that taking a risk to get the perfect shot is part of their job. It's correct that without video there is no story. That morning, Gilberto wanted to film whoever was shooting.

As we watched Gilberto run off, we realized that the white van, now stopped, was caught between the crossfire between soldiers of the Salvadoran army and guerrillas of the Frente Farabundo Martí de Liberación Nacional (FMLN) dressed as civilians. All of a sudden I heard a second round of machine-gun fire, and Sandra and I threw ourselves onto the floor of the van. It was then that I banged my head against hers. (Hours later, in the sanctuary of the hotel, Sandra would tell me that at first she didn't know if the pain in her head was from a bullet or something else. That's why she remained so still on the floor of the van.)

The gunfire continued, now with even greater intensity. "Let's get out of here," I said to Sandra. The driver was not behind the wheel anymore, and Sandra and I ran from the van, each going our own way. That's when I lost track of her.

Endless bursts of machine-gun fire from the rebels and soldiers could be heard all around me. I found the driver and we ran for protection, around the corner of a narrow street, but all of a sudden two helicopters from the Salvadoran army appeared, probably called to back up the soldiers on the ground. The noise was becoming more and more intense, and we watched as the helicopters bore down on us.

"Put your arms up," the driver said to me, "so they realize we aren't armed." In the confusion, I did what he told me, but the helicopters, instead of looking for their target, began to fire at us. Scared to death, we lowered our arms and ducked inside a shabby little house with a metal roof whose door was ajar. A woman was still in bed. She stared at us, but neither she nor her husband, who was standing next to the bed, said a word. What must they have thought? That we were guerrillas or that, like them, we were just afraid of the gunfire and in search of refuge?

At the same time, I had a lot of questions. Why were they shooting at us from the helicopter? Why us, who had nothing to do with this? Then it dawned on me that we were dressed just like the guerrillas (we were wearing jeans and T-shirts), and that from above it was impossible for the soldiers who were shooting from the helicopters to distinguish who was a rebel and who wasn't.

I knew how the young guerrillas that I had met on a previous trip felt, when airplanes and helicopters attacked them in the mountains in the interior of El Salvador. They were twelve- or thirteen-year-old boys, maybe even younger, who learned how to use guns and weapons as if they were toys. But in the game of war, the one who loses dies. I met the *"muchachos"*—as the villagers euphemistically called the guerrillas—at a shooting practice in a dense wooded area. The path to the forest was infested with antipersonnel mines, and thanks to a peasant we found out where to walk without getting our legs blown off.

The trip, with its bullets and shrapnel raining down on the little house where we had run for shelter, was certainly memorable. I was facing death without having done anything to deserve it. Never in my life have I been so afraid; I was paralyzed. I was stuck to the wall of the hut the entire time the air attack lasted, about twenty minutes. My muscles were tight as rocks and my mind ran with just one plea: I don't want to die. A good prayer might have helped me, but I couldn't think of any that would calm me down.

Finally, the circling of the helicopters began to subside, and they began to disappear into the horizon. "Thank you," I whispered to the owners of the house, and I ran back to the van. I found Gilberto there, and we tried to do a stand-up before the helicopters disappeared from the camera's lens. I was unable to speak properly; I was shaking, and my teeth were chattering. I tried several times, unsuccessfully, to briefly describe to the camera what had happened. When I was finally able to string enough words together to complete a paragraph, though, the helicopters were very far away, and they looked like harmless green mosquitoes. That is the only visual testimony I have of that moment. The guerrillas escaped, and a soldier died in the attack. Gilberto, unflappable, filmed him just seconds after he had taken a bullet in the chest.

That Sunday was the day of the presidential election in El Salvador, but the voting was marred by violence. When I returned to the hotel, exhausted, pale and with bags under my eyes, I found out that three journalists—two foreign correspondents and a Salvadoran—had been killed that day. One of them—a European cameraman—took a shot in the head when one of the soldiers or guerrillas mistook his television camera for a bazooka. Gilberto could have met the same fate.

Now I knew that animal fear that soldiers experience in war. That almost imperceptible but uncontrollable vibration that generates panic in the chest, mouth and hands did not leave my body until I got on a plane to return home.

SEPARATION AND PAOLA

The other war broke out in California. I knew that Gina and my daughter, Paola, were leaving to live in Madrid for good, but I still hadn't faced the reality. Under the circumstances, Gina and I tried to be as civil as possible to one another, and I even helped her prepare for the trip. After months of planning, it was time to say good-bye.

It all hurt so much that I remember the whole experience as if it were yesterday. I drove them from our home in Mission Viejo to Los Angeles International Airport. While we were waiting for the flight, Paola—who was only two years old at the time and had no idea where she was going—began to play next to the windows by the gate, all while the plane stood motionless on the runway, revving its engines.

Paoli laughed so innocently and happily that I was moved to tears. I used the last moments before she got onto the plane to play with her and hold her tight against my chest. I said to her: "I'll see you soon. I love you a lot." And when I turned to Gina to bid her farewell, I said something to her that we both still remember: "I hope you find what you're looking for in Madrid."

I was free again . . . but without Paoli. During the first months of our separation, I was zombielike. I would work all day in the newsroom, and when I got home, I would collapse in bed, and then as if I were hypnotized, I would lie there watching television until I would fall asleep. Amanda, Paola's nanny, who stayed working with me even after my daughter left, would talk on the phone with my mom in Mexico, and tell her that she was worried about me, since I was barely talking and the only thing I did was watch television. I guess it was a way of escaping. Instead of constantly crying over being so far away from my daughter, I emotionally disconnected so that the pain wouldn't paralyze me. On weekends I would play soccer, and then I would spend hours laying on a couch, reading the newspaper and waiting for the right time to call Paoli. After we spoke, I would sadly take a stroll through Ralph's supermarket, the closest one to my house. Now I understand how truly sad it was to look at me, alone and rudderless, walking down the aisles of a cold supermarket.

I lived in California, but I was homeless. Without my daughter, my yearning for a home turned to a lonely despair.

I made sure to keep in touch with Paola as much as possible, so that in spite of the distance between us, she would always be aware of who her father was. I called her every week, even when she didn't know how to talk yet. I would send her packages with presents and sweets, and I made sure that no more than three or four months would pass without me seeing her. Of course, I felt terribly guilty for having done something that would make her life so difficult.

The start was extraordinarily difficult, since we were all out of control.

I always kept Paola's room in my house impeccable, as if she slept there every night. I wanted her to feel a sense of stability that didn't exist. We finally managed to coordinate a system where Paola spent her summers, Christmas and Holy Week vacations in the United States with me. We still use this system. It's become routine, and it works well because we all know what to expect.

To this I must add the constant traveling that I did, and continue to do, to Madrid, and how superb it is to count on my amazing daughter to be my travel companion. Before she was ten years old, Paola had flown more times than most people fly in a lifetime. Although most of the times that she travels she does so because she has to, what she has learned from traveling—patience, openness, respect for diversity, the importance of prioritizing and the ability to fend for oneself—she practices perfectly. She is a very mature teenager. She is more considerate, polite and responsible than most fifteen-year-olds.

I never wanted to be an absentee or long-distance father. Therefore, the approximately four months a year that I spend with her are very intense. When I'm with Paola I feel like father *and* mother. Our talks, fun times, shopping and other activities that we can't do together during the year we condense into just a few weeks. So apart from our natural bonds, we have made an extra effort to enjoy every moment that we spend together. What has resulted from all of this is a unique father/daughter relationship. Whoever knows us knows that our relationship isn't typical. For years my relatives and friends used to complain that when I was with Paola, it was as if I had fallen off the face of the earth. That may be so. She is my priority, and nothing else is. Nothing else is more important to me than my daughter.

I have always been alert to and have tried to counter any negative result that Gina's and my separation has had on Paola. I think that we have compensated twofold. She has two parents who immeasurably love her, she has homes on either side of the Atlantic and she has two very different ways of seeing the world. Gina and I now get along better than when we lived together. We successfully sidestepped years of Paola's sweet attempts to get us back together. She once told me that when her mother and I were old, she was going to have us both live in the same house with her, but each with his and her own room.

In reality, Paola saved me. My separation from her has been, without a doubt, one of the most painful experiences in my life. It would not have been strange for me to distance myself emotionally from her in order to control that pain. But the exact opposite occurred with Paola: I am particularly bound to her, and I love her with all of my soul. My friend Edlin Ortiz, who left journalism for a spiritual life, used to tell me that everyone has someone who keeps us in touch with our feelings and spirits. That someone for me is Paola.

Apparently Paola is condemned to be a writer. Her mother writes, her maternal grandfather, Carlos Alberto, writes and her father writes. As a matter of fact, Paola wrote her first newspaper article when she was thirteen for the *Miami Herald* (I later included it in my book *A la caza del león* [*Hunting the Lion*]). Paola writes with the same smoothness, intellect and power that she uses to play basketball. She writes as she speaks, with excellent insight and emotional cleverness, always conscious of fine points and wit. I wouldn't be surprised at all if in a few years she will be telling a word processing program how she was marked by her parents' separation. The only thing that hurts me is if I unwillingly caused her harm by not doing more to rescue my relationship with her mother. But I think that Paola understands. She probably understands better than her mother or me.

The most difficult moments are still when we say good-bye in the airport. We hug, we remind one another of our mutual love—"I love you, Paoli," "I love you Dad"—and that we will see one another again very, very soon. But very rarely have we been able to control our tears. Whoever is looking at us would think that we would never see one another again.

When I return home after leaving her at the airport on her way to Madrid—I do it at least three times a year—I always used to find a note from her hidden underneath my pillow. But recently, instead of short notes on the bed, I find loving e-mails waiting for me on the computer. I think that Paola is the only person who can make me cry. That's how well she knows me. Every time I see her I recall that two-year-old girl playing by the windows of the Los Angeles airport, who innocently and full of love and trust, was smiling at me without having any idea how her future would change once she stepped on the plane.

RUFINA

I can't—I just can't—imagine what the pain of a father or a mother must be like being there at the moment that one of his or her children is murdered. I just can't think about it. Without a doubt, it must be one of the worst nightmares that any parent can have. And even worse, I couldn't think of not doing anything if one of my children were in danger. That's why Rufina's story touches me so deeply. And I still don't totally understand it.

I returned to El Salvador a few years after the end of the war. But the ghosts of violence that the Central American nation lived through still haunt Rufina.

Rufina had no last name. Everyone knew her only as Rufina. She is one of two survivors of the worst massacre carried out during the twelve-year civil war in El Salvador. (The other survivor was a boy known to all as Chepito.)

From the air El Mozote is not much more than an unpaved dusty brown speck with a bunch of shacks. In El Salvador's history, however, El Mozote is a large red stain.

On December 11, 1981, suspicious that the residents of El Mozote were helping the rebels of the Frente Farabundo Martí de Liberación Nacional, soldiers of the Atlacatl battalion stormed the town. They massacred more than six hundred people there, including babies, children, adolescents, pregnant women and the elderly. When the soldiers withdrew after their killing orgy, they thought they had left no survivors or witnesses behind, but they were mistaken. They didn't see Rufina, a thirty-eight-year-old mother of four who was hiding, shaking with fear, behind an apple tree.

"I am famous for my suffering," Rufina said to me when I went to El Mozote to interview her in March 1999. She had lost the ability to smile long before. She doesn't look you in the eye; she looks at the ground or up at the sky, as if asking for refuge. Her hair was almost completely gray, her hands full of calluses from working in the fields and her shiny purple dress, which she wore on important occasions, had been sewn in the middle to hide a missing button.

Rufina's real tragedy is that she witnessed the deaths of her four children and even today, two decades after the massacre, she still wonders if she did the right thing by hiding or if she should had come out of her hiding place to try to defend them. When I met her, she took me to the place where she had hidden, and there she began to recall how the soldiers of the Atlacatl battalion began the process of separating the townspeople.

"Did they separate the men and the women?" I asked her.

"Yes, they separated the men and the women . . . I was with my four children."

"How old were they?"

"The eldest was nine."

"What was his name?"

"José Cristino, María Dolores was five, Marta Lilian was three, and María Isabel was only eight months; I was holding her in my arms."

"What happened to your children?"

"They killed them . . . I had my baby girl in my arms, and the other three children were clinging to me. Two soldiers came and took them away from me. They snatched my baby girl out of my arms."

"Did they take all four children at once?"

"Yes, they took them all at once."

"What did you do?"

"I cried for my children and asked God to help me, since He is the one who can perform miracles."

There was no miracle. The soldiers had lined the women up and taken them from the town square to a small ranch to kill them. Rufina was the last in line, and in a moment of desperation she knelt down to ask God to save her and her children. In the middle of the chaos created by the screams of the women and children who were being killed, the soldiers were careless. Taking advantage of the confusion, Rufina, crawled off to hide behind an apple tree. Her refuge, however, soon became her torture, for from there she could hear her children's screams for help.

"The soldiers never realized you were there?" I asked.

"No," she replied. "If they had realized, they would have killed me. I tried to leave when I heard the screams of my children: 'Mamita, they're killing us. Mamita, they're sticking a knife into us.' "

"Your children said that?"

"Yes, my children said, 'Rufina they're killing us.' I couldn't bear hearing my children screaming, saying, 'They're killing us with knives.' I couldn't bear being there and I said, 'My God, what should I do when I hear my children screaming?' "

If Rufina had come out of her hiding place to try to defend her children, she would certainly have been killed like the rest of the inhabitants of El Mozote. Motionless, frozen by fear, Rufina made a promise to God. "If you save me, I am going to tell what happened here."

Rufina stayed hidden from five o'clock in the afternoon the day of the massacre until one o'clock in the morning the next day, when the soldiers finally withdrew. "We're done killing old people," she heard them say before they left.

Rufina kept her promise. She was saved, and thanks to her, we know what happened during one of the worst moments in the civil war in El Salvador. The pain, however, weighs so heavily on her that she drags it like an ox drags a plow.

Sometimes, she admitted, she loses the strength and the will to remember and to talk. She knows, though, that that is the deal she made with God; that until the day she dies she will remember and tell about what happened that December 11, 1981, El Mozote.

But I don't know how Rufina can keep living like that. I don't know where she gets the strength. I just don't know.

THE JOURNALIST AND HIS FAMILY

When Iván Manzano was about to accept a job with Univision as a cameraman in El Salvador, he came to me with a concern.

"What's wrong, Iván?" I asked. "Aren't you happy with the offer?"

"Sure," he said, "but just take a look around."

"What's the problem?" I asked him again.

"Everyone is either separated or divorced, and I don't want to end up like that."

Iván did not give up on us, though. After many years as a cameraman, today he works as a correspondent for Telemundo in San Salvador, and he is happily married. His concern, however, was a valid one.

Very few people with whom I work are still married to their first spouse, and we are no different from other journalists. The ones who suffer most in a journalist's life are his family members. Journalism is not a part-time profession. Covering the news is pure slavery. You can miss important information, an exclusive interview or the key to an investigation in the blink of an eye. We are constantly on the alert, as if nothing else matters, and sometimes, the price we pay is too high.

There are mornings when I get up without knowing if that night I will be sleeping somewhere thousands of miles away or in an airplane crossing the Atlantic. Journalists can be like kites, always drifting with the wind after a story. For us, naturally, this is extremely exciting. It is, in the words of Oriana Fallaci, a true privilege to witness history.

Journalists get high on news; adrenaline flows and fatigue disappears. We love new stories, and when an especially interesting story comes to an end, we are like bloodhounds searching for our next adventure. Who can resist a life like that? The pace can be dizzying, exhausting, but journalists never sleep better than after having sent a report off for publication or after going on air with a particularly difficult story. I had my best night's sleep in a hotel that had recently been destroyed by Iraqi soldiers.

Journalism is a passion that is nourished on the outside but that consumes you on the inside. You can live journalism day and night, and it's impossible to disengage. When I go on vacation, it takes several days before I can control the urge to read a newspaper or turn on the television to watch the news.

There is an old ritual journalists have of getting together in the evening, wherever the news is taking place, in the bar of a trendy hotel. Those conversations, full of exaggerations, alcohol, laughter and camaraderie, tend to recharge our batteries and our convictions. After comparing notes, I can honestly say that I have one of the best jobs in the world.

I believe, however, that there are few families that can survive intact the constant coming and going of a passionate journalist. "It's my job," is the most common explanation for the frequent absences at Christmas, birthdays and school plays. Maybe we should say, "It's my life." There are times when the demands of the job are so great that, combined with the fierce competition among the media, everything else becomes temporarily secondary, and there is no couple that can put up with that for very long.

I am no exception. I'm on my second mariage, and I know that many times I have put it to the test because of work matters. It's interesting how many reporters I know can live without their families but who could not live without journalism. I admit that at times we lose sight of our priorities.

My children saved me from falling into the claws of journalism, for it is a profession that demands complete loyalty. After the birth of my daughter, Paola, and years later the birth of Nicolás, I understood that there is a world where there are no deadlines or news sources, and where you don't have to compete with anyone to be a success. That world, far from the frenzied world of journalism, introduced me to Nicolás and Paola.

For many years I was doing two newscasts, one at 6:30 P.M. and the other at 11:30 P.M. That ate up my entire day. When negotiating my last contract, however, I decided to give up the late-night newscast despite a good offer to continue doing it. It wasn't worth sacrificing the childhood and adolescence of my children for a half-hour newscast. At another time, when I was just starting out, I wouldn't have hesitated to take on new responsibility. Not anymore.

Marriages are not made of gum. They can tolerate a lot, but not all the time. No matter how understanding the spouses of journalists are, it's still very difficult for them to accept a life of absences, sudden trips, beepers and deadlines; unless, of course, they too are journalists.

THE PERSIAN GULF WAR

Persian Gulf, February/March 1991. The military plane—a C-130 from the Saudi Arabian army—took a sharp turn in the air and began to lose altitude. You could hear a collective, agonizing "ahhhh" from the more than one hundred passengers. Most were Saudi soldiers, reinforced with Egyptian recruits, who were going to the battlefront in Dhahran, in eastern Saudi Arabia. The question now, however, was whether we would ever arrive.

Three journalists from Univision were on board—the American producer, Marilyn Straus, the Salvadoran cameraman, Iván Manzano, and me, as correspondent. There was also a group of twenty women and children confined to the front of the C-130. When we left Jidda, Marilyn was sitting next to Iván and me on a long, uncomfortable wooden bench that ran from one side of the plane to the other. There were no seat belts. We were tied to the wall of the aircraft in a web of green belts. When we stopped in Taif, near the holy site of Mecca, however, the Egyptian soldiers boarded the plane, and one of them sent Marilyn to the front with the other women. So as not to get into a discussion about the cultural differences between East and West, she got up and went.

The rude soldier turned out to be an air force pilot from Egypt. He didn't apologize to us for having sent Marilyn to the front, but he did want to talk. He spoke English fairly well, and he wanted to tell me about how great the C-130 was. "These are warhorses," I remember him telling me. His conviction about how great the aircraft was, however, vanished half an hour after we had left Taif for Dhahran. When the plane made a sharp U-turn in the air and we felt our stomachs in our mouths, the once courageous pilot turned pale. Nervously, he looked from side to side, and then he began to speak to himself in Arabic, uttering some type of prayer.

"What's going on?" I asked him. "Are we going to crash?" He did not respond and just kept on praying.

The cargo plane had tiny windows in the front part of the fuselage, so it was impossible to tell from where I was sitting how far we were from the ground. The only thing I could see was sky and more sky as the pilot did all he could to get control of the plane. It was terrifying; the cargo section was very dark, the airplane lost and gained altitude sharply, flying erratically. There was obviously something wrong. A deafening noise, like that of a giant blender, dulled the noise of the passengers' cries, with the exception of our cameraman, Iván Manzano.

Iván didn't speak English, so when we took off he had put on some headphones to listen to Celia Cruz on his portable radio. The plane's violent movements must have made him uncomfortable, but not enough to take off his headphones and ask what was going on. Celia Cruz's music was more powerful than fear.

All of a sudden I saw Marilyn. She looked scared and I thought she was coming to sit with us, in search of emotional support. Instead, she took a camera out of her bag. "I'm going to take the last photo of your life," she said with a smile that didn't convince anyone. She took my picture and returned to her seat with the other women.

My travel companion, the Egyptian pilot, did not even object to Marilyn's presence. He was too upset, too nervous. He got up and made his way as best he could to the cockpit. He disappeared for a few seconds. When he had returned to his seat I asked him again, "What's going on?" but he avoided my eyes, grabbing on to the wooden bench. So now he doesn't speak English? I thought.

People react very strangely when they're afraid. The Egyptian pilot became speechless, Marilyn starting taking photographs and I began to take notes.

Right now I am flying from Jidda to Taif on a military plane. I'm scared to death. I am definitely more afraid of these military transport planes than I am of Saddam Hussein's soldiers . . . Sometimes this profession turns into a game of suicide. It's about taking it to the limit, seeing how far you can get. Nevertheless, we quickly forget about the risks, we think we are indestructible, and this is when we make mistakes. The thing that keeps me strong and gives me the will to live is Paoli, my darling daughter, who of course does not understand what her father is mixed up in. I just looked at some photographs of her that I brought with me. I feel like crying when I see them. I would love to see her. Just thinking about her gives me the strength to go forward. The sun is coming through the windows of the plane. It's her.

I was hoping that these notes, which were almost unintelligible because of the turbulence, were not my last, when I felt a tremendous jolt under my feet. Everyone looked around, terrified. A few seconds later we realized that the plane had landed. The doors opened and we got out. We weren't in Dhahran, as we had expected, but rather we had returned to Jidda, our starting point. Once again, back where we began.

The pilot had requested an emergency landing, and he preferred to return to Jidda where there would be spare parts. Some mechanics went over to the plane's left engine and began to work on it. I suppose that was the engine that had failed. No matter whom I asked, no one was able to explain what had happened.

After a long while the repair was completed and we again boarded the same giant mixer. I had no choice. The logical thing would have been not to get back on and to look for another means of transportation, but a different logic operates in wartime. Besides, I was a journalist, and it would have been very difficult to explain to my bosses that I wasn't going to have a story that night because I was afraid to get back on a plane that almost crashed. Due to my nerves, my stomach was growling like a broken pipe. I climbed back onto the damned aircraft and this time the Egyptian pilot who was once again seated in front of me did not tell me that the C-130s were wonderful warhorses. The spell had been broken

WE ARRIVED IN DHAHRAN without further mishaps. Still in Saudi Arabia, relatively far from the battlefield, we were safe, or at least we thought so. As soon as we checked into the hotel, I went to my room and was getting ready to take a bath—to try and wash off the remnants of fear that still lingered inside of me—when the lights went out and an alarm went off. I knew what that meant; it was the first thing we were told when we checked in. Some Iraqi Scud missiles had been fired in the direction of the hotel, and we had to run as fast as we could to the shelter located in the basement. Again, terrified, I ran down the hallway and didn't stop until I realized that I only had a small white towel wrapped around my waist. Other correspondents who had already been there several days seemed to take the alarm more calmly, or at least they had taken the time to get dressed. "What am I doing?" I thought. "Should I go to the basement like this or return to the room to put some clothes on?" The embarrassment was worse than the fear, and I returned to the room, put on a T-shirt and jeans, and flew out of the room again.

It was a false alarm.

The surprises didn't end there. I returned to my room and discovered a huge bouquet of red roses. "How strange!" I muttered. "It must be expensive to get roses like these in the middle of the desert and in the midst of a war." Then I remembered that when we checked in, Marilyn had told me that it would be better if I stayed in the room that had been reserved in her name and that she stay in the one reserved for me. I didn't think anything of it and agreed. The roses, then, were for Marilyn, but who could have sent them? There was no card.

I soon had the answer. There was a knock on my door, and there were the two bodyguards of a man called Mohamed, a high-ranking government official from Saudi Arabia. "Where is Marilyn?" they asked me in an English that I could barely understand. "I have no idea," I told them, playing dumb. They stepped into my room and looked around, and when they were convinced she was not hiding in the closet or under the bed they left, visibly annoyed.

Later Marilyn told me what had happened. It turned out that the man called Mohamed had gotten the visas for us to enter Saudi Arabia. At that time it was almost impossible, but Marilyn was able to arrange the visas thanks to contacts that she had developed on a previous trip to the region. Who knows what Marilyn might have promised Mohamed so that he would give us the visas? Marilyn is one of the best producers with whom I have ever worked; she never fails at an assignment. Now, however, Mohamed wanted to collect on his little favor. The roses, obviously, had not worked. Marilyn had no choice but to spend two or three nights sleeping on the sofa in the hotel lobby so that Mohamed would not appear in her room with another bouquet of roses.

The only thing that saved Marilyn from Mohamed was the defeat of Saddam Hussein after the ground attack by the United States and its military coalition. The morning of February 28, 1991, U.S. Pres. George Bush announced a cease-fire. The Iraqi troops had been defeated, and they were in full retreat from Kuwait. The invasion of Kuwait—which had begun on August 2, 1990, and which had led to U.S. military participation—and the war, were behind us. Our work as journalists, however, was just beginning.

That morning we joined a caravan of foreign correspondents who were heading for Kuwait. We crossed Saudi Arabia to the demolished town of Khafji—where the only ground battle of the war had taken place—and we began to follow several military vehicles of the coalition that were headed to the capital, Al-Kuwait. I drove a good part of the way, and I have never followed the tracks of another vehicle more carefully; the Kuwaiti roads were filled with mines laid by the Iraqis, and we were in danger of being blown to pieces if we strayed from the marks. Therefore, no one drove more than twenty or twenty-five miles per hour.

When we were about halfway there it was still morning, but the sky had been growing dark. It was now completely black. I feared the worst, that Saddam Hussein, in a desperate act, had exploded a nuclear bomb. At that time no one had complete knowledge of the weapons that the Iraqi leader had in his possession. The temperature dropped considerably, and someone in the caravan mentioned the words *nuclear winter*. A little while later, we would find out that Saddam's troops, before fleeing, had set fire to more than five hundred oil wells. That was what was blocking the sun's rays and causing the temperature fall.

It was nighttime when we reached Al-Kuwait. A map of the city allowed us to orient ourselves and to head for the coast. A few Kuwaitis, surprised and dazed, were wandering the streets. We asked where the U.S. Embassy was, and instead we stumbled across the International Hotel. Its interior looked like a movie set. A few reporters, like us, and soldiers from the coalition had taken over the hotel rooms and transformed them into offices. *ABC News, CNN, British Army* . . . were written on pieces of paper, the ink still wet, and hung on the doors.

The reception area was empty. There was no manager, no employees. Strewn papers covered the marble flooring, and ceilings leaked because of broken pipes. Iraqi soldiers had occupied the hotel, and when they left they made sure they destroyed everything that was in their way. There was no electricity, and the badly damaged rooms smelled of sweat. There were paintings and nightstands on the ground that had been used as firewood to provide heat. We had to use flashlights and candles in order to see.

On one floor I ran into one of the anonymous heroes of the war. After almost seven months of Iraqi occupation, a Kuwaiti employee of the hotel told me how he had hid a Filipino friend in a closet in one of the rooms. Despite not having seen daylight for a long time, she was smiling. I must have been one of the first people she saw after coming out of her hiding place. She had survived. She was a Filipino Anne Frank. Elated, she offered me a small package that contained some fruit juice—for lack of champagne. Someone who was not quite as lucky was a Palestinian friend of the hotel employee who had been discovered. Iraqi soldiers immediately pulled him from the room, and arrested him; no one ever found out what happened to him.

After recovering from the shock of hearing the horror stories of the Iraqi invasion, I got to work. It was the first day of freedom in Kuwait, and I had to send a report to Miami as soon as possible so it could be broadcast on the Noticiero Univision. The problem was how to do it. The few telephones that worked were under military control, and there were long lines of journalists pleading to use them.

We had a report with exclusive testimonies and images of the liberation of Kuwait, and it was very frustrating to not be able to send it via satellite. Reports are often like fresh meat; if they aren't consumed immediately, they risk going bad. Besides, the best report is useless if it stays locked up inside a television camera. That was our position—on the other side of the world and with no chance of getting our story to anyone—when Marilyn, with her characteristic ingenuity, convinced our primary competitor then—CNN en Español—to send our report via satellite to the United States. (Later I would find out that that favor cost us nine thousand dollars, but no one ever complained; on a news day like that, any cost is justified.)

After a long journey that included an airplane that almost crashed, Mohamed's roses and bodyguards, a dangerous mine-filled road to

Al-Kuwait, a cold day that turned into night due to the smoke from hundreds of burning oil wells and a television report that almost didn't see the light of day, we were finally able to think about getting some rest.

Iván had stayed with the other Univision team that was covering the war, which was composed of the correspondent, Guillermo Descalzi, and Gilberto Hume, who was now a producer. Marilyn, cameraman José Pérez and I got in the car we had rented (which had once been white but was now an oily black because of the smoke stains from the oil wells) and we set out to look for a hotel. "The Holiday Inn near the airport is the only one in the entire city that has water," said one of the journalists who helped us send the report that night. We wanted to have a bath, and we weren't prepared to seek shelter in the ruined and foul-smelling International Hotel.

It was two-thirty in the morning, and we were lost in the city. We were immediately stopped by an urban commando from the Kuwaiti resistance, composed of Kuwaiti citizens who carried out attacks against Iraqi soldiers during the occupation. They were the law after the Iraqis fled and the coalition soldiers were taking control. One of them came over to us and pointed a machine gun at my chest. "ID," he said in English. Marilyn and José, more tired than fearful, showed them their journalists' identification, but I couldn't find mine. "Shit, I can't find it," I said out loud. "I can't find it," I repeated. I got no sign of sympathy in return. "ID," he said again. With my left index finger I pushed the barrel of the machine gun to the side. It swung right back, aimed straight at my heart. Despite the freezing air, my hands and forehead began to sweat profusely. In my desperation I offered a bag of chocolate kisses that I found among my papers to the boy who was aiming at me. I had brought them in case I was faced with extreme hunger. He shook his head no. "Damn it, where is it?" Finally, after what seemed like an eternity, I found my passport and my Univision ID. They let us pass.

Marilyn and José never noticed my distress. They could only see my back since they were sitting in the back seat. "What's going on?" they asked me calmly. "Nothing, nothing," I replied. The beads of sweat ran down my face, my hands had saturated the steering wheel, and my shirt, underneath my jacket, was soaked. As if that were not enough, we got a flat tire before we got to the hotel, and we had to change it, shivering in the cold.

The Holiday Inn must have been a good hotel before the Iraqis set fire to it. Two people in the lobby, who never identified themselves, asked us for $150 each. We didn't ask questions. We gave them the money, asked for the room keys and disappeared. In the candlelight I noticed a fine layer of soot on the rug, the bed and in the bathroom. I turned the water on. It came gushing out, ice-cold. I washed my face, leaving my features marked on the white towel, and I got into bed, fully dressed. That night I didn't even have the energy to dream.

"THANK YOU, THANK YOU," the Kuwaitis who had gathered in an impromptu parade on the highway that runs along the seafront of Al-Kuwait said to me the next day. Friday, March 1, 1991. The "thank you, thank yous" were accompanied by the sound of horns honking and guns being shot into the air. Men and children were kissing me, thinking that I was American. In their minds, the U.S. war effort had expelled the Iraqis from their country.

It was their first moment of recreation in seven months. A donkey, with a photograph of Saddam Hussein over its face, was taking lashes right and left. It wasn't all happiness though. A group of women dressed in black marched in silence. Each one was dragging her loss; some had been raped, others were widowed or looking for their children. Adael, a boy not more than eighteen, who was with his mother in the procession, told me how the Iraqis had taken his father from their home by force, and they didn't know what had happened to him. They assumed the worst. Henad, who was just as young as Adael, told me how his uncle was killed in front of his house, and that for three days the Iraqis prevented them from moving him. Whoever violated their orders would also be killed.

The procession took place in front of a beach in Al-Kuwait that was full of trenches, barbed wire, mines and antiaircraft artillery. The Iraqis thought, mistakenly, that the coalition's ground offensive would be carried out on the beach, and they had prepared to resist. The attack surprised them from the rear, and they were forced to flee, terrified.

Thousands of Iraqis, with cars and trucks loaded with jewels, works of art, clothing, money and anything else that would fit, tried to flee on the highway that led to Al-Mutla on the final day of the war. They didn't get very far. We went to see the so-called "highway of death" that very afternoon, and I was stunned.

Coalition planes had taken great pleasure in smashing the Iraqi army vehicles to pieces. There were ten kilometers of utter destruction: tanks that had flipped over and been smashed to pieces, burned-out trucks, weapons on the ground, demolished cars, mutilated bodies, all signaling chaos, a veritable cemetery. It seems that when the Iraqi soldiers knew they were trapped, they abandoned the tanks and Jeeps and fled. Many were captured or executed later, but others died right there. As a morbid souvenir, Marilyn and José picked up a dozen knives of the defeated. I didn't have the energy.

The following day we went to look for the dead and the survivors of the invasion.

"Look, look," the head of the morgue at the Al-Sabah hospital in the Kuwaiti capital said to me. He was pointing to the signs of torture on the Kuwaitis who had been killed by Iraqi forces during the final hours of the war. One of them had taken a bullet to the head: another's face had been burned. The one that shocked me most had had his eyes torn out and his tongue cut out. That was the punishment for those who collaborated with groups resisting the Iraqi invasion. Apparently the same executioner was responsible for these three Kuwaitis, for he had used a knife to carve his name in the victims' skin.

"Look, look," the morbid doctor said, enjoying our disgust. The smell of death permeated my clothes so much that later on I had no choice but to throw them out.

Off to the side of the Kuwaiti victims was a pile of bodies, fifteen maybe. Those were the Iraqis. Their bodies and legs formed a strange kind of purple octopus. None wore shoes, but almost all had a replica of Saddam Hussein's characteristic mustache. The doctors at the morgue paid no attention to them.

At a hospital nearby, a different kind of tragedy awaited us. "This ten-year-old girl," said Dr. Hishan al-Nisef, "saw Iraqi soldiers kill her four-teen- and seventeen-year-old siblings. She'll probably never be able to re-cuperate psychologically from the trauma."

Dr. Mariam al Ragem, head nurse at the Al-Sabah hospital, told me how one of her employees was forced to get into a car with an Iraqi soldier. She appeared hours later in the desert, beaten and raped. For me, that woman became of symbol of what the Kuwaiti people had endured during the Iraqi invasion. They survived, yes, but their honor would never be re-covered.

The plane coming from Jidda had just arrived. It was eight o'clock in the morning in New York, and the automatic doors at Kennedy Airport opened onto the street. A cool, rejuvenating breeze came in. I stepped outside, closed my eyes and took a deep breath. I felt the sun on my face and stood, just like that, immobile. "How great to be alive," I thought, "just great."

This was the first time in my life that upon landing on American soil I felt like I was home. Even if it meant that I had only arrived at the airport of such a busy city as New York. I felt the same way when I returned from the war in El Salvador: the fear of death morphed into a desire to live life at its fullest. At that moment, I couldn't imagine falling in love, although the conditions were perfect for it to happen.

LISA AFTER THE WAR

I met Lisa a few days after returning from the Persian Gulf War. Our rela-tionship blossomed in a series of wonderful coincidences. We met at a Univision anniversary party in Miami. She worked for an advertising agency in New York, but she had come to south Florida to go to the party and the Calle Ocho carnival.

When she saw me from far away at the party, Lisa told her boss: "There's the father of my children." He laughed, but she didn't. She was serious. We hadn't met yet, but we soon began to stare at one another. As I got closer to her, Lisa became nervous. She was afraid that her big-mouthed boss had told me about the "father of her children" comment. But I didn't hear about that comment until long after we were engaged.

Asking questions had become an occupational hazard that affected my personal life. So often instead of having a conversation, I just asked questions. Now I realize that I made many people uncomfortable since they felt that they were being interrogated. I guess it was a defense mechanism. That way, I knew all about other people without having to say anything about myself. But Lisa noticed right away what I was doing. "Stop asking me so many questions, and tell me something about yourself." We didn't stop talking all night.

That night I cancelled a date that I had, and I took Lisa for a spin around the city. I noticed that something special was happening because I didn't feel tired, although I had just returned from the Persian Gulf War. Lisa is always very honest, so she told me that she had a boyfriend, and that she was just about to be engaged and move to Boston. "Please don't get married," I told her, surprising even myself by how inappropriate I was. "Give me a little bit of time." And she did. We spent all of Sunday together. All of it.

The following weekend I went to see her in New York. There's where we clashed. We suddenly realized that although we barely knew one another, we were already seriously talking about a life together. We left her apartment and went to a bar to get some air. Lisa said to me: *Vamos a darnos un palito,*" and I started laughing. In Puerto Rico that may mean, "Let's have a drink," but in Mexico, that same expression carries such sexual connotations, that the accepted offer would end in a horizontal position.

Well, I still don't know what happened. It could have been fatigue from the Persian Gulf War or the effect of strong feelings. What did take place is that after two or three sips of a margarita, I got so tipsy that I could barely walk, and my words would get stuck in my throat. Lisa, who was well trained by her father in holding her liquor—he worked for the Bacardí Corporation—was laughing her head off. I was at my most vulnerable. I couldn't hold any liquor. Unfortunately, the serious and in-control image that I show on television fell apart. Thanks to that incident, Lisa and I were able to reconnect.

I remember sending her a card thanking her for some of the best days in my life. That sadness that followed me for years after separating from my daughter, Paola, was finally beginning to lift.

Without thinking it over much, we decided to vacation in Greece and Turkey. I bought the tickets at the now-defunct Pan Am, and off we went to JFK Airport in New York. We did everything in such a rush, that Lisa didn't even check if her passport was valid. When we got to the counter, one of the airline employees noticed that the passport had expired, and told us that Lisa couldn't travel. It was Friday afternoon, and there was no way of getting another passport. But I wasn't going to give up a week in Europe with Lisa over a stupid expired passport.

We got back in line, and we did such a good job confusing another airline employee that he didn't notice that the passport had expired. We got on the plane and celebrated with a glass of champagne. During our layover in Frankfurt, Germany, Lisa got a new emergency passport at the American Consulate. Case closed.

The trip really confirmed that we were not wrong. After visiting mosques for a few days in Turkey, we had an intensely romantic time in a hotel room built in a naturally formed cave of Santorini with a splendid view of the island's volcano, drinking a light and cool white wine. This sealed our relationship for good.

If there's one picture that captures the best of our relationship, it would be the one that we have of both of us, in a small seaside open-air restaurant, caressing one another under the table, and happy as larks. This picture occupies a very special place in our home.

After we returned, every time I would go see her in New York, she would play an old cassette recording of ocean waves, and then we would hug tightly, close our eyes in front of a window and make believe that we were back in Santorini.

DESPITE THE DISTANCE, our relationship was possible thanks to airplanes and telephones and because we loved each other so much. Lisa was living in New York and I was in Miami, and after a year we decided it would be more practical and economical to be in the same city. There have been few times in my life when I have been happier than during those first few months when my relationship with Lisa was developing. Everything seemed new, exciting and fun to me. I was revived.

Lisa did away with my fear of such an impressive city as New York. When I would I arrive to see her, I felt liberated and without any fear. It was that same sense of freedom that I felt when I first came to live in the United States. And then when she moved with me to Miami, we both missed New York as if we had lived there our whole lives.

The wedding, nevertheless, was disrupted by hurricane-force winds. We got married in San Juan, Puerto Rico, one day before hurricane Andrew devastated south Florida on August 24, 1992. It was one of the worst natural disasters in U.S. history. My friends, almost all journalists, had to leave before the religious ceremony so they could catch the last flight out to Miami and report on the arrival of the hurricane on U.S. territory. Again, journalism interfered in our personal lives. The only reason I didn't have to return was that I was getting married, but if that had not been the case, I'm sure that Guillermo Martínez—my friend and news director at the time who had given me some of the most important lessons in journalism—would have ordered me to cover the hurricane.

It's no secret that it wasn't the type of wedding that I wanted. I would've preferred to skip the religious ceremony, and elope with Lisa to Greece or the Caribbean, or to have gotten married in a small ceremony at home with our relatives and close friends. After a great deal of objections on my behalf, to the point of putting our relationship in danger, I understood that a big wedding—in San Juan Cathedral with dozens of guests that I didn't even know—was important for Lisa and her family. And so it was.

THE HURRICANE DID NOT ruin our honeymoon on the island of St. Martin in the Caribbean. However, my father had a heart attack, and Lisa and I had to return to San Juan a couple of days after the wedding.

It's not easy to be married to a journalist, which is why I remember one of the nicest moments of our relationship—besides the birth of our son, Nicolás—when she ran part of the New York City Marathon with me.

Among my obsessions in life was running the 42,125 meters or 26.2 miles in the New York City Marathon. I finally registered to run it in 1997, but I wasn't in very good shape.

A few minutes after the start of the race I noticed sharp pains in both knees—which were a little worn out from training—and with only twelve kilometers left to the finish line I couldn't bend my knees. I was walking at this point, not running. It was then that Lisa showed up. She wasn't even wearing sneakers, but she accompanied me, giving me encouragement until I crossed the finish line. It took me six hours, fifty-six minutes and seven seconds, probably one of the worst times ever recorded at the New York City Marathon. I finished number 27,841, but I didn't care. I had finished the marathon, and Lisa had shown me how deeply she loved me.

I admit that I'm not easy to live with. I am strongly opinionated, I am extremely independent and I am obsessively organized. Lisa laughs at me when I make my "orga-bags," which are perfectly organized bags or boxes full of important papers. I pay my bills punctually every week. Far from being a bothersome worry, paying my bills this way frees my mind to think about other things.

I make sure to answer all of my correspondence before going home. That way, I begin each day without carryovers from the previous day. I only have necessary objects on my desk, and it bothers me when someone leaves a fingerprint on my computer screen when he or she is pointing at something. Patsy Loris, my producer friend, says that I am "a man without a past," since I don't leave any trace of where I've been nor of what I have done. For years, when I left on vacation, I would take home the most important things on my desk, as if I were never to return.

I don't wear any rings, chains or anything that could bother me. I still don't wear a watch. I don't like knowing at all moments what time it is. Nevertheless, my typically Mexican lack of punctuality—arriving thirty to forty-five minutes late to all occasions—would nowadays be very problematic. I don't like to waste time, and I'm always in a hurry, like my friend Félix Sordo. And every time that I travel, I know all the ways of getting out of the place that I am traveling to. Before arriving I already know how to leave, and I know the availability of flights with such accuracy that I sometimes put even the most experienced travel agent on the spot. Just to be annoying, no doubt.

I don't keep anything. What ever I don't like, even if it's valuable, I throw it out or I give it away. I rarely admit that I'm wrong, and although I don't believe in astrology, my horoscope sign, Pisces—with its two fish swimming in opposite directions—reflects my many contradictions: I love spontaneity although I can be very inflexible in my way of thinking. I feel like a rebel but I have a very traditional lifestyle, and I am a public figure who's terribly bored with social obligations and get-togethers. And now, at this stage of my life, Lisa has had to take all of this.

Talking about food, the weather, cars, motorcycles, computers and other machines that I find unintelligible is terribly boring to me. My gift to myself on my fortieth birthday was to try not to do anything that I don't want to. Since then, I have been very successful at avoiding having to go to weddings, christenings, award ceremonies, lunch and dinner appointments, chamber of commerce breakfasts, medical conventions, or having to be on entertainment shows or interviewed for magazines. Most of all, I've been able to avoid events where the "TV Guy" is the star attraction.

My sense of freedom can be unbearable. Once Lisa gave me a kayak for two so that we could kayak together down the Coral Gables canals, but I exchanged it for a kayak built for one. Deep down, I wanted an escape mechanism, a few moments of solitude. I know that this incident makes me look bad, and talks volumes about her sense of generosity.

Lisa is the one who has surely had to withstand countless inconveniences and frustrations: dates broken by breaking news or emergencies, nights without sleeping while I'm off covering a war, and not being able to make any significant plans. Everything can change with one newsworthy event. Sometimes I really don't know how she can stand me.

But the worst must be when I retreat into my cave. My biggest weakness is my distancing, that occasional lack of interest in establishing contact. There is nothing worse than not recognizing the presence of others. That's why, more and more, I admire my mother's ability to pay attention to everybody, even in the most difficult or tension-filled moments. I still can't learn from her example.

There are long periods of time—for instance, when I am writing a book or after returning from a particularly difficult trip—when I am absent and distant. It's true that I dedicate a lot of time to projects that have nothing to do with work in television. But rarely can I free myself from the newscast. Lisa has no doubt that I am a workaholic.

My excuse is that I do what I please, and they pay me well for doing it. But this almost childish attitude is not exactly the most convenient way of maintaining a stable and committed relationship. I know that it's not. Nevertheless, Lisa has withstood it all and makes an enormous effort to keep our paths of communication open.

And of course, she was right, and very perceptive, when she saw me that evening and said, "There's the father of my children." What made her so sure that we would end up married, without even knowing me? It's due to that hunch, which would be too difficult to explain in a rational manner or in words, that we're together.

Our son, Nicolás, has kept me young, and has become my great daily joy. I laugh with him, play with him and pay more attention to him than I do to those who think that they're important. This is all thanks to Nicolás. I have been able to experience him on a daily basis, something that I was never able to do with Paola.

There's something wonderfully comforting about waking a child, still warm from bed, to give him breakfast and later take him to school. And nothing compares to a pair of little arms wrapping themselves around your neck, right before saying: "Good night, Papá." What I was missing in life was seeing a baby's hair grow and its babbling becoming first words. I have enjoyed Paola by fits and starts, which may have been intense and rich, but they've had painful pauses. On the other hand, I have not stopped seeing Nicolás since he was born, except for when I have been away on business. I've also kept a diary of the funniest phrases he's said.

I'm always on Nicolás's trail, and thanks to that, I have recouped a little bit of my sense of direction in life. Wherever Nicolás and Paola are, together, that is home.

THE CHILDREN OF KOSOVO

When I arrived at the Kosovo war refugee camps in Macedonia, I was grateful that my children were not there. Nicolás had just turned one, and Paola was a thirteen-year-old teenager. I saw hundreds of minors, some of them orphaned, others lost, others injured, all of them living through a tragedy.

While I was there, I couldn't stop thinking of my children. And what if they had been born in Kosovo? And what if the Serbs had killed their father, mother or both? What would Nicolás do, on an unknown street, without even being able to say his last name? How would we have found him? And what if one of those bastards had wanted to rape my daughter? What would I have done? How could she defend herself with a gun to her head?

I saw my children in every Albanian Kosovar child that I encountered. In every single one. And so I wouldn't forget it, before I left for Macedonia, on the first part of my video camera, I recorded Nicolás playing with my suitcase. Every night, when I returned to my hotel room, I would play the video with Nicolás. And when I did so, I felt embraced. Fortunately, my world was not the one that I was covering.

SKOPJE, MACEDONIA, APRIL 1999. "Free, free, set them free . . ." sang the vocalist of the Wild Bunch Band at the top of his lungs. The Sting song held up well despite the peculiar accent of the Macedonian singer. After all, the Wild Bunch Band was one of the best groups in Skopje. If they weren't, they would never have been invited to play at the Marakana Club, the trendiest spot in the city. It was so trendy, in fact, that the discotheque had a unisex bathroom, just like the one made famous on the now-canceled American television series *Ally McBeal*. A waitress, who was selling shots of tequila, was having a hard time trying not to spill her tray of imported drinks onto the young people dressed in black. It was just like any trendy bar in London or New York; the place was packed.

When the band took a break, I asked the singer if it was hard to play in a disco when you could hear NATO planes on war missions overhead. "We're at war, but not tonight," he said. "We have to have fun." The con-

trast was fascinating. That same afternoon I witnessed NATO planes attacking zones controlled by the Serbian army in Kosovo, and hours later I
was being passed shots of Mexican tequila to the music of Sting in the
background.

The young Macedonians didn't seem to have any moral conflicts about
having a good time in the middle of a war. I spent my first night in Skopje
to the rhythm of "burn, baby, burn . . ." Sanco, my guide, thought it
appropriate to take me to the Coliseum Club, a discotheque that had two
levels, "so I could see how young Macedonians felt with respect to the
war." I wasn't really able to talk much, though, over the sets of American
music from the eighties.

The girls in their Wonderbras and the young boys with their heads
practically shaven who had packed into the disco were clear indications of
the cultural globalization that had crossed the Macedonian borders long
before. The most popular television program in Macedonia was a
Venezuelan soap opera, *Cassandra*. It was so popular that not even Pres.
Gupcho Georgievski dared interrupt the show; he would wait until it was
over to give his speeches on the war. It was also common to hear songs in
Spanish on the radio by Thalia *(". . . amor a la mexicana . . ."),* the
Colombian Carlos Vives and Cuban Celia Cruz. A couple dancing on top
of a table brought me back to Macedonia.

"Welcome to the war," I thought.

I HAD ENDED UP in Macedonia because I'm stubborn. Some of my bosses
at Univision thought that the war in Kosovo was of no interest to the Hispanic community in the United States. I didn't agree, but I couldn't force
them to send me. So I withdrew money from the bank, bought an airplane
ticket and asked for two weeks' vacation to go to the war. Alone. On
my own.

How could I remain seated, comfortably, at my desk in Miami with the
twentieth century coming to an end while one of the worst cases of racism
and ethnic discrimination since the end of World War II was taking place
in Europe? The Albanian Kosovar refugees fleeing Serbian violence gave
me a serious case of journalist's itch.

My friends and family thought it was crazy to take vacation time to risk dying in a war. The frustration, however, of seeing the main story of the moment from so far away and out of reach got the best of me. Neither Serbia nor Albania would give me a visa. Macedonia did. I would not be reporting for television, but I would report for the radio and the newspapers. I equipped myself with a notebook, camera and video camera, and I left.

I traveled to Athens—the airport in Skopje was closed—and I headed north by car. When I got to the border between Greece and Macedonia, an immigration officer got right to the point. "You're not a terrorist, are you?" he asked me. It was probably the first Mexican passport he had ever checked. Before I could respond, the officer let out a cry, "Ah, Pancho Villa," and he began to laugh and let me by. I still don't understand what's so funny about the name Pancho Villa, but thanks to the laughter the Mexican revolutionary provoked, I was able to enter Macedonia and reach the border with Kosovo.

The war was just a few kilometers away. You could easily see military airplanes and the columns of smoke caused by the bombing. The consequences of the war were in plain view. Macedonia, which had become independent in 1991, was receiving almost half of all Albanian refugees coming from Kosovo.

The expansionist desires of the Serbs were no secret. Under the orders of leader Slobodan Milosevic, a military commando had demolished the small Kosovar town of Racak on January 15, 1999. Forty-five bodies, including women and children, were found scattered in the streets and yards of Racak. That was the first sign. In order to stop Milosevic, it would be necessary to act quickly and without hesitation. The United States, however, was preoccupied elsewhere.

At that time, the U.S. Congress was trying Pres. Bill Clinton for lying and obstruction of justice in the Monica Lewinsky case. Kosovo was too far away. It wasn't until after February 12, 1999—when they were unable to get two-thirds of the Senate votes required to remove Clinton from office—when the United States really began to worry about the fate of the Kosovar refugees. After the failed peace talks in Rambouillet, outside of

Paris, Clinton ordered the first air strikes on Wednesday, March 24. Monica Lewinsky was left behind. NATO bombing, however, only intensified the defiant attitude of Slobodan Milosevic's army.

Every day thousands of Albanian Kosovar refugees were crossing the border into Macedonia, filled with horror stories. I saw them arrive with their bundles and their suitcases. Some had only what they were wearing: the lost look, dragging feet, the sweater or jacket soaked from the rain and the muddy shoes. The Macedonian authorities would wait until there were one hundred or two hundred and then they would direct them to some tents for a couple of days, so they could recover physically from the journey, before sending them on to refugee camps in Stenkovec or Blace.

In the refugee camps in Macedonia, the first thing I noticed were the children. Children, children, children everywhere. I had no choice but to listen to their stories. They were children of war, the real innocent victims.

Yolanda, a Spanish woman who was working for the Red Cross, was in charge of tracking the children lost during the war. "Today there are about eight hundred parents searching for their children," she told me without much emotion, accustomed to this type of human tragedy. "At the same time there are about four hundred children looking for their families."

"Jehona Aliu, five years old, Urosevac." I found Jehona's name on the list of more than a thousand lost children that the Red Cross had in the refugee camp in Stenkovec. Jehona was living in tent number D-289. I caught her by surprise, playing with other children in the middle of the canvas tents that NATO had provided for the hundreds of thousands of Albanian Kosovar refugees. She stared at me with her big brown eyes. Her hair was very short, and her ears were too big for her slender face. She laughed easily.

The only thing the Red Cross knew about Jehona was that one night Serbian soldiers had entered the Kosovar town of Urosevac at gunpoint and taken the Alieu family from its home. Apparently, shortly after crossing the border into Macedonia. Jehona was separated from her parents, and she was found by a group of British soldiers.

We spoke a little, but the communication process was complicated. Jehona only spoke Albanian, and an adult was translating her words into

Macedonian. Sosa, my translator, would then translate them into English. I didn't need to speak Albanian, though, to understand the anguish in her eyes. They shouted, "I'm lost, help me."

Jehona lived in the same tent as Xhavit, a thirty-four-year-old man who looked ten years older than that. Xhavit was also forced by the Serbs to leave his house in Vucitrn. He lifted his two-year-old and his three-year-old, Agon and Ardin, onto the wooden cart driven by his neighbors, "so they would be more comfortable," he recalls. He and his wife would go ahead of the cart in their tractor. At an intersection, however, while still in Kosovo, Serbian soldiers forced Xhavit and his wife to keep moving straight ahead, and the neighbors — with Xhavit's children on board — to turn off down another road. Neither Xhavit nor his wife dared complain to the Serbian soldiers. The slightest provocation and they would be killed.

When I saw them in the refugee camp, both Xhavit and his wife were emotionally devastated. Their only comfort was to take care of Jehona until she could find her parents, and until they could find their children.

There were stories like these everywhere that touched me very deeply. But this wasn't the only one. Julia Dangond, a born adventurer, who I have admired for years for her gusto for life, told me with tenderness and feeling how her experiences in the Albanian refugee camps had forced her to give more meaning and intensity to everything that she does. "We only have one life," she would say, with that sparkle in the eyes of someone who has dared to go her own way. Although born in Santa Marta, Colombia, Julia has the gift of feeling at home in any part of the world, and with people from the most varied backgrounds imaginable. Julia's experiences are intertwined with mine.

While I complain about not having a place I call home, these people at the refugee camps in Macedonia not only did not have a home but, also, did not have a future. Like Lumnie, Blero and Fatos.

Lumnie Feta, an eighteen-year-old girl, had to take care of five siblings: Samer, Mustafa, Imer, Nebi and Feribe. They had been living in Penu with their parents. It's a small town that doesn't even appear on most maps. In early 1999, the Fetas were forced to immigrate to the city of Podujevo, and there the parents were separated from the children. The children—four girls and two boys—walked alone for more than one hundred kilometers until they reached the border with Macedonia. They were living in tent C-114 in Stenkovec, and they were the attraction of all visitors and journalists. "Party of six," they would say, recalling the television program *Party of Five,* in which five children lived alone, without their parents.

Blero's story was very distinct: he escaped death. Literally. His only crime was being young—twenty-four—and an Albanian Kosovar. When his family was forced from their home in Urosevac, south of the capital Pristina, Blero left for the mountains. Serbian boys of his age entered the army as soldiers. Albanians, however, were killed; it was easier to get rid of them before they were trained in guerrilla tactics. Blero spent two weeks hiding from the Serbian soldiers. He didn't eat, but thanks to the constant rain, he had water. I met him in the Blace refugee camp, just a few minutes after he had crossed the border of Kosovo into Macedonia. "If they had found me, I'd be dead," he told me. "It's like Vietnam." The first thing this former student of the University of Pristina did was get hold of a cellular telephone; he wanted to find out if his parents and four siblings were alive. The voice on the telephone was unable to give him an answer, and when I asked him what he was going to do, he just looked off to the north, toward the mountains of Kosovo.

Sometimes more common stories, unlike Blero's, are more touching and, at the same time, brutal. That is why I remember Fatos. Fatos couldn't stop urinating. Since the Serbian soldiers had forced their way into his house in Podgraje, no medicine had been able to control this nine-year-old boy's incontinence. What more, he had diarrhea, maybe because of his nerves. His parents were desperate, so they took him to see the doctors of Doctors Without Borders in one of the refugee camps in Macedonia. One of the doctors, instead of giving him medicine, sat him down to draw. His father thought it was ridiculous, but he didn't dare complain. I met Fatos during his second appointment with the doctor who had prescribed drawing instead of medicine, and the change was notable. I couldn't help but look at his pants, and they were dry. Then I looked at his face and he was smiling. He had a drawing in his right hand, which he showed me, proudly. It was a simple house with two walls and two windows very close to the roof. There were no doors or windows in the lower part of the house. You didn't have to be a psychologist to understand. Fatos saw the Serbian soldiers coming from a window on the first floor of his house in Podgraje, and they forced their way in through the front door and destroyed his world. In the house that Fatos had drawn, no one would be able either to come in or leave.

Hundreds or maybe thousands of Albanian children who crossed from Kosovo into Macedonia received the same therapy as Fatos. At first glance, the drawings were not very different from those I had seen in classrooms in other countries; bright colors, green gardens, smiling suns and sleeping moons. When you looked more closely, however, other things jumped out: a soldier shooting, a child thrown to the floor, a house on fire and bombs, many bombs, exploding. Abbreviations, indecipherable but familiar to these children, also jumped out in the drawings: NATO, USA, UCK (Ushtria Clirimtare and Kosoves, or the rebel Army for the Liberation of Kosovo). These, after all, were not just any children; they were children of war.

"Some are very sad when they arrive, they can't smile," Yoav, one of the Israeli volunteers who was coordinating the children's activities, told me.

"How do you realize that these children are carrying the trauma of war inside them?" I asked him.

"It's very easy," he replied. "They touch you a lot."

Before I left the camp in Stenkovec, Ardiana, a six-year-old girl, approached me. The interpreter had remained behind, and I was left, looking into Ardiana's eyes. My stare did not frighten her. She just stood there, like a little soldier with her arms hanging straight down at her sides, smiling. She was curious about my video camera, and I handed it to her. Like any little girl her age would do, she began to play with it and to touch the different buttons. Ardiana, her parents, four siblings, two uncles and her paternal grandparents, had been living in Pale. For six days they were at the railroad station in Pristina, until an old train car brought them to the southern border. Despite Ardiana's long journey, she still trusted a stranger and had the energy to smile and to play. We made a connection without even saying a word. I saw my daughter, Paola, in her eyes. I took a photo of Ardiana that I later put in my office.

"Is that your daughter?" I've been asked.

If they only knew. Somehow, I took my children with me to that war. For days I couldn't avoid the questions: "What if Paola was Ardiana? What would Nicolas had done, lost in the street of Kosovo . . . ? "

On my last night in Macedonia, my guide, Sanco, wanted to leave me with a good taste in my mouth, and so he took me to have dinner at Urania, which was supposed to be the best restaurant in Skopje. Three violinists softened the atmosphere. They even ventured to play "Las Mañanitas," a song that in my native Mexico is dedicated to those celebrating birthdays. "That's a Mexican song," I told Sanco. "Of course it's not," he said. "It's an old Macedonian song."

The moment was completely surreal. As I was having dinner with Sanco, his wife and a group of journalists, accompanied by violins and red wine, the Serbs carried on with their brutal campaign of ethnic cleansing in Kosovo, NATO airplanes continued to bomb Serbian positions and just a few kilometers from the restaurant, Ardiana and Fatos and Blero and Lumnie and Jehona and Xhavit were cold and hungry in their tents. The contrast was too much for me. I excused myself for a minute and went to the bathroom. When I returned to the table, dessert was being served.

GROUND ZERO

On September 11, 2001, four commercial airliners—two from American Airlines and two from
United Airlines—were hijacked in the northeast by
nineteen Muslim fundamentalist terrorists. Two of
them were crashed into the twin towers of the World
Trade Center in New York, one was flown into the
Pentagon in Virginia, and the other, after a struggle
between passengers and hijackers, crashed in a field
in Pennsylvania. Thousands died. Never before had
the United States lost so many people in one single
day. It was the worst terrorist attack in history, and
the only one on U.S. soil since the Civil War, with the
exception of Pearl Harbor in 1941.

Everything changed that morning. The United
States declared war, a few days later the stock market
plummeted (signaling a recession) and the confidence of the only military and economic superpower
as an invulnerable nation vanished. The United
States had been hit. Our lives would never be the
same.

WE HAD GOTTEN UP LATE that morning, and Nicolás
was happy. Just days before, my son had begun
school, and he was starting to get over the fear of

spending a few hours away from his parents. Every time I would take him to school, he would point his little finger up toward the sky and say. "Look, Papá, that's my flag." That morning, the thirteen horizontal red and white stripes and the fifty stars seemed to float, abandoned in the blue sky. He was talking, of course, about the flag of the United States of America.

That Tuesday, September 11, 2001, I stayed a little bit longer at the school and I watched as Nicolás put his hand on his chest, just like hundreds of his grammar school classmates, and recited, "I pledge allegiance to the flag of the United States of America . . ." I was moved to see a child who was barely three years old recite, even if mechanically, the salute to the flag of the United States. I am Mexican (or rather, very Mexican), but the United States has given me opportunities that I could not find in my country and, besides, my two children were born in this nation of immigrants.

I left the school happy, and to get some exercise I ran home, followed by my dog, Sunset. After a light rain, the sun fought its way through the clouds and burned my face. It was a morning typical of the American dream: a house in the suburbs, a good job, two wonderful children and a secure future.

I was right on all accounts, except for the secure future.

When I got home, I went to the kitchen to get some water while my wife, Lisa, answered the phone. It was a friend. She immediately hung up and ran to turn on the TV. I didn't pay much attention until she cried out, "It can't be!" The TV was broadcasting the bizarre images of an airplane buried in one of the World Trade Center towers in New York. We froze, speechless, in front of the television, and right there, dumbfounded, we watched as another commercial airliner crashed into the second tower, causing an enormous explosion. It was nine-thirty in the morning.

"What is this?" I said aloud. "What's going on?" The possibility that it was an accident disappeared with the crash of the second airliner. An error on the part of the control towers of one of the three New York airports could have been detected and corrected by any pilot. The only plausible conclusion was that it had been a terrorist act.

I made a couple of phone calls to the office—as a journalist I live off the unusual, sudden occurrences—and I went to take a shower. The plan was to go directly to the airport and get on the first flight from Miami to New York. Lisa surprised me as I was getting out of the shower. "They attacked the Pentagon too," she told me, and she began to cry.

The linear, secure, peaceful world that only minutes before I had glimpsed for my son, Nicolás, had turned into a chaotic, unpredictable scene full of fear. The United States, which was so used to fighting outside its borders and feeling practically invulnerable to international terrorist attacks, dropped to its knees for a few agonizing moments. The attack had been bold, cruel and well planned. The bipartisan displays of patriotism and the counterattack would come later, but innocence had been lost.

I was, of course, unable to fly to New York. All the airports in the entire country were closed, and the city that Frank Sinatra had said never sleeps, slept, terrified, disillusioned, without song.

Twelve, thirteen, fourteen, fifteen hours of television coverage went by as I reported, on the worst day in the history of the United States, on the number of those who had possibly been killed by the terrorist act, or the act of war. I described a hundred, two hundred, a thousand times how an airplane had crashed into the twin towers in New York, and how a few desperate souls jumped out of the windows so they wouldn't burn to death.

From nine-thirty that morning until eight-thirty that Tuesday night, George W. Bush practically disappeared from the map. There was "credible evidence," a presidential spokesman would later say, that the White House and the presidential jet were also on the list of terrorist targets.

So, Air Force One, like a supersonic grasshopper, jumped from Sarasota, Florida (where Bush was at the time of the first attack), to an air base in Louisiana, to another one in Nebraska and finally, to yet another in Virginia. The president, absent but safe, reappeared on live television at 8:32 P.M. that Tuesday evening to talk to the nation from the White House, where he had arrived that afternoon.

Maybe there was no vacuum in authority during those long hours when we did not see or hear from Bush or anyone from his administration. Maybe all the orders were being given from the airplane. Maybe the president was in full control. Maybe. Code Delta—an antiterrorist emergency operation—was in full effect. Security was a priority, but power not seen is power not exercised.

No one dared even to think that while President Bush took his thirty-two days of vacation that summer, terrorists were actively planning their attack. Where were the U.S. intelligence services? Maybe they, too, were on vacation.

The night of September 11 ended with the same airplanes destroying the same towers, and the same images of desperate human beings throwing themselves out of buildings. When I finally left the studios that night it was raining. I didn't open my umbrella, and I walked slowly to my car. I put on the radio to listen to more news. I couldn't take it anymore, I pressed the CD button and listened to Madonna sing, "Hey mister D.J. . . ." My mind, I admit, found relief.

I got home, ate some bread with butter, prepared a chocolate milk, like when I was a little boy, and got into the shower. When I got out, I went into Nicolas's room and touched his stomach, a ritual that I have done since he was born.

Yes, he was breathing, and I took a deep breath, relieved.

That very Tuesday that the United States lost its innocence, I lost the conviction that the future for my son would be better than mine. I ran my fingers through his hair gently while he slept, and I remembered that that very morning he had said to me so proudly at school, "Look, Papá, that's my flag."

IT WAS WORSE THAN WAR. I had not seen anything like it in the mountains of El Salvador or in the invasion of Kuwait or in the refugee camps in Kosovo. Death was certainly part of all of those wars that I had covered as a war correspondent, but I had never been in a place where there was such concentrated destruction.

It was not, either, anything similar to what I had witnessed in Oklahoma City when a terrorist act destroyed the federal building in April 1995. Two blocks were devastated, ablaze, covered by ash similar to what I had seen after the eruption of Chichonal in Mexico in the early eighties. Here, however, there had been no volcanic eruption. Two commercial airliners, converted into missiles, had destroyed the two tallest buildings in the world financial center in minutes. The remains of almost three thousand people were buried among the ruins of what had once been the twin towers.

They call it ground zero. It is the exact spot where the towers fell. I was able to slip into ground zero shortly after the terrorist attack one night when surveillance was still poor and army reinforcements, the National Guard and police from every corner of the country had not yet reached Manhattan. I was expecting to see bodies strewn everywhere, but I didn't see a single one.

"Where are the bodies?" I asked, rhetorically. Both the cameraman who was with me and I were surprised at the dimensions of the tragedy. Half a million tons of debris were on fire right before our eyes, which were reddened by fear and by the white particles of asbestos that stung like needles in your eye. "I don't see a single body," I said to Angel Matos, who had accompanied me to the bloodiest places in the world. All of a sudden we realized what had happened, and a chill ran through my body.

The dead were there, but I couldn't see them. I was inhaling them, but I couldn't see them. I smelled them, sickly and caustic, but I couldn't see them. I was stepping on them, but I couldn't see them. The dead were everywhere, pulverized, burned, in little pieces. I didn't see a hand or a finger, not even a face, but the dead were there. They were in my lungs, stuck to my clothing, tangled in my hair . . . until I was surrounded. They were in the air. They were the dust that flew about with the cold breeze off the water and jumped up in the air with the shovels and pickaxes of the rescue workers. I did not resist; I closed my eyes and let the dead embrace me.

Some of the damaged steel structures suggested that they had been there for almost thirty years, supporting the two giants of the World Trade Center. They could not withstand, however, two blows that broke their spinal columns, and they came crashing down, just as architects and engineers had planned. If those towers fall someday, those who built the twin towers thought, they will do so without bringing down the surrounding buildings. And that is what happened. The tragedy could have been much worse. I moved away, but the giants moaned. They emitted smoke from their thousand mouths of cement. They thundered inside. They were in agony.

The streets surrounding ground zero were deserted. Clumps of ash covered the roses and carnations in a nearby flower shop. The newspaper stand, now empty, still had tall stacks of newspapers from that Tuesday, September 11, 2001, waiting to be read. A car that had once been blue, now covered by a pile of rocks that had collapsed the roof onto the steering wheel, still had its left blinker on, indicating the left turn it was never able to make; the driver did not have time to escape. The police, stunned by the magnitude of the tragedy, let me leave ground zero without a single question. I tried to make eye contact with one of them, but he was staring off into space.

I got back to the hotel at three in the morning. I got into the shower and washed off the twenty-one hours it had taken me to drive from Miami to New York. Then, with a wet, soapy towel, I scrubbed away the ashes of the dead. I fell into bed, clean, defeated. I turned out the light, took a deep breath and smelled them again; those who had fallen in the twin towers were still with me.

I tried to return to ground zero, but I was not allowed in. My press passes and professional tricks were not enough to let me get as close as I had already done the first time. I did manage, however, to get one block away from the disaster site.

Security was now very tight, and the city had been taken over by an impressive military operation. "We're at war," said Pres. George W. Bush, and no one doubted it. The enemy still had no face, but the United States was on a war footing. There was a new nationalistic resolve in the alert eyes of the police and troops.

It was no time for recriminations. These would come much later, no doubt, during the 2004 presidential campaign. Democrats and Republicans were showing unprecedented unity. Everyone supported President Bush, and his level of popularity, which stood at 90 percent in some surveys, even surpassed that of his father during the Persian Gulf War. Flags flew around the country. Patriotism was reborn. No one even wanted to recall that while Bush took thirty-two days of vacation at his ranch in Crawford, Texas, terrorists were preparing their fatal blow.

The consequences of the terrible oversights in intelligence and in airport security systems were in front of my eyes. From a distance I saw the smoke rise from the rubble, and shortly after a cloud of ashes, blown by a gust of wind, enveloped me. It was them—the dead—embracing me once again, an embrace from which I could no longer escape.

The night was for the dead, but the morning was for the living. On every street corner of a fallen New York, the city was trying to get up. Family members of the victims stuck photographs of the disappeared to walls, cars, windows and mailboxes. When they learned I was a journalist, they would repeat the name of the person they were searching for. "Don't forget him, don't forget him," they said time and time again. "I know he's alive." I didn't dare tell them that since Wednesday, one day after the terrorist attack, they had not found any more survivors.

I heard dozens and dozens of stories. All New Yorkers felt like talking, as if it were a huge group therapy. Some of the things I heard were stories of genuine heroism, like the firemen who entered the twin towers while their terrified occupants were fleeing. Others, however, were truly horrifying.

Elda, five months pregnant, was sure that José had escaped alive. Convinced of this, she told her children, Sasha and Miguel, "He might be in a coma and unable to talk, or maybe he got hit in the head and can't remember his name." "What floor was José on?" I asked Elda, and after hearing, "on the one hundred and . . ." I stopped listening and turned to look at Sasha and Miguel. They smiled at me and I tried, poorly, to reciprocate. I was crying inside. I didn't want to be the one, with tears, to inform Sasha and Miguel that their daddy had died. When I said good-bye, Elda was still insisting. "I know he's still alive," she said. "Besides, José always wanted another boy, and today the doctor told me we're expecting a boy."

José didn't make it, but Jesús Noel Barral did. He was on the ninety-seventh floor of tower number two when he felt the crash from the building next door. He immediately began to go down the stairs, stopping on the seventy-eighth floor. He hesitated, wondering if he should take the express elevator to the lobby or not, and then he got on. The doors opened, and he went out into the street. There, three minutes later, he saw an airplane embed itself into the second tower.

"If I had kept walking down the stairs," he told me, "I wouldn't be here." The day I met Jesús, just a few blocks from ground zero, he was hugging his nine-year-old son, Yashua. "I was thinking of him," Jesús told me, "when I was coming down the stairs of the World Trade Center."

Bolívar Arellano saw it all from his apartment. He was one of the first photojournalists to arrive at the disaster site. His photographs are cruel testimony to what happened. Several of them show people throwing themselves out of windows; another powerful one captured the pile of flesh and blood when one of those bodies hit the ground; one more showed an arm that had been separated from a body.

Bolívar was on crutches, for as he was taking the photos, he injured his leg. His eyes, too, were injured from witnessing such pain and desperation.

YES, I WAS AFRAID. Even a week after the attack, I was still nervous. It was the first flight I had taken since September 11. How did they pull it off?

In short, it can be attributed to a very serious oversight on the part of U.S. intelligence services and very clear problems with airport security systems. How were so many terrorists able to falsify their identities, pass through metal detectors with knives and box cutters, violate all security inside the airplanes, overcome the crew and then, take control of the four airliners, converting them into missiles loaded with civilians? How? Could it happen again?

I was thinking about all of this as a taxi was taking me from downtown Manhattan to New York's La Guardia Airport. I was used to arriving just one hour before a flight, but now, with stricter security measures in place, I gave myself a minimum of two hours. That proved to be more than enough; the airport was practically deserted.

At the American Airlines counter, I was asked the typical questions:

Did you pack your own bag? Have your bags been out of your control at any time? Has anyone given you anything to carry on? No more or less than before; that ritual had not changed. I would have liked them to ask for extra identification or check through my bag and briefcase. I would have felt safer had this been done, but it was not.

I did notice a change in the small coffee shop where I like to have a hot chocolate in the morning before boarding. I know La Guardia Airport fairly well, since I travel there on business five or six times a year. Instead of finding the half-dozen or so Hispanic boys waiting like bees on hurried customers, I saw only two sad employees preparing cappuccinos and lattes. "Where are your coworkers?" I asked them. "They were all laid off," they replied. The cup of hot chocolate burned my hand.

As I sat there, blowing on my hand, I met Cristian. He was no more than seven years old. He and his mother were on the same flight to Miami as I was, but their final destination was Quito, Ecuador. Cristian, however, did not want to board the airplane. "Mama," he said before getting to the airport, "I don't want to get on those airplanes that crash." Me either. The image of those planes crashing into the twin towers, one after the other, was unforgettable, for Cristian and for me. I calmed him down as best I could and said, "I'll see you on the plane."

As I was heading for the door I passed two U.S. immigration officers who were patrolling the corridors. That, I thought, is something new. When I reached the metal detectors, I was again asked for my identification, and seven people—seven—watched on a screen as my three pairs of underwear, four pairs of socks, two dirty shirts and a wrinkled suit passed through the machine. They let me through, and I was worried. Shouldn't my electric razor, shaped like a pistol, have been inspected?

I kept going, passing empty stores, and I sat down in a corner to write a couple of reports for the radio. It wasn't long before two police officers approached me. They heard me speaking Spanish, and it probably seemed strange or suspicious to them. I greeted them with a nod of my head, and nothing came of it.

I waited, and waited, and waited. The plane was at least a half-hour late, but no one complained. When the time came to board, the passengers all seemed to look at each other suspiciously. Who among us could be a terrorist?

The man sitting next to me on the flight was a white businessman, about sixty years old. I could see him looking at the notes I was writing down in Spanish out of the corner of his eye and see that he was nervous. A polite smile and a "hi" calmed him down. Good manners, I thought, will now be fashionable.

The plane taxied to the runway, and there was complete silence in the cabin. I turned around and saw several people clutching their seats. I looked down and realized that I, too, was doing the same thing. We passed over Manhattan, and the island was missing the two gigantic teeth of the twin towers. Smoke was still rising from the spot which changed our lives forever.

Breakfast was served, without the usual metal utensils. I ate my tasteless omelet with a plastic fork. My life, along with everyone else's, had changed that September 11. Plans of retiring at age fifty, buying a new house and getting a new car every two years now seemed so trivial. All of a sudden we found ourselves struggling for our survival. In eighteen minutes—the time separating the two plane crashes into the twin towers—the world had been turned upside down.

I tried to philosophize, think of other things. Francis Fukuyama was mistaken when he thought that the breakup of the Soviet Union was the end of history. No, the United States was no longer an invulnerable superpower, nor would globalization be the preferred way to extend its empire and ideas. On the other hand, Samuel Huntington was right when he suggested that a clash of civilizations would mark the future and the United States, the leader of the West, would be threatened. A woman who had gotten up to go to the bathroom cut off this mental game. We all watched her.

There was not a single cloud or any turbulence whatsoever that day, but every time someone went to the bathroom or got up to take something out of the overhead bin, all the other passengers, including myself, became nervous. In a climate of terror, diarrhea can make the calmest and sickest of travelers a potential terrorist in the eyes of other passengers.

Two and a half hours later, we landed in Miami, relieved. I can now say with certainty that the flight was one of the safest flights I have ever taken. Cristian walked off the plane holding his mother's hand, smiling.

Almost three weeks after the terrorist attacks I was finally able to cry. I was driving in the pouring rain when the music from the CD took me back to another September, two years ago, to another car on another highway and another job and to another future that was much brighter. The contrast was dramatic.

Alone, I cried. I shouted.

I felt off balance. While I was in New York I had repressed what for most people was natural in a situation like that. I didn't cry, I didn't scream. I kept my composure. I am convinced that they hired me as a television reporter not to express my feelings or emotions on camera. I was now sick, however, from holding back.

I lost four or five pounds. That is my problem: stress, far from giving me an appetite, makes me lose weight. For weeks after the attacks, I felt weak, I couldn't sleep and I had nightmares of the planes crashing into the twin towers over and over again. I had bags under my eyes, my skin was dry and my hair looked even grayer. I was slumped over as I walked, had a difficult time concentrating, even on the tennis court or soccer field, and every little thing made me angry.

After crying that afternoon in my car, however, I began to regain balance in my life. I went back to writing without distraction, made a goal in the Saturday soccer games and won my first set in a tennis match in a long time.

The weather was improving. "It's only drizzling," I thought, as the sun poked its way through the clouds.

Sun.

Sun.

Even journalists need to vent their emotions.

WAR AND SOCCER. Attacks and calls for normalcy. The United States was living with these contradictions on Sunday, October 7, 2001, when

George W. Bush ordered the bombing to begin in Afghanistan. It was ab-solute schizophrenia.

A few hours after the attacks, the mayor of New York City, Rudolph Giuliani, asked all New Yorkers "not to stay locked up at home." "Get out," Giuliani urged, "be courageous." That was the first time in the United States that tasks as simple as going to the market or the movies, taking the kids to school or driving to work had been considered acts of courage.

Whom should we listen to? Americans were wondering. To the presi-dent, George W. Bush, who was encouraging citizens to fly so that airlines did not go bankrupt? Or to the attorney general, John Ashcroft, who was warning about the real possibility of new terrorist attacks in the United States?

The second Sunday after the attacks demonstrated clearly what it is like to live in times of war here in the United States. Spanish-language television split the screens in two in order to broadcast the soccer match between Mexico and Costa Rica at the same time bombs were falling on Kabul and Kandahar. The more purist English-language television chose a different approach: some channels broadcast the war, bomb by bomb, while others opted to show the battlefield between the New York Giants and the Washington Redskins. After all, American football is a war con-tained in a hundred yards.

That same day that Bush ordered B-2 bombers from a military base in Missouri to attack the Al-Qaeda terrorist camps in the Afghan mountains, Barry Bonds of the San Francisco Giants hits his seventy-third home run of the season, rewriting the history books. Everyone fights with what he can, some with bombers worth $2 billion each, others with baseball bats.

This was the new "normalcy" in the United States, bombs and bats.

The twenty-first century really began on September 11, 2001. That is the definitive date. In few places were the contrasts felt more than in New York, where thousands of people died.

I had to return to New York to accept the Maria Moors Cabot award for journalism, after spending a week in Miami reporting the tragic events of that fateful day. Despite the enormous effort on the part of businesses, restaurants, government agencies and ordinary people to get on with business, the enormity of the catastrophe dominated almost everything.

There was a new phobia in New York: the fear of entering very tall buildings. We'll have to find a name for it. A friend told me how one morning she ran out of her hotel in Manhattan shortly after getting to her room on the seventeenth floor. Visits to the Empire State Building—once again the tallest building in New York after the collapse of the World Trade Center towers—were now made only by a small group of masochistic tourists.

Early October 2001 was a wonderful time to visit New York, if, of course, you were able to conquer the fear of getting on an airplane, sleeping on the fifty-first floor and feeling that terrorists might strike again. There were few people on the street, the traffic was reasonable, the generally rude and abrupt New Yorkers were now pleasant and kind, and getting into the most popular shows on Broadway didn't require buying tickets on the black market for five hundred dollars apiece.

Some time ago, to cite an example, I had wanted to eat at Nobu, a Japanese restaurant in TriBeCa, but it was impossible to get in. Reservations had to be made weeks in advance. Finally, due to a cancellation, I was able to go. The meal was, in a word, extraordinary. Nevertheless, before getting to the restaurant I had to go through the area affected by the terrorist act, and the odor of burning and of death still lingered in the air. How could sushi or tuna tataki be enjoyed when pieces of violence and death are lodged in your lungs?

Likewise, a lovely walk along Fifth Avenue at once turned distressing when I stumbled upon the funeral of a fireman at St. Patrick's Cathedral. So many people died that Tuesday, September 11, that there were not enough churches to accommodate all the funerals, many of which were being held without a body.

Before I left the city, I visited the Museum of Modern Art. The few people who were visiting the museum were crowded in front of Jasper Johns's avant-garde painting of the American flag. Tourism and patriotism. I, on the other hand, stood in front of Claude Monet's wonderful water lilies from 1920. It is an enormous painting that covers an entire wall.

That's life, I thought, complex and contradictory. It is like Monet's painting: if you look at it close up you can only appreciate the brush strokes of color and pieces without direction. You have to move back to give it meaning. In times of war it is also necessary to step back a little in order to try and understand what is happening. That is what life in America has become: war and soccer games.

AFGHANISTAN: A VACATION AT WAR

It's absurd and not easily explained, but I wanted to go to the war in Afghanistan. After the exhaustion of covering the terrorist acts of September 11, 2001, in New York, I needed to go in order to put the final period on the story.

It all began Thanksgiving night. I was watching television at my sister-in-law's home in Leesburg, in northern Florida, after having eaten the typical Thanksgiving turkey, when Christiane Amanpour suddenly appeared on the screen, in a CNN broadcast from Kabul. I watched her—I admit— somewhat enviously, and I said to myself: what am I doing here? The world is in chaos in Afghanistan, and I was eating turkey in Florida. At that moment I decided to go to the war, by myself if need be, but I would go.

I didn't say anything to my family so as not to worry them, but the following Monday I began to make arrangements for the trip: tickets, visa, contacts, etc. For security as well as economic reasons, Univision had decided not to send any journalists on our staff to cover the war, but this seemed unthinkable to me. The war in Afghanistan was, without a doubt, the most important piece of news in the last decade, and I had to be there.

I have never blamed anyone for the things that I do or do not do. So instead of getting angry with my bosses or fighting with others at the company, I asked for a few days off and informed everyone that I was going to Afghanistan. This way, no one could stop me.

I know it sounds strange, but I spent my vacation at war.

In the Mountains of Tora Bora in Eastern Afghanistan I heard the boom again and again. BOOM! I couldn't see the battlefield, but I could hear it. The U.S. bombs and the bullets from the machine guns and the Russian-made Kalashnikov rifles were muffled; the explosions created an echo in the mountains and could be heard kilometers away. BOOM! BOOM! BOOM! . . . and three mushroom clouds formed. Every time I tried to scribble something in my notebook, the vibrations from the bombs prevented me from writing inside the lines. BOOM! Again and again. BOOM! BOOM!

For several nights in mid-December 2001. I couldn't sleep because of the continuous flights of the U.S. B-52s over the mountains of Tora Bora, where some believed Osama was hiding. (In the Arab world he is called only by his first name.) In fact, no one in the region had been able to sleep during that time. The soldiers from the Eastern Alliance, which was composed of three tribal groups, had been gaining territory on the more than one thousand Taliban and members of the terrorist organization, Al-Qaeda, who were entrenched in those inhospitable mountains. But not even the U.S. air strikes had been able to completely defeat the Taliban, who counted among their ranks well-trained and fierce Arab, Chechen and Pakistani soldiers. The bombing I witnessed, though, didn't matter, nor did the conditions of surrender imposed on the Al-Qaeda members. What mattered was if Osama bin Laden was hiding there.

Commander Malang Yar of the Eastern Alliance assured me that Osama was hidden in the area. In this he was in agreement with suspicions of the Pentagon and statements by the Chairman of the Joint Chiefs of Staff, Richard Myers, even though the soldiers under Yar's command were not so sure.

"Osama is like a bird," Janmohd told me as he caressed his machine gun like a baby. "And the mountain is very big." "Only Allah knows," confirmed his exhausted colleague, Maselkhan, stroking his beard during one of the many breaks in the fighting. Ayabgul, another warrior from the Agam tribe, then suggested they look for Osama near the Afghan border with China. The truth was, no one knew.

I couldn't find a single person who knew someone who had seen Osama in the mountains of Tora Bora; not a one. I asked dozens of times, with the help of my translator, Naim; he would ask the warriors in Pashto, the language that dominated in that region, then translate what they said for me into English, and I would jot it down in my notebook in Spanish. Rumors that Osama was in the area came from radio communications in Arabic that were intercepted by Taliban enemies. In other words, they knew about Osama from hearsay. In the end, Osama got away once again, but the hunt wasn't over.

No one, including myself, saw Osama bin Laden during the final days of 2001, but the winding and dangerous road from Jalalabad to the mountains of Tora Bora—it took me two and a half hours to make the trip of only fifty kilometers in a four-wheel-drive vehicle—opened my eyes to the legendary misfortunes of the Afghan people. On that journey I met Mohamed, a man of thirty-five who looked fifty, who had lost his left leg when he stepped on a mine. Even so, Mohamed was lucky. "The two friends who were with me," he told me, "died." Near the Jalalabad airport—well, it's really an uneven runway full of holes—there were red signs in English, Arabic and Pashto warning of the mines that had been placed there during the Russian occupation from 1979 to 1989. Afghanistan, which had been at war for twenty-three years, had more antipersonnel mines on its land than any other country in the world. In that, Afghanistan was number one. It was also number one on the list of poorest nations in the world. The intense drought of the last four years had allowed only the strongest to survive.

Before reaching the mountains, I ran into the dust-covered children of the plains of Chapliar, a desert area with a fine sand that prevents tears and mucus from running down the children's faces. After I saw a four-year-old girl covered in dust from head to toe—who was as surprised to see a foreigner like me as I was to see her heartrending appearance—it was easy to see why one in four children did not reach the age of five.

As the Jeep passed by, blowing up more dust on those children of the desert, I was struck by the feeling that they would not last very long, standing there, without water, without food and without dreams. All those children, without exception, were holding out their hands asking for money, or they held their fingers together and were raising them to their mouths. The message was unmistakable: we're hungry.

The houses in the Afghan countryside are like small, square fortresses of mud and wood, with no water, telephone, electricity or imagination. They were crowded together like in those biblical illustrations that try to portray life as it was two thousand years ago. Those houses I saw were hiding some of the poorest people I have ever seen; I have visited more than fifty countries on five continents, and nothing prepared me for the poverty and violence that had ravaged the people of Afghanistan.

I CROSSED THE AFGHAN-PAKISTANI BORDER on foot. No border is without its conflicts. But Tijuana (on the U.S.-Mexican border) is heaven on earth compared to Torkham. A Pakistani soldier opened an enormous, rusty gate so I could cross the border, while another two or three guards, throwing punches and shouting, were trying to prevent a group of Afghan refugees from slipping through. I was literally shoved into Afghanistan.

I was carrying a letter that would supposedly allow me to get to Jalalabad safe and sound in the company of guerrillas under the command of Haji Zaman, one of the three tribal leaders who had divided up Nangahar province after the Taliban fled. But his people were nowhere to be found on the border.

But when one of the lieutenants of Haji Qadir—another one of the leaders—saw I looked lost, he came over to me and offered to have his guards take me to Jalalabad for a hundred dollars. I had no choice. So, surrounded by three perfect strangers, I rode the eighty kilometers in a beat-up Toyota. Kafir, a twenty-year-old soldier, sat down next to me in the back seat. I was not very comforted by his Kalashnikov rifle, on the floor of the van, which jumped up every time we hit a hole in the road and which sometimes wound up aimed right at my chin. Afghan roulette, I thought. My hands were sweating profusely I thought, "What the hell am I doing here!"

Kafir asked me in very basic English what I thought of Osama bin Laden, but sensing it was a trick question I refrained from telling him that Osama was an unpresentable, cowardly criminal. Shortly after, I applauded my prudence when I heard that Kafir was a follower of the terrorist leader. "I am a follower of Osama," he said. I froze and managed to reply, "Okay." We both looked straight ahead as the rifle continued to dance on the floor, between his knees.

"At any moment this guy might turn around and blow my brains out," I thought.

And instead of waiting for the shot, I presented him with a proposal. "If you take care of me, I'll take care of you." The questions about Osama bin Laden were over, and when we arrived, Kafir got a fifteen-dollar tip.

Life was worth very little in Afghanistan. Very little.

During the ride, I couldn't stop thinking about the four journalists who had been killed on November 19, 2001, on a road in Afghanistan. The reporters in this war had died not because of combat, but because of robberies or attacks on the country's little-traveled roads. Visa and American Express were not accepted in Afghanistan, and for the guerrillas, the journalists wore a cash sign on their foreheads. For someone accustomed to earning just twenty dollars a month, a foreign journalist's wallet was a big haul.

Nowhere in the world have I felt so fragile and vulnerable as I did in Afghanistan. Despite our political differences, Kafir and his followers helped me pass through all the checkpoints without a scratch, before dropping me off at the filthy Spinghar Hotel in Jalalabad, the unofficial meeting and lodging place for foreign journalists in that part of the country.

It would be a gross exaggeration to call Jalalabad a city. In Jalalabad the problems that postwar Afghanistan would face were visible. This was no-man's-land, or rather a place that many were fighting over but that lacked a strong government, efficient police and a certain sense of order. That was the danger. The fleeing of the Taliban left a thorny vacuum of power in Afghanistan.

In the market in Jalalabad (amidst sickly looking carrots, piles of recently sheared wool and plenty of hashish) the illiterate and armed boys of the three tribal leaders walked about nervously. They were constantly fighting over small pieces of territory: the market, the road from Jalalabad to Kabul, the entrance to the only hotel. And they tried to impose their authority with weapons and frequent checkpoints. Fighting was a daily occurrence, and it wasn't unusual to hear shots being fired in the air. Afghans love to argue, but I always had the feeling that their shouts in an atmosphere so filled with tension could have been the prelude to an armed confrontation.

Besides, the now ex-Taliban were mixed in with the rest of the population and it was impossible for me to take a step without feeling the curious stare on the back of my neck of someone who had never seen a foreigner before . . . but who has been taught to hate him, or at least resent him. On the streets of Jalalabad I received a couple of strong shoves and, I think, insults in Pashto (which of course I didn't understand and all the better).

It upset me to see that the women in Jalalabad were still as repressed as in the days of the Taliban. For starters, the women didn't appear in public. I saw little girls and old women, the latter completely covered up in the traditional burka, but I didn't see a single young woman for days. In post-Taliban Afghanistan you could now listen to music, watch TV and fly kites, but women had no voice or vote.

The province of Nangarhar—which takes in Jalalabad—is more conservative than the capital, Kabul. Afghanistan, though, was decades behind in the equality of the sexes in income, job and education opportunities. Suffice it to say that before the war, only six of every one hundred grammar school children were girls.

In the part of the world where I come from, this kind of blatant discrimination is called machismo. Not here. In Afghanistan, I was assured, the submissive and secondary role of women is an age-old tradition. Unfortunately, I was unable to speak with any women; the men did not allow it. "The only possession many Muslim men have is their wife," one man who had never let his wife go out alone explained to me.

If Jalalabad was a microcosm of the poverty, violence and sexual discrimination that awaited Afghanistan, it was easy to see that peace would be much harder to win than the war against the Taliban.

THEY WERE AS CURIOUS about me as I was about them. They saw me look at them and I saw them look at me. During six years of Taliban rule, foreigners had been prohibited from entering Afghanistan, and it was obvious that the children in a refugee camp outside of Jalalabad had never seen one.

They looked curiously at my jeans, my boots and the cameras that hung from my neck. I'm sure that one of those Afghan children must have thought: this guy wears some pretty strange necklaces. I, on the other hand, was trying to read the maps of anguish and poverty drawn on their faces.

Sand-children. Their skin, cracked like dried dirt, looked as if it were about to break open. These were children who had never seen a comb; their hair had become tough from years of wind, desert sand and the absence of shampoo and soap. Their hands were brown and rough, like sandpaper. Their faces said five, six or seven years old; their eyes, though, transmitted the anguish of an old person who had seen death close up. They had never had a glass of milk or washed their faces with clean water. Their toys were pieces of paper cut in the shape of cars hanging by a thread from a piece of wood. The hunt for the most wanted man in the world—Osama bin Laden—was far from their worries, as was the installation of the new prime minister, Hamid Karzai, who had the impossible job of uniting Afghanistan. No, the immediate concern of those children of war was survival.

In this town of warriors, I saw many blue and green eyes, hair made blond from the sun and dust, and empty stomachs crying out desperately. The war in Afghanistan had provoked an exodus of more than four million refugees, most of whom settled in Pakistan. There were also, though, many who were internally displaced; one of every five Afghan families had to leave their house and flee with their children. And the children I found here, who are the poorest on earth, were still smiling. I couldn't understand it.

I was astonished by the violent treatment of the children in Afghanistan. Scenes of fathers, guerrillas and guards driving away children with sticks and long pieces of thick rubber or by merely raising a threatening hand, as if they were pesky flies, were common. It saddened me. They are children whose curiosity and happiness is quickly stamped out by violence.

However, the worst violence these Afghan children of war experience is hunger. Fawad Haider of the United Nations Development Program told me that two out of every three children under the age of fourteen have to leave school and work in order to help their families survive. That is his estimate as an expert even though there is no reliable study on the subject. The reality could be worse. Afghan children lose their childhood, and sometimes their lives, shortly after they're born.

The camp I visited, on the road from Jalalabad to Torkham, consisted of hundreds of tents. There was no water, electricity or bathrooms. "Watch out for the mines," my guide warned me, half-jokingly, referring to the human excrement everywhere. The winter filtered through their plastic tents easily; a child who was lucky enough to escape from hunger during the day could easily freeze to death at night.

My visit was short, not even an hour. Among the thousands of resident at the camp were many ex-Taliban who were bothered by my presence and by the photographs I was taking of the children. They suspected, mistakenly, that I was photographing their women, in burkas from head to toe, an unforgivable offense.

Furthermore, the residents in the camp blamed me for the slowness with which humanitarian aid was arriving, as if I had something to do with it. However, I did see dozens of trucks loaded with food, stopped on the Pakistani border because of bureaucratic red tape, while here in the camp, there were children and old people who were literally starving to death every day.

"We have to leave," my guide said, frightened, when some of the men in the camp began to shout at the armed guards who were protecting me. My presence had become a topic for discussion and was threatening to create a disturbance. I put my cameras away and quickly headed for the car. But when I turned around, dozens of children were following me, smiling, maybe waiting for another flash from my camera or a coin. Despite my initial impulse to open my wallet and give them some money, common sense stopped me. If I had given money to some of the children—the exchange was fifty-five thousand Afghanis to the U.S. dollar—

the others, including adults, would have surrounded me leaving me no escape, and I would have lost more than my wallet.

When I got in the car I felt my tongue, which was rough and full of sand. It was hard to swallow. The refugee camps of the Albanian Kosovars that I visited in Macedonia were almost luxurious compared to what I saw in Afghanistan. These were desperate people prepared to do anything to survive. We can't forget that they were survivors of many wars. The first to fall in this battle, though, were the sand-children I met in that refugee camp.

MORE JOURNALISTS DIED in the war in Afghanistan in 2001 than U.S. or British soldiers in combat there. Eight. I know exactly how each one died: I had brought with me the newspaper clippings reporting each of their deaths. For me it was a terrible reminder: a dead reporter can report nothing.

The most important thing for any journalist in a war zone is survival, but we are at a distinct disadvantage. In Afghanistan, everyone seemed to be armed (Taliban, soldiers of the Northern Alliance, U.S. Marines), except for us. No news is so important that it justifies the death of a journalist, though at times we take risks because it's our job to be the eyes and ears of those who are not there.

The interesting thing is that the same journalists who risked their necks during the day to cover the fighting in the mountains of Tora Bora, searched for the illusory protection of being in a group at the Spinghar Hotel in Jalalabad at night. At our four-dollar dinners—white rice with raisins and cauliflower with chicken legs fried in oil black from being used over and over, nan bread and Pepsi—I heard the most fascinating stories from journalists: "The Taliban shot at me and I had to hide under a tank . . ." "When I got to Kabul we were surrounded by corrupt guerrillas eager for a few dollars . . ." "My hotel room, which had recently been bombed, was fine, except it had no roof . . ." In these adventures, if something went wrong, you wouldn't show up for dinner to tell about it. And eight journalists never showed up for dinner.

The Spinghar Hotel could have easily been mistaken for a battered psychiatric hospital from the Soviet era; two floors, walls stained from humidity and long, cold, dark hallways. But in the middle of the war it was hard to find another spot that was better protected from the gunfire. I was put in a room with the correspondents from the *Miami Herald* and the Knight Ridder newspaper chain. "We'll leave you there with Osama," they said to me, in hysterics. "Osama" was an annoying mouse that made noise all night long, and that first night damned Osama took a bite out of a chocolate bar I had brought in case of emergency, and I had to throw it out.

My thirty-dollar-a-night room smelled liked a battlefield. Several journalists before me had already slept on the same mattress full of holes and covered with the same gray sheets that hadn't been washed in more than two months. The shared toilet had no water, and the layers of filth and excrement suggested another kind of war. This forced me to learn a legendary Afghan technique that requires a lot of balance and aim, and it goes without saying that I didn't bathe for days. But in the middle of a war I was thankful, believe it or not, for my foul hotel room.

My guide and translator, Naim, slept in the same room. Naim was a Pakistani "fixer," meaning that he could fix anything. For two hundred or three hundred dollars a day, these fixers would arrange transportation to the war zone (one hundred dollars), hire bodyguards or armed guerrillas (twenty dollars a head), translate from Pashto into English, buy food (nothing cost more than a dollar) and assure that your reports would arrive where they were supposed to arrive. Sometimes these fixers even saved your life.

"Don't go over there, Mister George," Naim warned me calmly. "Mines." He called me George because Jorge in Pashto meant "younger sister," and there was no way I was going to convince Naim to call me that; I suppose the Mister was because I was the one paying. Naim earned in one day what a poor Pakistani family would earn in five months. They were prices inflated by war, but I don't regret a cent of what I paid. The important thing was that I was safe and sound.

Naim was recommended to me after he had saved the life of a U.S. television journalist. The reporter, who was black, had been mistaken for a member of the Al-Qaeda organization from Sudan or Yemen, and he was about to be killed by soldiers of the Eastern Alliance and angry Afghans. Naim courageously saved the CNN journalist from the furious mob ready to stone him to death. For me Naim was also a great companion. The only problem was that his snoring—added to the squeaking of Osama the mouse and the B-52s overhead—never let me sleep more than three hours at a time.

In a war journalists form alliances and friendships that would be unthinkable in peacetime and ratings time. They share toothpaste and toilet paper, share medicine for coughs and diarrhea, give each other candy, exchange information and interviews, and maintain a strict code of silence: the affairs, indiscretions and abuses of drugs and alcohol are always a professional secret. However, the most appreciated correspondents, without a doubt, were those who lent you their satellite telephone (for six dollars a minute) so you could call home every night and let your loved ones know you were still alive. (Thank you Daryl from CNN; and many, many thanks to Enrique Serbeto of the Spanish newspaper *ABC*.)

The lobby of the Spinghar Hotel (which means "white mountains") was full of young, armed Afghans, members of the correspondents' security teams; after the death of four journalists on November 19, many reporters had decided to hire guerrillas for their protection. In the garden of the hotel there was a boy who, instead of saying "good morning" would ask: "Are you going to the war zone today?" as if it were like going to the market to buy carrots. In addition, there were groups of little boys who would follow you like a swarm of wasps, asking for money and saying over and over again, "I'm a poor boy, I'm a poor boy."

I left the hotel with a mixture of nostalgia and relief. The news of the war was dwindling, and quite frankly, I had never stopped being afraid during my time in Jalalabad and Tora Bora. I felt fragile, vulnerable. The danger was not dying in combat but rather being attacked or robbed by one of the many different armed groups of bandits and guerrillas. The fear, I'm sure, kept me alert and prevented me from getting too comfortable in a place where you couldn't trust anyone.

I paid Naim a small fortune, hugged him like a brother and got in a taxi that for one hundred dollars would take me from Jalalabad to the Pakistani border. But the danger was not over.

One of the people riding in the taxi with me—there were five of us—stopped to buy hashish in the Jalalabad market and then made another similar stop on the border at Torkham. I would later find out that if the Pakistani police had found drugs in the vehicle, I could have spent the rest of my days in jail or have been sentenced to death, even though I didn't even know the person who had bought the drugs.

All this was more than enough for me. It was time to go home. I could have stayed in Afghanistan a couple of days more, but I didn't want to push my luck. They were waiting for me at home for dinner.

Before leaving for Afghanistan I weighed a thin but energetic 145 pounds. I weighed myself because every trip I take or during times of stress I tend to lose weight. This time was no exception. In order to fit in during my stay in Afghanistan, I reluctantly had to respect the holy month of Ramadan.

Foreigners, of course, were not obligated to stop eating, drinking, smoking or having sex from sunup to sundown during Ramadan. The last two prohibitions didn't bother me, but I didn't want to eat or drink anything in public and take the risk of being attacked by an ex-Taliban or a Muslim who thought my action showed a lack of respect. I ate very little and poorly, and I only slept a few hours each night, much less than what I was accustomed to. However, I never felt tired. I ran on pure adrenaline.

At the end of my trip the scale confirmed what I had suspected: I lost five pounds due to nerves and stress. In addition to my forced Afghan diet, I brought back with me an Afghan virus that didn't leave me alone for several weeks after my return. With each sneeze I left the war behind.

The mental impact was much more complicated. Months would pass before I was able to regain a certain balance in my life and return to my routine. But I still haven't been able to shake off that feeling of vulnerability I acquired in Afghanistan and that made me see life as though it were a piece of glass ready to shatter.

One of the first photos of me, when I was six months old. I am sitting on my grandfather Miguel's shoulder; he's one of my heroes, a marvelously talkative man who was born with the century and from whom I heard the tragedies of the Second World War and the adventures of the Mexican revolution.

Me, at the age of three. I still hadn't broken my nose.

With my classmates at the Colegio Tepeyac (later named Centro Escolar del Lago). I was seven years old, and had a triangular face. I am first (*left*) in the first row, squatting, with a carefree smile.

Playing with my favorite toy at my grandfather's house in Mexico City.

In Florida, with my wife, Lisa, our son, Nicolás, and my daughter, Paola.

With Benjamím Beckhart and Gloria Meckel, two good friends and confidants, in good times and in bad.

My friend Felix Sordo, who died in the 1985 earthquake in Mexico City. Here we were photographed after interviewing the rebel priest Marcel Lefebvre.

With my uncle Armando and my mother in Puttaparthi, India, in Sai Baba's ashram.

The entire Ramos Avalos family at the 10 Piedras Negras Street house: my father, Jorge, my mother, Lourdes, my brothers Alejandro, Eduardo, and Gerardo, and my sister, Lourdes. I'm in the far right corner. At the bottom, my grandmother Raquel, my aunt Tere, and my uncle Miguel.

This picture was taken during my days as a classical guitarist. I gave up the music of Bach, Tárrega, and Albeniz when I started college. I was better with words than I was with music.

When I was an athlete, I managed to become a part of the pre-Olympic Mexican team. In this picture, I am jumping "Fosbury" style. A back injury permanently kept me from my dream of going to the Olympics.

In 1996, I was one of the last ones to finish the New York Marathon. It took me six hours, fifty-six minutes, and eight seconds. Quite a record.

In Chiapas, 1982, when we were covering the eruption of the Chichonal volcano, we were almost buried under the ashes. In this photograph I am with the rest of the crew. I am to the right, thin, dusty, and holding a hat in my hand.

During my first days as a reporter at Televisa in Mexico. The picture was taken right before the censorship incident that made me resign and move to the United States.

On January 1, 1984, I started working for Channel 34 in Los Angeles,
California. It was my first TV
opportunity in the United States,
and I had more desire to succeed
than actual experience.

Angel Matos, chief of operations,
an extraordinary cameraman, and
Patsy Loris, the executive producer
of the Noticiero Univisión, the person who knows the most about my
work. Both of them have been with
me on the most important stories I
have ever done. Here, we are in
Bogotá, shortly before I received
two death threats.

Courtesy The White House, Nov. 29, 1990. Photo: Carol T. Powers.

George Bush was the first American president I ever interviewed. This was taken in the White House, days before the beginning of the Gulf War.

With Bill Clinton, the eternal teenager. I have never been able to understand how he could have sacrificed so much for so little.

Courtesy The White House, Dec. 8, 1994.

With George W. Bush, when he was still governor of Texas, and he was slightly over Al Gore in the polls in the presidential elections of 2000.

Fidel Castro, the Cuban dictator, tried to put his hand on my shoulder during an interview as we walked together in Guadalajara, Mexico, 1991. After taking his arm off me, when I asked him about the lack of democracy in Cuba, his bodyguards took me aside and pushed me away.

With the Venezuelan president Hugo Chávez, after he won the presidential election of 1998. Back then he still listened. And Carlos Bardasano from Univisión didn't miss a word. Four years later, in April 2002, after the massacre of unarmed civilians, Chavez was overthrown for forty-eight hours. "He's back, he's back, he's back," yelled his supporters. "Never forget the massacre," yelled the opposition.

Carlos Salinas de Gortari has been one of the most controversial presidents Mexico has ever had. After six years requesting an interview with him, I was finally able to meet with him in October 2000 and ask about the serious accusations against him.

In the Lacandona jungle, Chiapas, with Subcomandante Marcos, the leader of the Zapatista guerrillas.

With Vicente Fox, winner of the historic July 2000 presidential elections in Mexico. It was the end of seventy-one years of authoritarian PRI governments. This picture was taken a day after his victory.

In Moscow, 1991, during the breakup of the Soviet Union.

In Nicaragua, covering the disasters caused by Hurricane Mitch.

Flying to Caracas in a cargo plane, not exactly first class. The airport had been closed to commercial airlines due to the flooding.

In Kuwait, during the first days following the allied victory against the Iraqi invasion.

In Macedonia, near the Albano-Kosovar refugee camps in 1999.

With the Eastern Alliance guerillas in Tora Bora, Afghanistan, December 2001. At that time, it was thought that Osama bin Laden was hiding in those mountains.

On one of the Eastern Alliance tanks.

In New York, September 2001, covering the consequences of the terrorist attacks on the World Trade Center.

OF COURSE IT WAS DIFFICULT, but I don't regret having gone to the Afghan War; or any other for that matter, since wars have given my life an amazing amount of perspective. I have seen horrible things. Dead people, and bodies turned into smoke and dust. After seeing those kinds of things, an embrace, a kiss and even an afternoon lying on the couch take on a new dimension, honestly. I appreciate life and all I have a lot more. That's easy to do, especially when violence and war are your points of reference.

When I go off to cover a war, nobody needs to tell me how it was. I am what I wanted to be all my life: a firsthand witness to history. What other profession can offer you something like that? I've already said it: since I was a teenager, I wanted to visit places where changes were taking place, and meet the people who were leading the changes. Journalism gave me that opportunity. I couldn't imagine doing anything else. There is such a big world out there with so much to see that it would be a waste to be locked up in just one place. I did well by picking the profession that I liked the most, and not become what my father thought I should have become.

I have been able to live through interesting episodes of history. I can't complain. It has been so intense—sometimes too intense—that sometimes I have felt like a candle burning at both ends. Still, I wouldn't change it for anything.

AN (INQUISITIVE OR PREGUNTÓN) JOURNALIST IN LATIN AMERICA

> We all have to hunt down a lion. Some have done it, but trembling.
> —GABRIEL GARCÍA MÁRQUEZ
> (AQUELLOS TIEMPOS CON GABO)

> Of course we must disrupt everything . . .
> question everything, and not just sit down and contemplate the countryside.
> —ELENA PONIATOWSKA (LA PIEL DEL CIELO)

Eloísa Ortiz, the grandmother of Alejandro Escalona, a journalist and good friend of mine, once complained to her grandson about me: "That Ramos asks too many questions." People had already tried to define me in a lot of ways, but for a journalist—who always tries to ask difficult questions of those in power—to be told that he asks too many questions is very satisfying. That means that I'm doing my job right. If the grandmother of Alejandro, the publisher of the Chicago weekly *Éxito*, would have told him that my interviews on television were boring or that they looked phony and staged, then I would be worried. Fortunately that is not the case. My career as a journalist could be summed up in just a few lines.

60 presidents
2 terrorist attacks
4 wars
2 death threats
2 emergency landings
4 political conventions
2 assassinations
2 decades as a reporter
and thousands of reports, both written and on
the air. Thousands.

It is, in fact, much more than a to-do list—been there, done that—and a map covered with blue pins to identify the countries I have visited. Journalism has permeated my being so deeply that it has changed the way I live.

The novelist Mario Vargas Llosa said, "Fiction is a lie that conceals a profound truth." It is the journalist's job to peel away that truth like an onion. That is precisely what I have tried to do for more than twenty years, peel away the news.

Although I have been the anchor of the Noticiero Univision for more than fifteen years, I still feel like a street reporter. I am sure that I'll be judged by my last interview or report, and not for the whole of my career. That is why I never stop asking questions, questioning the obvious or looking for the impossible.

I think that I have interviewed some of the most influential presidents and political leaders of Latin America, and I have developed a very good technique for interviewing them. First of all, I try to know more about specific topics than the interviewee does. That's the only way to be equals. Second, I prepare many more questions than I will ask, so that toward the end of the interview, I start getting rid of the easy ones, so then I only have difficult ones left. Third, and probably most important, I base the interview on the most relevant and controversial subjects. I think that it's a waste of time to ask a president how his family is doing, when what people want to know is if the president made money from drug trafficking, or if he allowed his brother to enrich himself while in office. You then have to search for the point when the person interviewed contradicts him or herself, or he or she lies. Every politician has his or her weak point, and it's up to us journalists to find it. And four, there is no such thing as a silly question. Sometimes even the most naive questions lead to important matters. For instance, when you ask a politician how much money he or she makes, sometimes you get the most implausible responses. Curiously, most politicians answer this question with an "I don't know."

Once I've done my homework, and I've prepared for the interview, I like to play a psychological game in order to calm my nerves and humanize the person with whom I am going to speak. When I interview presidents or people with lots of power, I especially like imagining them with their big bellies and backaches, bags under their eyes, balding, with hair coming out of their ears, and dirty nails that haven't been cut. In other words, I like lowering them to a manageable and realistic level. If you let them stand on their untouchable, superhuman laurels, you will never have a good interview.

Then comes the fun part. Among journalists, I have been in more bathrooms in presidential palaces than most. Bathrooms reflect the personality of a head of state much better than impressive meeting rooms or the state dining rooms. Of course, I have never been in the private bathroom of a president, but I have been in almost every bathroom that I could find in the executive mansions where I have done interviews. And those bathrooms say a lot about a country.

There are some truly embarrassing and dirty bathrooms. I have been in a couple of them in Central America and the Caribbean. They symbolize a great deal of poverty, low budgets and a lack of attention to details. After all, these are the bathrooms that are used by a majority of guests, and that is the impression that they take home.

For example, the White House is conscious that every guest wants a souvenir, and since JFK and Jackie's portrait is far too big to fit in a briefcase, the executive mansion offers in its bathrooms paper hand towels emblazoned with the Great Seal of the United States engraved on them. It's funny that my colleagues and I consider this petty robbery acceptable, so we have several paper towel souvenirs from the White House. (Jack and Jackie's portrait still hangs there.)

But the bathroom that impressed me the most was the one at the Moneda Palace in Santiago de Chile. Like any reporter answering to nature's call, I asked where the bathroom was, and off to the lavatory I went. But imagine my surprise when I discovered a soldier standing right in front of the door of the bathroom, in what seemed to me a poor attempt at undercover espionage. Are the Chilean government's intelligence agencies interested in monitoring the renal failures and stomach problems of its guests? The government of dictator Augusto Pinochet was long gone, but it frightened me a bit that in a democracy a soldier would follow me all the way to the bathroom.

This bathroom routine before my interviews helps calm my nerves, washes the sweat off my hands and makes the visits to executive mansions all the more interesting. Apart from the answers that I will get from my interviewees, I am always curious to know what I will find in the presidential bathroom.

OF COURSE, MY INTERESTS go beyond my findings in the hemispheric "dirty war." Although fragile, democracy has been driven into Latin America. And while the regional trend toward democratization is inspiring, there is no doubt that the region's economic disparities there are creating deep problems that can endanger democracy in several countries. Our democracies are not made out of steel.

I am worried by the fact that when things aren't going well, there is a sad and reactionary tradition of looking for solutions with caudillos, coups d'état and strong-arm governments. Regardless of the terrible consequences of a host of authoritarian regimes in the region, we seem not to learn the most important lesson: human rights violations are unacceptable, as is the taking of a life in the search for a specific order. It's the beginning of the twenty-first century, and we still don't learn.

It's true that democracy—long awaited for decades by the majority of the countries in the region—wasn't a magic wand nor did it solve the most pressing problems in Latin America. With the exception of Cuba, all the countries of the Western Hemisphere have some type of democracy. But the main problem for the region—poverty—only tends to grow. In each one of my trips I see that there is now more poverty in the region than anytime before in its history, and it's growing. Granted, neoliberal policies have created more solid governments and balanced budgets, but it hasn't addressed the appalling distribution of wealth—the worst on earth—from which this hemisphere suffers. I have never seen such injustices and disparities even in Africa!

Bad governments tend to be an endemic condition in the region. It doesn't matter where I go, the most frequent criticisms I hear are hurled against presidents or useless and crooked officials who are never punished. Apart from each situation's particulars, the essence of the problem is that Latin American governments tend to base their leadership on personalities, and not institutions. Where the law doesn't rule, corruption does.

As a journalist, I have covered an endless number of flashy social events where the money raised regularly ends up in the politicians' bank accounts. Some people who have lost all hope say to me: "Let them steal. But they shouldn't steal too much. They should leave a little for the people."

Furthermore, our development cycle is continually ruined by crises that push us back two or three decades. The best example is Argentina, whose unreal economic circumstances used to allow for its citizens to visit the United States without a visa. Many would ask: "Why would an Argentine leave his country? He has it all right there."

But Argentina was living off credit. Like someone that lives off his or her credit cards, there inevitably comes the time when you have to pay the bill. Argentina's grace period ended during the last months of 2001, but the country had nothing to pay with. The Argentine peso's artificial parity with the U.S. dollar collapsed, and then Argentina had a whole stream of interim presidents parade through the Casa Rosada.

A government based on the rule of law and well-established precepts, and not on populism and improvisation, would have averted the present

Argentine crisis, the Mexican crisis of 1994, and most of the crises that came before that.

Of course, ill-informed, and in some cases resentful, sectors of Latin American society often blame the United States for everything that is wrong with Latin America. The U.S. position when confronted with frequent Latin American crises has little to do with foreign policy concerns, and mostly to do with internal political ones. The United States went to bat for the Mexican economy in 1994, but it didn't do the same for Argentina eight years later. This doesn't mean that the United States likes Mexicans more than Argentines. No. It's not the same thing to experience an economic boom—as occurred during the Mexican crisis—as it is to be in the midst of a recession and a war against terrorism, as is Argentina's case. Furthermore, the transitional Argentine government has not yet offered a convincing plan for economic recovery.

What has really caught my attention during these last two decades of covering the hemisphere is that the United States's relationships with Latin America have been historically made up of contradictory and very markedly different cycles. Sometimes the United States hugs you so tightly that it smothers you (like a bear does), and at other times it behaves as Latin Americans didn't exist. There are obsessive periods—like during the Central American war—followed by periods of isolationism.

The predictable manifestations of anti-Americanism in Latin America (more pronounced in countries with strong nationalistic traditions like Mexico and Argentina) are a response to both a tactless and offensive history of invasions and interventionism, as well as to a totally hands-off approach by the United States in critical moments. The United States mostly exists without looking at or thinking about the south.

On the other hand, Latin America cannot live without thinking about the United States, at least as its reference point. They do no have that luxury, since the majority of the region's nations export their goods to American markets, and they also depend on the giant of the north in cases of emergency. The simple existence of the world's only superpower in our own hemisphere forces a constant internal debate over the wishes and designs of the United States for the region. What does the United States want, and how do we respond?

It's interesting to note that at an official level, American politicians with whom I cross paths often have three very clear objectives for the region, which they repeat as a sort of mantra: the expansion of democracy, free trade and respect for human rights. However in practice, what shapes the United States's Latin American policies are the obvious and not so obvious threats to American security—terrorism, drug trafficking, leftist guerrillas—and the desire to expand American economic influence.

I live in two worlds: the United States and Latin America. From here, be it Miami, Los Angeles or New York, I constantly look south. And when I'm down there, I look north. But I am never totally accepted in either. In Latin America they dismiss me by saying: "Oh, but you live in the United States," as if that would keep me from understanding what is going on. And in the United States, some are still suspicious of my place of origin and accent.

Journalism, however, is the conduit that combines these two worlds.

I'm convinced that governing systems built on a personal leadership style, instead of on institutions, encourage abuses and the amassing of power and wealth in the hands of the few. That's why I believe that a journalist's main societal role is to ask hard questions that can prevent—or at least expose—abuses of power. I think that's the task of Latin American journalism.

I must recognize that for me it's easy to go out and cover a story, confront a president and return to my trenches in Miami. Nobody censors me, and I have means of transportation and a good salary that keeps me from being tempted by political pressures and economics. But for example, a reporter in Colombia runs the risk of dying or being kidnapped for doing exactly the same thing that I do every day in the United States.

It's one thing to refuse demands from a multinational corporation or an authoritarian government when you are well paid. The issue is very different when you're making a pathetic salary—as is the case with many Latin American reporters—and you barely have enough to eat and to send your children to school. If we add to this the close friendships and alliances among the ruling classes—politicians protected by the media, businessmen supported by public officials, servicemen tied to drug traffickers and criminals—then we must conclude that being a critical journalist in Latin America is a rebellious act, and in some cases, truly revolutionary.

TWO BOOKS HAD A TREMENDOUS influence on my choosing journalism as a career and as a way of life. One is *La Noche de Tlatelolca*, by Elena Poniatowska, which is a compilation of accounts of the massacre carried out by the Mexican army on October 2, 1968. The other is *Interview with History*, by Oriana Fallaci.

I have had the pleasure of interviewing Elena a couple of times in Mexico City. The strength, honesty and sensitivity with which she explains the world have always touched me deeply, both in person and in her books. I do not know Fallaci. "Journalism is an extraordinary and terrible privilege," wrote the Italian writer and reporter. "Terrible" because it brings us closer to wars, destruction, violence, the lowest expressions of the human condition. It is extraordinary, however, because it allows us to witness history in the making.

I fell into journalism almost by accident. I wanted to make news, not cover it. I soon realized, however, that journalism would allow me to be in places where the world was changing and to meet the people who were changing the world. Wonderful! So I could be a man of my time and experience the world. That is precisely why journalism is a genuine privilege.

One of the things I regret is not having the courage to approach the legendary Italian journalist in Saudi Arabia. We were staying at the same hotel in Dhahran during the Persian Gulf War, but I didn't want to bother her. I left it for later, but then we were both swept up in trying to be the first journalist to enter a liberated Kuwait, I wanted to tell Oriana that from her book I learned that the principal job of an interviewer is not to be liked but to ask the difficult questions, to get to the heart of the matter, to reveal the contradictions of the interviewee, particularly those who wield a lot of power. Her aggressive style of interviewing, without holding back, made an impact on mine.

Perhaps this is why I approach an interview like a war. Everyone has a vulnerable spot. Concealed in the dialogue is the fight for control. What controls the interview, the questions of the interviewer or the agenda of the interviewee? What prevails, the interest the interviewee has in hiding his errors and contradictions or the insistence and insight of the interviewer in drawing out what hurts and what defines that person?

I am convinced of what the correct attitude of the journalist in an interview should be: if I don't ask this question, no one else will. It's about unmasking the interviewee, revealing a new feature or expression. In the end it is preferable to confront the interviewee as you would an enemy and not a friend, and to do so with the conviction that the first interview could also be the last. I have had many encounters like these.

Some interviews I have done have gone more smoothly and have been more satisfying than others. I recall a moving conversation about death with the Chilean writer Isabel Allende, and a wonderful exchange with six Nobel prize winners (at a conference of the Organization of American States in Washington). "We also say stupid things," said the only woman and only American in the group, Jody Williams (peace, 1997), in order to calm my nerves in front of the impressive group of thinkers: Argentine Pérez Esquivel (peace, 1980), Costa Rican Oscar Arias (peace, 1987), Derek Walcott from the Caribbean island of Saint Lucia (literature, 1992), Mexican Mario Molina (chemistry, 1995) and Canadian John Polanyi (chemistry, 1986). I learned more from them than from any president, but what they said was not necessarily news.

The opposite generally occurs with presidents. They don't say many memorable things, but their comments are news, even when they are lies. That was the case with former president of Colombia, Ernesto Samper, when he denied having any knowledge that his election campaign received $6 million dollars of drug trafficking money, or when Ernesto Zedillo pretended not to know about the antidemocratic way in which he was elected president of Mexico in 1994, and his absurd denial of having attended a much publicized meeting in March 1995 with former president Carlos Salinas de Gortari, or when Salinas de Gortari denied that he had any knowledge that his brother Raúl was involved in suspect business transactions while he was president, or when Daniel Ortega said he didn't know how much he paid for a house in Managua that he had, in fact, appropriated.

During my career as a journalist, I have interviewed about fifty rulers and heads of state, and with very few exceptions, the powerful public image rarely compares with the imperfect being made of flesh and bone that I have to meet. From my interviews in Latin America, I think that I've done five interviews that clearly illustrate the abuse of power throughout the region. Three of them were with presidents, but the most dramatic was with a victim of Augusto Pinochet's Chilean dictatorship, and the last one is with a dreamer whose only demand is that the United States allow his island—Puerto Rico—to stop being a colony.

I guess I know why Alejandro's grandmother complained that I asked too many questions. I'm still proud of doing so, though.

ERNESTO SAMPER: WHEN A PRESIDENT LIES

Bogotá, Colombia, January 24, 1996. It was one o'clock in the morning, and Pres. Ernesto Samper had interrupted an emergency meeting of ministers in the Palace of Nariño to speak with me. More than special deference, Samper wanted to be sure that the world would hear his version of the scandal that was on the verge of costing him the presidency.

Five hours earlier I had heard the accusations of Fernando Botero, the former director of Samper's electoral campaign, who was being held in a cell at the Escuela de Caballería in Bogotá. The accusations were overwhelming. According to Botero, President Samper "knew about the large sums of drug money received by his campaign," and he participated in the administration of those funds and in a "cover-up operation." In short, Botero was accusing the president of having received $6 million from drug traffickers from the Cali cartel during his electoral campaign, with the goal of defeating the opposition candidate Andrés Pastrana.

Botero, just like former treasurer Santiago Medina, had been arrested for suspicion that he had allowed the infiltration of drug money. Now, however, Botero had turned his back on his old boss and was ready to tell all; first, to save himself, and second, according to him, out of a moral commitment to the country.

My interview with Botero, which had been organized in complete secrecy, took President Samper, who had defeated Pastrana in the recent elections, by surprise. Now it was he who wanted to tell his version of events.

"Regrettably, Mr. Fernando Botero is lying," Samper said. "He designed the campaign himself so that the administrative side would be completely autonomous from the political side."

"But aren't you the one who is responsible in the end for the campaign? How can you say: 'I am a candidate but this isn't my responsibility, this doesn't concern me'?" I asked him.

"I didn't receive the checks, I didn't hand over the receipts."

"Either you are lying, or Mr. Botero is lying. One of you has to be lying, you can't both be telling the truth."

"Yes, I agree completely, which is why I am pointing out today that Mr. Botero—who is in a rather difficult situation from both an emotional and a legal point of view—is lying in order to save himself."

"But how can it be that your campaign director knew about having received drug money, that your treasurer knew about it, other people knew about it, and you, the candidate, did not know about it? Don't they tell you what's going on?" I persisted.

"No, I had no responsibility for the finances," he concluded sharply.

"Don't you think you should resign?" I asked.

"Of course not," Samper said. "Considering that I am not responsible for the campaign events, and that that blame was analyzed and I was exonerated, why would I resign?"

That's where it ended, or so I thought, Samper was never going to accept his share of the blame nor would he resign the presidency. We sent the interviews of Botero and Samper via satellite to Miami. Then I went with Patsy Loris, the producer, and Angel Matos, the cameraman, to El Nogal, a private club, to spend the night, for reasons of security. Very few people knew where we were staying.

The following morning, when I came down from my room to meet the driver who would take us to the Univision office in Bogotá, a pale receptionist told me that the head of security for the club was looking for me. I ran into him in the lobby. "We received a death threat against you," he said, getting right to the point. "Is it that serious?" I asked. "We always take these things very seriously," he responded.

Nervous, I asked the receptionist what the threat was. She looked at the head of security as if asking permission to speak, and then she told me that she had received a call around nine o'clock that morning. The message was, "Tell Ramos we're going to kill him." When she asked the caller to identify himself, he hung up.

The police arrived shortly after and installed a system in the main telephone exchange to intercept calls. A second threat was received around eleven o'clock that morning. According to the receptionist, the man's voice seemed to be the same as the one from the earlier call, and he also used the word *"quebrar,"* a synonym for death in Colombia. According to one of the police investigators, "the phone call was traced to a cell phone tied to a government official." It was unfeasible for me to substantiate that information, but the look of worry on his face was quite convincing. He told me, "We cannot guarantee your life here in this country." At that moment it seemed really stupid to me that someone would threaten me on a government phone, so for years I ineffectively searched for whoever was behind the threats. Nevertheless, it was clear that my presence in Colombia made the government uncomfortable, since we were broadcasting all the facts about the Samper scandal to the United States and Latin America. In the end, whoever it was that wanted me out of the country, he or she got his or her way.

The police and the head of security of the club led me to a room and drew the curtains until they could organize a convoy of patrol cars and motorcycles, reinforced by agents from the public prosecutor's office, to take us to the airport to catch the first flight bound for the United States. We entered the airport via the runway. I boarded an American Airlines plane, and once back in Miami I spent several weeks under the protection of bodyguards and members of the Dade County Police.

Angel Matos, one of the best cameramen in the industry, and the executive producer Patsy Loris, accompanied me courageously and with great poise during that trip to Colombia. Angel never lost perspective as to what was important in the most critical moments, besides ensuring our physical protection: he used a bulletproof vest to carpet the floor of the van that we shared with correspondent Raúl Benoit, he organized the final details of the delicate transfer to the airport—"You can never let your guard down," Raúl said in response to the multiple threats I received—and he established possible escape plans in case of an armed attack.

Years later, when Angel and I were recalling this incident, he smacked himself on the forehead with his two gigantic hands and said, "It's scary not to be scared," and he was right. Angel acted like an experienced soldier on that occasion, without an ounce of fear. "The real danger," Angel recalls, "was that among the three different security bodies that accompanied us to the Bogotá airport were the gunmen who wanted to kill you."

Raúl Benoit was not totally convinced that they would have wanted to kill me. "I think it would have been a tremendous publicity stunt if they had kidnapped you," Raúl told me one afternoon in Miami, long after the threats occurred. "You were worth more alive and kidnapped than dead." We never did find out what the ulterior motive was behind the threats or who exactly was behind them, although I do have my suspicions.

Patsy, just like Angel and Raúl, maintained her composure until we took our seats on the plane. A couple of glasses of champagne relaxed us, and I saw a stream of tears run down Patsy's face. "Do you realize what happened to us?" she repeated, in disbelief. "Do you realize? They could have killed us all."

In addition to that experience in Colombia, Patsy has been a true guardian angel throughout my career as a journalist. She has made possible countless exclusive interviews and important news stories for which I ultimately got credit. Television is very unfair; those who work behind the camera like Patsy—indispensable and irreplaceable in the production of the Noticiero Univision—are rarely in the public eye. Without her, a wonderful journalist, and the Univision team, my career would have ended in a ball of fire.

In mid-1996, the Colombian Congress exonerated Samper for a second time from accusations of having received money from drug traffickers during his presidential campaign. Ironically, several members of congress who voted to acquit Samper were also accused of having received money from drug traffickers.

After the two unresolved death threats, I did not have the slightest desire to return to Colombia, but President Samper offered us another interview in order to try to regain his honor, and it was difficult to resist the temptation to interview him again. We took extreme security measures; I traveled to Bogotá wearing a bulletproof vest, and I was transported from the airport to the presidential home lying down in the back of a heavily guarded van.

There had been a significant change at the Palace of Nariño. A beautiful painting of a fat woman by Fernando Botero, the father of Samper's former associate, no longer hung on the walls of the presidential palace, and Samper was breathing a little easier.

Before the second interview began, I asked Samper if he knew who was behind the death threats I had received. He told me he was unaware of the threats, something I thought strange since they had been reported in the Colombian and international press. I dropped the subject and focused on the questions.

Very early in our conversation, I showed President Samper a photograph in which he appeared with two drug traffickers. Both had been killed. One of them was Elizabeth Montoya de Sarría, whose alias was *"la monita retrechera* ("resourceful blonde"). Elizabeth Montoya had been arrested in April 1986 in Los Angeles for drug possession and trafficking.

"Don't people have a right to suspect that something strange is going on when you appear—" I began when Samper interrupted me.

"If the photograph were real, yes," he said.

"It was in 1989, wasn't it?"

"It's a photomontage, my dear Mr. Ramos." Then, pointing to the photograph he said, smiling, "You see, I have one arm that is going around the room and then returns, and the hand you see here . . . is not my hand."

Samper was not going to give in. Fernando Londoño, Botero's lawyer, sent the original photograph that I showed Samper to a laboratory in the United States to see if it had been altered and was, in fact, a photomontage, as the president suggested. A former intelligence officer of the U.S.

government determined that the photograph was probably real, even though he couldn't give a definitive conclusion.

Samper never acknowledged that the photograph in which he appeared with two drug traffickers was real, or that he was aware of and participated in the administration of $6 million of drug money given to his election campaign, or that his presidency was an embarrassment for Colombians who were upset to have a president like him. Samper continued to insist that the mistakes in his campaign and his presidency occurred behind his back. I decided not to remain in the capital after the interview; that very night I left for Quito.

I greatly admire the Colombian character and culture. Colombians enjoy a party like no one else; maybe because historically they have lived so close to death. That's why, among other things, I regret not being able to visit Colombia more often. In 1998, I tried to return to cover the presidential elections that Andrés Pastrana won. However, a few days before the trip, some wreaths or floral arrangements for the dead arrived at the Univision office bearing the names of all the journalists who were planning to be there for the election. I haven't the faintest idea how they found out about our plans, since they had not been made public. It was perfectly clear that for a certain sector of the population we were not welcome. Just in case, in the end we decided not to go.

I NEVER INTERVIEWED Andrés Pastrana while he was in the presidency. To begin with, I thought that it would be unethical for me to interview someone whom I held in high esteem. I always thought that both Pastrana and I fought against Samper from the same side, but he in politics and I through journalism. It's difficult to criticize someone with whom you have many things in common.

Nevertheless, I must recognize that Pastrana made a colossal mistake when he handed over to the guerrillas of the Revolutionary Armed Forces of Colombia (FARC) a piece of Colombia the size of Switzerland, without the guerrillas agreeing to a cease-fire, an end to kidnappings or attacks on civilians. Three years after the experiment was put to work, Pastrana had to reverse himself at the beginning of 2002.

Things in Colombia will get worse before they get better. The reason is quite simple. None of the armed groups has enough firepower to beat the others. The Colombian army doesn't have the military strength to defeat the FARC and ELN (National Liberation Army) guerrillas. The guerrillas cannot defeat the Colombian army and the paramilitaries. And the paramilitaries can never militarily dominate the guerrillas nor the Colombian army.

Colombians have a lot to learn from the peace processes in El Salvador and Guatemala. Only though negotiations will Colombians—as the Salvadorans and Guatemalans before them—find peace. Meanwhile, Colombia will go on destroying itself in an all-out and meaningless, war.

HUGO CHÁVEZ: WHEN A PRESIDENT STOPS LISTENING

"I am not the devil," Chávez told me in our first interview. He was still listening then. His hands were raw from greeting so many people. I spoke with him the day before he won the presidential election on December 6, 1998. It seemed incredible that a man of the military who rose up in arms seven years earlier and who was thrown in prison because of it was about to achieve with votes what he could not achieve with bullets.

A presidential pardon by former president Rafael Caldera freed him from prison, and a populist campaign of revenge had him siding with the poor, which was about 80 percent of Venezuelans. His clear electoral victory put an end to forty years of domination by the two traditional Venezuelan political parties, Acción Democrática and Copei. Even before his election, however, there were already serious doubts about his democratic convictions.

"How can someone who tried to stage a military coup be called a Democrat?" I asked him.

"It's possible," he replied. "But do you know what's going on here? A system that was called democratic degenerated into tyranny. On February 4, 1992, when I and many other members of the Venezuelan military headed out with rifles in our hands, we did so in search of democracy."

"But the government that you wanted to overthrow had been democratically elected," I argued.

"Yes," he said, "but in the name of a democratic election, Pres. Carlos Andrés Pérez massacred an entire town and used the same troops to gun people down at close range. You saw that, the world saw it: the *Caracazo.*"

Ironically, the same criticisms of authoritarianism that Chávez had hurled at Pérez came back to haunt him years later. I spoke to the commander again—"That's my job," he said, pleased—on February 18, 2000, and his attitude toward the press had changed dramatically. I accompanied him on a business trip to the state of Táchira near the Colombian border, and he forced me to trail after him the entire day before agreeing to talk to me for a few minutes. I guess he wanted me to see him with the people, as that is his strength.

Eight of the twenty-four journalists who accompanied Chávez on the trip were Cuban, emphasizing Chávez's recent closeness with the Castro dictatorship. "The course that the Venezuelan people are following is the same course, and it is heading toward the same sea that the Cuban people are heading toward," the president had said previously, continuing to call the Cuban leader "brother Fidel."

"Cháaavez! Presideeente!" cried the residents of La Fría and Guarumito as the president gave out kisses, handshakes and received hundreds of letters and pieces of paper with all kinds of request: help *mi'jito* who is sick, I need work, the mayor of my town is a crook . . . and Chávez, right there, instructed the ministers who were with him to solve the problems of a boy without an eye, a school without teachers and those victimized by the worst rains in half a century.

In the meantime, his bodyguards were sweating blood. Without any apparent concern for his security, Chávez threw himself into the crowd and disappeared. I have never seen a Latin American leader do something like this since the assassination of the Mexican presidential candidate Luis Donaldo Colosio in 1994. Chávez, though, whether for show or out of populist conviction, was doing it.

When I sat down to speak with him in the open courtyard of a rural school, he insisted on being surrounded by his ministers, bodyguards and hundreds of La Fría residents. So every time I asked him something he didn't like, the people would boo, and when the president responded, his words were followed by applause. Never in my life had I conducted an interview with fans cheering and booing.

Chávez's language was still loaded with references to Bolívar, and the way he compared himself to Jesus Christ was alarming. The first significant change I noticed in Chávez, however, was that he was no longer listening. He felt powerful, and it was little wonder: he was in the process of changing the constitution in order to allow for his immediate reelection, and he had the Congress, the court, the army, the media and the unions under his control.

I asked Chávez about the accusations of corruption against two of his main advisors, his closeness with the Cuban dictatorship, the abuses of the army that he led, the criticisms about the management of the crisis during the devastating floods in late 1991, about his broken promises to improve the economy and about the way in which he was cornering all the power in Venezuela. Chávez, however, didn't want to be challenged, much less by a foreigner in his country, and instead of answering me he decided to attack me.

I asked him if the rumors that he had solicited Fidel Castro's personal advice for managing the floods were true.

"You are repeating garbage, *hermano,*" he responded, annoyed.

"That's why I want to ask you . . ."

"I will respond with my dignity, and for the dignity of the people," Chávez insisted in an accusatory tone. "Only garbage is coming from your mouth."

"I'm asking you a question. My job is to ask questions."

"Fine, fine. But you are collecting garbage, manure. Why don't you collect something else?"

"Well, it's a legitimate question as a journalist, don't you agree?"

"Am I obligated to respond only to what you ask me?" Chávez asked me now.

"No, of course not."

"I have the right to express myself too, don't I? So I will repeat myself, *hermano,* with all due respect. You are carrying around a load of garbage. It seems that only garbage reaches you journalists. It seems that you gravitate toward garbage, and if there is something worthwhile, you either ignore it or you just don't know how to collect it . . . What kind of questions are these?"

The Chávez I was interviewing was very different from the candidate seeking the presidency. He no longer listened, he no longer remembered. When I reminded him that two years earlier he had told me that Cuba "was indeed a dictatorship," he avoided the subject. "It is not my business to condemn the Castro regime," he responded abruptly.

Our contentious interview ended with a typical Chavista gesture. Right there, in the middle of the cement courtyard with its sad basketball court and surrounded by his enthusiastic followers. Chávez made a dramatic pause. "Give me a *cafecito,* please," he said to one of his assistants.

He was brought two cups of *guarapo,* a very weak coffee. He gave me one, took a sip of his, and then raised his hand in the air.

"Viva México," Chávez cried out, as he clinked his cup against mine.

"Viva Venezuela," I countered. It was the only time all afternoon that I received applause.

That is precisely what Chávez wants: that nothing happen in Venezuela without his approval. He even wants to control applauding. Chávez's is an adventure doomed to failure.

There is no real democracy in Venezuela. What there is in Venezuela is Chavism. President Chávez, after achieving through the ballot what he couldn't get with the gun, broke his election promises and amended the constitution so that he could be reelected. Not only did Chávez dictate the new constitution to his followers, he also controls the army, the Congress, the judiciary and the Supreme Court. Only the workers and businesspeople have rebelled against Chávez's governing style.

Chávez's popularity is declining sharply. He promised to govern in the name of those with the least in Venezuela, and now there are more poor people than ever in the country, even though Venezuela makes millions of dollars from its oil reserves. Chávez is a populist and demagogue, with a soft spot for dictators like Fidel Castro and Saddam Hussein, and who also suffers from illusions of grandeur; Chávez constantly compares himself to Jesus Christ.

As the internal opposition in Venezuela grows, several scenarios for

Chávez's departure have emerged. From my point of view, it would be very dangerous if Chávez were removed by force. A coup would make him a martyr, and it would seem doubtful that the democratic governments of the region could support a junta—either civilian or military—that over-threw a legitimately elected president.

Chávez is falling under his own weight. His economic policies are clearly improvised, and the government functions at the whims of his con-stantly changing moods, sometimes combative, other times conciliatory, and always highly paternalistic.

Chávez is a caudillo of the twenty-first century, who arrived late for the dictators' party.

HUGO CHÁVEZ: WHEN A PRESIDENT STOPS LISTENING, PART 2

"Finally, Chávez isn't in power anymore," I thought to myself as I arrived in Caracas that same Friday morning, April 12, when the Venezuelan pres-ident was escorted out of Miraflores Palace by the group of military men behind the coup d'état. The passengers on board the American Airlines flight began clapping when the plane landed in Maiquetía Airport. Yet they weren't applauding the pilot's skills. A businessman who was happily returning to his country from Miami said out loud, so that all could hear: "We've arrived in a free country."

I also couldn't hide my enthusiasm at being able to witness the fall of one of the most authoritarian presidents that Venezuela has had in fifty years. The unpleasant experience that I had when I interviewed Chávez two years ago had turned me into a frequent critic of his from abroad. I was not all disturbed with his departure. "One less to deal with," I thought. "Now we only have to get rid of Castro."

That same Friday night I had dinner with the Univision team that ac-companied me in a restaurant in Las Mercedes neighborhood of Caracas. The atmosphere was festive. An executive who had drunk a little too much and whose tie was a mess offered to buy us a round of drinks, which we graciously accepted, as we all laughed together. Why shouldn't we accept the offer? The tragic populist experiment known as *Chavism* was finished.

Or at least that's what we thought. We greeted the new day drinking margaritas.

The day before, Thursday, April 11, Venezuela experienced one of the bloodiest days in its modern history. A peaceful march by hundreds of thousands demanding the resignation of President Chávez turned into a massacre after the leaders of the march led the people toward Miraflores Palace. Only a few blocks away from the president's home, where Chávez was shielding himself from the crowd, members of the so-called "Bolivarian Circles" began shooting into the crowd.

Later on, the Chávez administration would try to give its own version of the events by insinuating that the ones responsible for shooting into the crowd were the members of the opposition. But the televised images recorded by a cameraman from Venevisión—Venezuela's largest network—did not allow for the president's lies. The video was chilling to watch. Over and over again, Chávez's sympathizers were shooting wildly from a bridge over Baral Avenue into the crowd below, then loading their weapons again and shooting some more. The majority of the dead died from a single shot to the head, and the only people who can shoot so accurately are marksmen who have been trained by the army or the police. I crossed that same bridge and saw for myself how easy it is to shoot someone marching below. But the killers were cowards: they shot their victims as if they were in a carnival shooting gallery. They killed in cold blood from a vantage point. It was a heinous criminal act. It is unforgivable.

Chávez lost his authority because these images were shown over and over again in both the Venezuelan and international media. It was a "video-coup." The armed forces establishment, frustrated at having to accept the inevitable truth that those responsible for shooting at the crowds were people tied to the Chávez administration, turned against the president and were able to remove him from Miraflores Palace in the wee hours of the morning of Friday, April 12. Chávez was detained, toppled and defeated.

We would later learn that Chávez was transferred to five different places until he finally ended up in the military base on Orchila Island. Right before he left the executive mansion, the same group of servicemen who negotiated Chávez's departure named Pedro Carmona—a business-man and president of an umbrella organization for all business concerns in Venezuela—as leader of the provisional government. But Carmona, naive and ill advised, made the terrible decision that in a few hours would cost him his position: he dissolved the National Assembly and removed judges and governors.

The American ambassador in Caracas then tried—with the help of a Venezuelan businessman tied to the media—to make it known to Carmona that this type of government could never be recognized by the administration of George W. Bush. But the message arrived to late: Carmona had already crowned himself "king of Venezuela." Or as Teodoro Petkoff of the newspaper *Tal Cual* told me in an interview: what Camona did was conduct a "Pinochet-type coup *lite*." Carmona had hurdled over the Constitution of 1999 in an Olympic fashion. Granted, the Constitution may have been controversial, but it was indeed approved by a majority of the electorate.

When I read the news of what Carmona had done, as I was lying on the bed in my hotel room, something didn't make sense to me. I thought: "This guy is going to be left all alone and very fast." I put on the television, and my suspicions were confirmed. None of the presidents who were in San José, Costa Rica, for a meeting of the Rio Group was willing to recognize Carmona's new administration. I said to Rafael Tejero, a producer with whom I have shared some of the most interesting news events in this hemisphere: "This doesn't look good." Rafael just bit his lip and shook his head from side to side.

We went to work all day covering the arrests—or almost lynchings—of former officials of the Chávez administration. When the regional headquarters of the "Bolivarian Circles" was raided, large caches of weapons were found, alongside posters of Che Guevara and Fidel Castro. The weapons were shown to the press as irrefutable evidence that those close to Chávez had the means to carry out the massacre of Thursday, April 11.

When I returned to the Caracas Hilton Hotel in the afternoon of Saturday, April 14, I put on the television—it's become a type of necessary reflection each time that I travel—and I noticed that all the channels were broadcasting movies, cooking shows and variety programs. It left me with the erroneous impression that nothing important was going on in Venezuela, so I called the Univision offices in Miami so they could get me out of the country on the next available flight. I told them: "Nothing's going on here."

Rafael and I left with our cameraman, Frank Ramírez, for the studios of Venevisión—a corporate affiliate of Univision—in order to edit that day's report. We found that the people at Venevisión were very nervous. Network executives walked in and out of the editing room with worried looks on their faces. In his Cuban accent, and with his fine-tuned ear. Rafael said to me: "This is not right."

When we walked into a room where all the programs being broadcast throughout Venezuela were simultaneously monitored, I realized the root of the problem: CNN en Español was interviewing military leaders and Chávez's officials who were assuring the public that the former president had never resigned and that he, Hugo Chávez, was still the legitimate president of Venezuela. But more worrisome than that were the images of thousands of Chávez sympathizers literally taking over Miraflores Palace. None of these were broadcast in Venezuela, where the only things on television were movies and game shows. I turned to Rafael: "This is shocking. The new government is falling apart on CNN, and no one here is saying anything."

We finished editing our report, and just as we were going to send it to Miami via satellite, we came across the first logistical obstacle: due to security concerns, Venevisión couldn't beam it to Miami. All of the satellite transmission equipment was being hidden in several locations throughout the city. We tried to leave the studios, but the security guards didn't allow us. They didn't even have to say a word.

An angry and defiant mob had surrounded the headquarters and studios of Venevisión. They were all Chávez supporters. There's no doubt about it. They came on motorcycles, armed with clubs and stones, and maybe, guns. There were around 200 to 250 of them. That's when I realized why the reporters from Venevisión, Radio Caracas TV, Televen,

Globovisión and other media couldn't go out to the street to cover the takeover of Miraflores Palace: the hordes of Chávez supporters would've beaten them without mercy.

That's also when I recalled the statement of an official at the Interamerican Press Society: "They have no freedom of expression in Venezuela. But they do have brave journalists." That same group of Chávez sympathizers became so infuriated at the tight security surrounding Venevisión, as well as at the building's solid masonry construction—it looked like a castle on a mountain top—that they moved on to the more vulnerable Radio Caracas TV building and destroyed its windows.

We also got a good scare. While we were reporting via satellite during the quickly changing events on Saturday night, a hail of gunfire forced us to turn off our lights and go off the air. These perilous circumstances—and groups of Chávez sympathizers riding around on their mopeds beating journalists—stopped us from going back on. In Miami many people erroneously thought that I had been arrested, or that they had shot me. Meanwhile, my relatives and friends went through real moments of anguish until I was able to leave our improvised hiding place and find a phone to tell them that I was fine. I was really frightened, but okay.

Chávez's return to power was now just a matter of time. One by one, the military leaders and officials who had betrayed him were doing their acts of contrition on channel eight of the Venezuelan Broadcasting Company, the state-run network that was back on the air after two days of silence. In other words, *Chavism's* leadership regrouped on channel eight.

In the end, several dynamics came together to bring Chávez back to power: the clumsiness of Carmona's provisional government, the loyalty that Chávez inspired among the lower and middle ranks of the army, the slowness with which the military personnel who led the coup negotiated the never-signed resignation and probable departure of the overthrown president to Cuba, and the thousands of Chávez sympathizers that retook the streets and Miraflores Palace.

It was incredible. Never in my journalistic career had I seen something like it. A "video-coup," followed by a countercoup forty-eight hours later.

As a journalist, I felt privileged to report this event firsthand. Who has ever been witness to a coup and a countercoup all within two days? That's why I became a journalist. But on a personal level, I was filled with despair when I saw that a "crazy chatterbox"—the nickname for Chávez coined by the Mexican author Carlos Fuentes—would again rule with a lethal combination of repression and populism.

"Render unto Caesar what is Caesar's, unto God what is God's, and unto the people what is the people's." This was President Chávez's opening line of a long-winded address that he gave shortly after returning to Miraflores Palace in the early morning hours of Sunday, April 14. That day there were no newspapers or newscasts, but there was a lot of looting.

I wrote in my notepad: "This country is again fucked-up." It was four thirty in the morning, and Chávez was on television. I took the remote control and I clicked a button. Suddenly Chávez disappeared from the screen, but only for a short period. He'd be back again, in full force.

DANIEL ORTEGA: WHEN A PRESIDENT HIDES IN HIS HOUSE

I try to find the right strategy that will make the interviewee bend, especially if he has a lot of power and influence. There is no such thing as a leader who doesn't have contradictions. Some of them indeed are innocent enough. But in other cases, these contradictions tend to reflect mega-abuses.

Every interviewee reaches a point where he breaks, where he is vulnerable. And you don't have to do exhaustive journalistic research in order to find that breaking point. The issue that breaks most presidents and politicians is money. I recommend to my journalism students that they should "do the president's arithmetic." Add up how much money they've made as public officials, and then go check how much more they really have in liquid and concrete assets. Very few presidents, very, very few, pass the money test. Basically, simple arithmetic doesn't work for them. Almost all of them end up with a lot more money than their modest public servant salaries would suggest. And the most egregious example of this that I have ever found is the case of former Nicaraguan Pres. Daniel Ortega, who says that even he doesn't know how much he paid for the house he lives in.

ONE CANNOT UNDERSTAND the recent history of Nicaragua without Daniel Ortega. Not only was he the president of the country after the Sandinistas toppled Somoza's dictatorship, but for years he tried to regain the presidency that Violeta Chamorro had snatched from him in the 1990 elections. It's impossible not to recognize the merit and the importance of the Sandinista revolution in ending decades of dictatorships. It's also necessary, however, to shed light on their abuses when they were in power.

Nicaraguans know one of the clearest examples of this abuse as *"la piñata."* It refers to property that was confiscated by the Sandinistas and used for their personal benefit, and the house in which Daniel Ortega lives falls into this category. It is actually a three-thousand-square-foot fortress with six bedrooms, six fountains, two living rooms and several dining rooms. The house originally belonged to Jaime Morales, who later would be one of the main advisors to former president Arnoldo Alemán. He laid the first stone, and as time passed he made it more beautiful with valuable wood and works of art, until it had practically become a museum, according to what I was told.

The Sandinistas took power on July 19, 1979, two days after Jaime Morales traveled to Mexico City as the head of the Red Cross in order to obtain urgent blood donations. Morales's wife and three children were on vacation in Miami. What a surprise when they found out that two days after the victory of the revolution, Daniel Ortega and his companion Rosario Murillo had taken possession of their house.

"For absenteeism," was the argument used by the Sandinistas to confiscate property. However, Morales was not in the country because of a mission ordered by the Sandinistas themselves. Since then there has been a prolonged legal battle between the Morales family and Daniel Ortega over the house.

Morales calculates that when the Sandinistas took the house, it was worth over $1.5 million, including the works of art, maybe even $2 million. Ortega, however, according to receipts of the Banco de Inversiones Nicaragüenses de Desarrollo, which Morales had in his possession, only paid fifteen hundred dollars. That first and only payment was made in

April 1990, after Ortega's defeat in the presidential election, and supposedly it was made to assure that the property would remain in his name.

Ortega maintains that the house is a "symbol" of the Sandinista revolution, acquired "within the legal framework" and that if he were to return it to Morales, he would endanger the homes that were confiscated and handed out to the Nicaraguan people after the fall of Somoza. The interesting thing about the case is that when I spoke with Ortega in late 1996 in Managua, he didn't recall what he had paid for "his" house.

"ALLOW ME TO SPEAK directly to you about your house," I said.

"Yes."

"They say it's worth $2 million. How much did you pay for the house?"

"Well, the truth is . . . first . . . it's not worth $2 million. That is an exaggeration."

"How much is it worth? What's your estimate?"

"Eh . . . it's not worth that much; it's worth much less."

"A million?"

"No, no, no."

"How much did you pay for the house?"

"Well, I paid a price of . . . of . . . of . . . I paid a price in line with what was being paid back then for houses in this country."

"How much? How much was it then?"

"Well, the truth is that I don't have the exact figure, I don't have it. Perhaps if I had it . . ."

"But more or less."

"It was very little, very little."

"Yes, but I'm asking you because many people fear your return to power because of this."

"Well, for me it would be very easy to leave the house . . . But on the other hand it would be a bad signal to thousands of Nicaraguans who would feel defenseless if I do that. That is to say, they would feel that if I leave my house they too will lose their houses, especially the humblest people, the poorest people."

ORTEGA NEVER DID TELL ME what he paid for his house. The hospitable phrase that is so often repeated in Latin America, *"Mi casa es su casa,"* became unspeakable for the Sandinista leader. He represents the old rebel who never understood that the Nicaraguan revolution was fought for all the people and not only for the very few who replaced the previous dictatorship with an authoritarian regime. Ortega, however, has made the history books by becoming the only candidate in Nicaragua who has lost three consecutive presidential elections. Perhaps one day he will realize that his time in power is long gone.

LUZ DE LA NIEVES AYRESS MORENO:
TORTURED DURING THE PINOCHET DICTATORSHIP

My hatreds are shared equally. I am as bothered by dictatorships of the right as I am by those of the left. The same way that I didn't allow Fidel Castro to put his hand on my shoulder, I would never accept an embrace from Augusto Pinochet. But I would have liked to confront him before he slipped into dementia. I never had the opportunity to do so. I used to enjoy hearing his puny, whining voice when he defended himself against the denunciations of massive violations of human rights during his murderous regime.

Ironically, leftist dictatorships such as Fidel's have gotten all types of help from all kinds of governments, while the brutal right-wing regimes quickly lose the international public relations battle. But I don't think that there is such a thing as good or bad, soft or hard, dictatorships. As far as I'm concerned, a dictator is a dictator is a dictator.

I HAVE NEVER LOOKED into Nieves's eyes. Of all the people I have interviewed, Nieves is the only one whose face I don't know. I know the sound of her voice, though, and it's a voice in pain.

"I didn't kill anybody, I didn't steal. My crime was being young, against the dictatorship, and rebelling against the military," Nieves told me by phone.

She was twenty-three years old when she was arrested for the first time. Gen. Augusto Pinochet, in September 1973, had just overthrown the democratically elected regime of Salvador Allende in a military coup. Nieves was freed, but a few months later, in January 1974, the military arrested her again, and what followed were the worst three years of her life.

When she recalls that time, Nieves's mother, Virginia M. de Ayress, says, still distressed, "What good is this shitty life if I can't even defend my family."

I found out about Nieves much later, in 1998, several years after democracy had returned to Chile. Her testimony, however, given on tape and smuggled out of the prison in the vagina of a friend and first made public in February 1975, tormented me:

> This is how Pinochet tortured me: I was taken prisoner along with my *papá* and my fifteen-year-old brother, Tato . . . it was an impressive operation, and they moved us to one of those houses of the SIM (Servicio de Inteligencia Militar) . . .
>
> They threw me on the floor where there was a lot of water, then they turned the force of the water on my body, primarily on my breasts, in my vagina, anus, eyes, mouth, and on the back of my neck . . .
>
> Then they called Papá and began to torture him in front of me so I would talk, and they kept hitting me at the same time . . . then they called my brother and did the same thing to him . . .
>
> They pulled my nipples and made these cuts on me with knives or razors. They stuck their filthy hands in my vagina, as well as bottles, fingers, sticks and metal objects, and then they applied electric shock again.
>
> They pulled me outside and pretended they were going to execute me.
>
> In Tejas Verdes I was one of those who was tortured most often, along with another woman who was five months pregnant . . . they left me for dead. I think a lot of people died in Tejas Verdes, but I don't know how many or their names; I was always in solitary confinement.
>
> Among the new forms of daily torture I experienced . . . they lay me on top of a table, tied my hands and my feet, and stretched me . . . they opened my legs and stuck mice in my vagina, and all the while they kept stretching me.

Nieves is a survivor. Her testimony was recirculated because at the end of the century many people did not know or did not want to remember the horrors of Pinochet's dictatorship, especially the young people and the Chilean politicians.

Nieves spent forty months in prison, and then she was banished from Chile in December 1976 for being considered "a danger to national sovereignty." She lived in Germany, Italy, Africa, Mexico City and New York. "I was born in Chile, but I am from the world," she told me. She never stopped denouncing the atrocities committed during the Pinochet regime, particularly when the former dictator was forced to face justice in London and in his own country.

Despite her grief, Nieves is convinced that she beat the military that carried out the coup. When they stuck mice up her vagina, their goal—in addition to torture—was to sterilize her, causing toxoplasmosis. They were not successful.

Nieves has a daughter who turned twenty at the new millennium. Her strong, unbreakable, courageous voice melts when she speaks about her. "My daughter is my triumph over the military," she said proudly before hanging up the phone. She is the triumph of life over death.

RUBÉN BERRÍOS: DREAMING OF INDEPENDENCE

Vieques, Puerto Rico. At some other time or in some other place, Rubén Berríos could have been a guerrilla, but he was born in Puerto Rico and decided to be an independent. Like many Latin Americans, Berríos cannot understand that someone might prefer a life in a colony to one of freedom, even if that colony belongs to the United States. That is why he has dedicated his intellect and his energy into fighting for what, it would seem, very few in Puerto Rico want: independence.

A Puerto Rican journalist once described Puerto Rico's ambiguous political status with the following words: "There are birds that remain in the cage, even when the door is open." Berríos has tried to make the bird less afraid so he will fly.

In the most recent election and in most of the surveys, the independence movement did not receive even 5 percent of the vote. The options of statehood and the associated free state are buried in a bitter equilibrium that has left Puerto Rico in a permanent state of ambiguity. Maybe Vieques will disrupt that balance.

On April 19, 1999, two five-hundred-pound bombs accidentally killed Puerto Rican guard David Sanes in Vieques. The bombs had been dropped from an F-14 of the U.S. Navy. Since then, the proindependence fervor—which had much support in 1914, 1936 and 1945—has reappeared with uncommon strength.

"Not one bomb more," was the battle cry of politicians, activists and Puerto Ricans in general who were demanding an immediate end to U.S. naval exercises in Vieques. In other words, they were telling the navy: get out of my house. What few failed to consider was that running the United States off Vieques implied the risk that they would leave Puerto Rico for good. That is precisely what Berríos and other independents were looking to achieve: to do away with a century of colonization. The United States—difficult to believe in this era—still insists on imposing by force its position in Vieques.

I met Berríos in Vieques the day before he was arrested. On Thursday, May 4, 2000, FBI agents and local police removed more than two hundred demonstrators who for 361 days had made Vieques an independent territory. A problem with diverticulitis had caused him to lose thirty pounds, but at the age of sixty he looked strong and determined. Almost a year camped out on the island had not affected his appearance: he had impeccably clean nails, a white beard that was well trimmed, and he wore a loose fitting shirt, green pants and no socks. In the small hut with its metal roof where he lived, I found, next to plates of *yautía*, rice, bananas and carrots, many books on Latin America. "Puerto Rico is not, has not been, nor will ever be American. It is Latin American and will take its place in concert with other free Latin American nations," he said to me as I shuffled through the books, including a biography of Kemal Atatürk (1881–1938), the founder of the new Turkey.

This was all an unmistakable sign of the historical vision that Berríos and his followers had for Puerto Rico. Colonization was a thing of the past.

The future meant independence. There is no question that Berríos is a dreamer, but all revolutions begin with a dream.

"Do you think the issue of Vieques is raising the possibility that Puerto Rico could be independent for the first time in a century?" I asked him on the beach, as we protected ourselves from the scorching sun.

"Well, the independence of Puerto Rico depends on the respect we Puerto Ricans have for ourselves and on losing our powerlessness," he said, "and the powerlessness is dying away with the issue of Vieques because we have the U.S. Navy at bay."

"Is Vieques responsible for that change? Is Vieques the catalyst that will lead to independence?"

"I think that in a few years we will see that Vieques is the catalyst for Puerto Rico's sovereignty. I haven't any doubt about this. Puerto Rico's history will be written in terms of before and after Vieques."

For Berríos, Puerto Rico is a nation with a language, identity, culture and history that are very different from the United States. Therefore, he does not see any chance of it becoming the fifty-first state.

"Do you think that statehood is now farther away than ever in the history of Puerto Rico?"

"Precisely. Statehood is a nightmare. It is not advisable for the Americans, the Puerto Ricans or Latin Americans. Puerto Rico is a different nation. There is an old saying in the countryside here: *"Ningún jíbaro se echa un guabal al pecho."* That is to say, no peasant would put a spider in the middle of his chest, and the American peasant is not going to put that spider on his chest.

Berríos was arrested and thrown off Vieques a few hours after our interview. On Monday, May 8, 2000, exactly one year after Berríos had set up his camp on the island, U.S. Navy military operations resumed on Vieques.

Those who thought that the issue of Vieques was going to die because of the events of September 11 are quite mistaken. But there has been a change of strategy to get the U.S. Navy out of Vieques, and eventually — for those whose goal is independence — take sovereignty over Puerto Rico away from the United States.

After the death of more than three thousand people at the World Trade Center in New York, at the Pentagon and in Pennsylvania, it just did not look right to hold violent protests against the U.S. naval presence on Vieques. Nobody wanted to give the impression of being anti-American, or of having ties with the terrorists.

What changed was the tone of the protests against the U.S. Navy, but what did not change was the decision by the majority of Puerto Ricans (according to polls) to put an end to the naval exercises, and to get the navy out of Vieques. Or so Rubén Berríos, the leader of the Pro-Independence Party, told me during a heated conversation in his old offices in San Juan at the end of 2001.

Berríos sounded optimistic. I have never doubted the authenticity of his struggle to see Puerto Rico become an independent country. And I was surprised to see that even after the terrorist attacks of September 11, his convictions are as strong as ever.

Looking me straight in the eyes, Berríos said to me: "One day, Puerto Rico will be independent."

"But will you be around to see it happen?" I asked him a little rudely.

"Of course I will!" he answered. But then Berríos qualified his answer: "I hope I will."

THE LAST TIME that I saw Berríos was on the island of Vieques, right before he was arrested, the independence leader's skin had lost some of the color that it had gotten after spending one year under the Vieques sun, but his mind had not stopped devising thousands of ways to find the right formula that will gain Puerto Rico its independence.

In a speech that he gave shortly after the terrorist attacks on the United States, Berríos said: "At the dawn of the twenty-first century . . . Puerto Rico is not a sovereign nation. And the reason is simple: we were turned into a colony of the United States in the twentieth century." But Berríos doesn't think that this has to be permanent. He is convinced that the Vieques situation has awakened Puerto Rican nationalism and the uncomfortable feelings that many Puerto Ricans have about being a colony. The war cry seems to be: "Puerto Rico for the Puerto Ricans!"

But Berríos isn't delusional either. He's very aware that in the last elections, his party—*el Independista*—didn't even get 5 percent of the vote. And with well-financed campaigns of those who want Puerto Rico to remain as is—a commonwealth—or of those who want it become the fifty-first state of the United States, it's doubtful that proindependence Puerto Ricans will reach their objective through a referendum.

So what to do?

Berríos proposes a change in strategy. This gray-haired independence leader with a pleasant smile loves to say: "The United States will do what we force it to do. We Puerto Ricans have to design a strategy for the twenty-first century."

Berríos's strategy consists in convening a constitutional convention dedicated to the issue of Puerto Rico's status, or something along those lines, in which all the political parties will come together to "force the United States to take into account the will of the Puerto Rican people." The question is: what is that will?

It's not hard to understand the fear of those Puerto Ricans who think that independence would turn Puerto Rico into a poverty-stricken third-world island. But Berríos responds by saying that the transition to national sovereignty would be a long one, and that nothing should stop Puerto Rico from signing very beneficial treaties (commercial, immigration, cultural) with the United States. For Berríos, the most important thing is to take Puerto Rican sovereignty away from the Americans.

Berríos's bet is that when Puerto Ricans lose their fear of being without the United States, there will be a viable political alternative available. According to him, the Vieques issue continues to be fundamental. For Berríos, if Vieques (*"la isla nena"* or "small island") manages to free itself from the United States, the big island will follow.

In other words, after the terror of September 11, the struggle for Vieques is more alive than ever.

Berríos goes against the current because he knows that great changes in history begin with an idea and a lot of determination. And that's why he piques my curiosity so much. If Berríos had been born in another country, he would have had no alternative but to become a revolutionary. But he was born in Puerto Rico. He is, without a doubt, the most urbane rebel that I have ever met. The only thing that he wants is the same thing that the Americans wanted for themselves: to live in a free and sovereign country.

Berríos's struggle interests me so much because he is looking for home. The difference is that he knows where his is. Nevertheless, his problem is that others occupy his home.

Berríos may dream the impossible dream, but he is at a colossal advantage, since he is on the right side of history by trying to put an end to the five hundred years of colonization over Puerto Rico. Is this too much to ask for?

These have been some of my wars and some of my loves. And in my mind, I cannot separate one from the other. They have all left their scars.

FOUR | THE ETERNAL RETURN

MÉXICO ME DUELE

Out of place everywhere, at home nowhere.
In my own country, also, sometimes, I have
an exile's feeling.

—JAWAHARLAL NEHRU

(THE GLOBAL SOUL OF PICO IYER)

The Mexican is like one who goes into
retreat and protects himself;
he masks his face, he masks his smile.

—OCTAVIO PAZ (THE LABYRINTH OF SOLITUDE)

Mexico: hands without bread but a head
filled with dreams.

—CARLOS FUENTES (INÉS)

I am standing in the *zócalo* in the capital, right in the center of Mexico. It is December 1, 2000. I am not alone. Thousands of Mexicans are listening to a speech by Vicente Fox, the first president from the opposition in the last seven decades. After seventy-one years of abuses by the PRI, a change had finally come, and with that change came representative democracy.

"Mexicanos al grito de guerra . . ." Here I am in

the very center of my country singing the national anthem. It's a strange feeling. I hadn't sung it for twenty or twenty-five years because I hated anything that showed loyalty or association with the PRI governments that illegitimately took control of everything: power, the colors of the flag, the verses of the national anthem.

Today it's different. I am singing the national anthem, and I have goose bumps. Despite the cold, I feel warm tears running down my face to the corners of my mouth. I am truly moved.

FOR TWELVE YEARS I was famous among my fellow journalists and some politicians for always asking the presidents of Mexico the same question. Since 1988, when I interviewed former Pres. Carlos Salinas de Gortari, and later, in 1996, with Ernesto Zedillo, and most recently in 2000, when I interviewed Vicente Fox, I can't recall having a conversation with these Mexican leaders without asking them about the *dedazo*.

The *dedazo* was the practice all PRI presidents had of designating a successor. It was a decision that was both personal and final, and one that coincided with the fraudulent, fixed election results. In my opinion, this was the main obstacle to the establishment of true representative democracy in Mexico, and this is why I insisted on bringing it up. Besides it being my responsibility as a journalist, I felt it was my duty as a Mexican.

Times have changed, and Mexican journalists now have the well-earned luxury of asking any official whatever they feel like without suffering punishment or retaliation. Prior to 2000, however, many journalists would have jeopardized their jobs by asking the president of the Republic a blunt, aggressive question.

The fascinating thing about the *dedazo* was that everyone knew what was going on, but no one wanted to talk openly about it. With the publication of the book *La Herencia*, by Jorge G. Castañeda in 1999, in which all the living former presidents of Mexico—Luis Echeverría, José López Portillo, Miguel de la Madrid and Carlos Salinas de Gortari—spoke about the personal and antidemocratic way in which they were elected, the subject of the *dedazo* was finally demystified. Prior to 1999, however, the subject was virtually banned in the high circles of power in Mexico. That's why my questions on the matter always made people feel uncomfortable.

I felt safe from my trench in Miami. Every question I asked about the *dedazo* helped guarantee my job, not jeopardize it. The growing Mexican community in the United States made sure I was aware that they greatly appreciated it when a journalist questioned the president of Mexico about his abuses.

In the elections on July 6, 1988, I had a thirty-eight-second conversation with the then presidential candidate Carlos Salinas de Gortari who, no matter which way you looked at it, had been designated as winner by the president at the time, Miguel de la Madrid. When I found Salinas de Gortari he was cornered, waiting on line to vote with his daughter and his bodyguards.

"They say that the president of Mexico is the one who chooses his successor. In this case, did Miguel de la Madrid choose you as his successor?" I asked him.

"The line is long," he replied, referring to the dozens of people in front of him waiting to vote. "That means that it's the Mexicans who vote and choose their president."

Salinas clearly did not want to tell the truth. His response was part of an old political game in which it was necessary to cover up the selection process of the new president. Hours later, one of the most scandalous electoral frauds in the history of modern Mexico would be carried out.

Early results after the polls closed indicated that the leftist candidate Cuauhtémoc Cárdenas was surprisingly out in front. Soon, however, the computerized system of vote tallying stopped working. "The system broke down," said those in charge of the tallying. In fact, the system was silenced for several days until they could come up with a way to fraudulently award the election to Salinas. For example, 100 percent of the votes in 1,762 boxes were for Salinas, like in the good old days of the Soviet Union; no one was sick, no one failed to vote, no one voted for the opposition. Everyone supposedly voted for Salinas.

On August 29, 1994, shortly after Salinas left power, I had the opportunity to interview him in the official residence of Los Pinos. I asked him once again about the *dedazo* that had given him the presidency.

"[Former president] Luis Echeverría said in September 1990, "The tradition in Mexico is that the president at the time choose his successor.' Is that still the case?" I asked him.

"I would say that each one looks at it based on his own experience," he replied, avoiding the subject.

Salinas de Gortari left Mexico after his brother Raúl was arrested and accused of being the mastermind behind of the death of PRI leader Jose Francisco Ruiz Massieu. There were and continue to be many questions about Raúl's fortune and how he amassed it without the then president knowing.

Years later, on October 6, 2000, taking a break from his long exile in Dublin, Ireland, Salinas and I touched on the subject again in a long conversation we had in Mexico City. I asked him about how he had personally chosen Luis Donaldo Colosio and later Ernesto Zedillo (after Colosio's assassination in March 1994) as presidential candidates. This time he had a different response.

"You chose Zedillo, didn't you?"

"I played a key role in assuring that Mr. Zedillo would be the PRI candidate for the presidency of the Republic," Salinas said, publicly admitting his role in the matter for the first time. "And I also played a key role in assuring that Luis Donaldo Colosio would be the PRI presidential candidate."

"You personally chose who the candidate would be twice?"

"Twice I played an essential role in assuring that the PRI would nominate Donaldo Colosio and Ernesto Zedillo as candidates for the presidency of the Republic."

Ernesto Zedillo, elected president of Mexico in 1994, never wanted to admit what everyone already knew; that thanks to Salinas de Gortari's finger, he got to Los Pinos. It was there, in the Vicente Guerrero reception room, that María Elena Salinas and I had the chance to speak with Zedillo on October 29, 1996. The conversation was filled with tension.

"It's no secret that the tradition in Mexico is for the president at the time to choose his successor, in what Mexicans refer to as the *dedazo*. Many Mexicans think that you would not have won the candidacy of the PRI without Salinas de Gortari. Do you owe your candidacy to Salinas de Gortari?" I asked.

"Look. In the first place I want to correct something you said. The president of Mexico does not choose his successor. The oral, political tradition of Mexico says that the president at the time has an enormous, although not decisive influence on the candidate . . ." Zedillo said, trying to hide the obvious.

"It's not decisive?"

". . . on the candidate that the Partido Revolucionario Institucional chooses."

"I am talking about the candidacy . . . I was here [in 1994], there was no congress: in fact, former Pres. Salinas de Gortari, in a letter made public, spoke clearly about how he defended your candidacy in the face of pressure from other politicians, including former Pres. Luis Echeverría. I recall having spoken to Santiago Oñate, the president of the PRI, on February 26 [1996] in Washington, and he said, word for word, 'The presidential candidate is chosen with the direct intervention of the president.' What we want to establish—and you promised to speak truthfully—is that the Mexicans know how you were chosen as the candidate," I argued.

"No. Better yet, go and ask the PRI. I was told by my party that I would be the candidate, and I assumed that responsibility."

A complete denial. Zedillo's discomfort with that and other questions was such that he never wanted to speak with me again.

Manuel Clouthier, the late leader of the Partido Acción Nacional (PAN) used to say that "the pig won't drop the ear of corn, even when he's hit," referring to the antidemocratic behavior of the PRI to stay in power no matter the cost. At the end of the century, however, something changed in Mexico.

The party of Salinas de Gortari and Ernesto Zedillo lost the presidential elections when, for the first time, an independent entity—the *Instituto Federal Electoral*—and not the government, was put in charge of organizing the election and tallying the vote. Seventy-one years of cheating, fraud and lies that allowed the PRI to continue in power came to an end with the elections on July 2, 2000. On his fifty-eighth birthday, Vicente Fox became the first democratically elected president since 1911. Sixteen million Mexicans voted for this rancher and former president of Coca-Cola.

I spoke with Fox on Monday, July 3, one day after his victory over PRI candidate Francisco Labastida. He was tired but still enthusiastic. He wore a suit, tie and cowboy boots. What was emphasized in our conversation, of course, was the arrival, finally, of true representative democracy.

"Did the PAN win or the PRI lose?" I asked him.

"Well, I think Mexico won," Fox said. "First of all, there was strong competition, sometimes even bitter and rude, in the electoral process, but in the end Mexicans won and democracy won. We had the same government for seventy-one years. In fact, this is the first time in the history of this country where political power is being transferred from one party to another. It has never happened. So, every minute and every day, we are making history, and we are walking along PRI paths that we have never before set foot on."

"Was it a rejection of the PRI?"

"Yes, and an important one. I would say that maybe close to half the votes could have been because of that. People are fed up. On the other hand, we also had a platform that interested many citizens. Our platform, above all, was to be an inclusive government, a transition government, and a pluralist government. We were the only ones to propose this, and I think this was an important point in our victory."

Before even beginning his presidency, Fox had made the most important achievement of his political career: being the catalyst for democracy in Mexico. It was the end of the *dedazo*, and he would have a hard time in his six years as president equaling what he did on July 2, 2000.

The problem with Fox is that nothing that he can do can dismantle seventy-one years of authoritarian rule. Fox also brings with him the inevitable disappointment that comes when one realizes that democracy is not a little magic wand that whips up jobs and solves financial crises.

Fox's victory was the last step of a democratic movement that swept the whole hemisphere. The disappearance of Pinochet's dictatorship in Chile, the conclusion to the Somozas in Nicaragua, and the end to frequent coups d'état in Argentina, Brazil, Uruguay and Paraguay, and even the humiliating fax resignation of former Peruvian dictator Alberto Fujimori, were obvious signs of which path Latin America was moving. Cuba is the exception. But even today it isn't easy being a dictator. Fidel Castro, who was received with applause and confetti during the Latin American Summit of Guadalajara in 1991, was virtually expelled for the Monterrey Development Conference, held in Mexico in March 2002. In less than one decade, Castro became an unwanted guest and a terribly out of fashion one. When I think about Castro, I recall *The Autumn of the Patriarch*, probably my favorite book. The funny thing is that Gabriel García Márquez wrote it with Augusto Pinochet in mind. I can't however, help but think of García Márquez's Cuban friend, Fidel.

Even if it is so that democracy has taken root throughout almost the whole hemisphere, there is no hope in sight for the problem of poverty. Today there are more poor people in Latin America than ever before. Neither neoliberal formulas, nor multimillion-dollar American aid, nor sometimes-suicidal loans from the World Bank or the International Monetary Fund, have been sufficient to create wealth and distribute it in an egalitarian manner. The main threat to the stability and survival of the region's new democratic regimes is the painful and pulsating growth in poverty rates. Having balanced budgets and paying off foreign debt is worthless if the majority of Latin Americans just get poorer. Also, the arrival of democracy has not meant more justice. When Fox was running for president, he promised to investigate, try and imprison the "fat fish," as the criminals from past administrations are called. I liked Fox much better as a candidate than as president. In varying degrees, unpunished crimes and corruption still are brutal characteristics of the new Latin American democracies. The old is dead and the new has been really born in Latin America. It's not easy to run with one of your feet tied down.

In these circumstances, critical and investigative journalism is of the essence. In Latin American countries, journalists compensate for the lack of justice by playing the role of the police, prosecutors and human rights officials. Meanwhile, in countries such as the United States and those within the European Union, an ever-vigilant press gives voice to those groups that are traditionally discriminated against or marginalized.

Nothing can compensate for the lack of justice, but sometimes journalism is able to level the playing field. Just sometimes.

The PRI was in power when I was born, and I often feared they would be in power when I died. Fortunately, that didn't happen. I was so happy that my country would have a future without the PRI that I went with a group of friends to play soccer at the metropolitan Cathedral, next to the *zócalo*. This was a clear sign of irreverence. However, it was also like saying that this country is ours. A couple of policemen watched us from a distance, astonished. In other circumstances they would have ordered us to get out of there. "Here, next to the Cathedral in the *zócalo*, in front of the National Palace, you may not play soccer," they would have pontificated. "These places must be respected." If we had refused to leave, the police would have called security reinforcements and they would probably have scored the final goal. These, however, were different times. They saw us playing, and they left us alone. The rules of democracy were beginning to undo Mexico's authoritarian past.

Mexico was beginning to change, and Fox's victory stirred up powerful personal questions within me. I had always thought I would return to Mexico if democracy were to come, in order to help in any way I could. Now that it had come, the question was what to do? Should I follow through with my plans of returning one day? Consider the opportunity to become involved in Mexican politics? Or better yet, should I plan to continue in journalism?

The fact of the matter was that as a journalist I sometimes got tired of just observing and I felt like jumping to the other side of the camera and doing something, anything. The questions are: what, and where?

These doubts consume me. I know that I am going through a transitional period, yet I don't know where I am going. The same questions that I asked myself when I was young—Who am I? What do I want to do with the rest of my life?—have returned to haunt me. But the problem is that now I have a trajectory. Should I keep doing the same thing, anchoring the news, interviewing people and writing books? Are Walter Cronkite and company the model to follow for a Spanish-speaking journalist? Or should I change careers and risk it—as I did when I left Mexico—and jump into the political arena? Even if the answer to the latter were yes, I would have to think about where I would enter politics. Do I want to return to Mexico and enter the political scene in a country that I recognize less and less? I have kept my Mexican citizenship should the opportunity arise and I decide to enter the political realm in the country I was born.

I have taken this so seriously that I got a master's in international relations at the University of Miami in the little free time that the newscast allows. I did this so that I wouldn't be at a disadvantage with so many Mexican politicians who have graduate degrees from abroad. Ironically, this course of study helped me put my job in its proper context, instead of giving me the tools with which to dive into the world of politics, as I had expected. For the moment, I have discarded the idea of politics. But new doubts have arisen, since I may decide to remain in the United States.

Would it be preferable if I became an American citizen and ran for a congressional or Senate seat? I have even thought of the alternative of getting involved with UNICEF, the United Nations or some organization that defends immigrants. Sometimes it's obvious to me that my job as a reporter is not enough as far as my future is concerned. But before deciding on what to do, I have to know which country is mine and where my home is.

Another realization I have is that every day I know less and less about the country where I was born. It's not enough to visit Mexico three, four, five times a year. Even ten times wouldn't be enough to know what's going on. Nothing can replace living somewhere. When I write about Mexico in my articles—which are published on the Internet and in newspapers around the continent—there are now overtones of remoteness. It's the vision of someone looking from the outside in, and that hurts. Slowly but surely my country is ceasing to be mine.

When I write about Mexico now I do so almost as a foreigner. There are ten, fifteen, twenty Mexican journalists who have probably written about the subject before I do, and with a detail that I cannot replicate from afar. But I have also used that in my favor. I have learned to ask shorter and more direct questions—as is customary in the American press—and not to concern myself with whether an interviewee is annoyed or uncomfortable. This style might make for good television, but I have to admit that it doesn't have the depth, context or topicality of a conversation between two people who are living under the same circumstances.

When I arrived in the United States in 1983, I was intrigued by the stereotypical vision of Mexican Americans with respect to Mexico. Their points of reference—food, fashionable hotels, local politicians, their favorite soccer teams—have very little or nothing at all to do with the present. Now the same thing is happening to me.

The Mexico I left behind is very different from the Mexico of today. The music I used to listen to can now only be found on vinyl albums. The writers I used to read have arthritis and some even refuse to use a computer. The soccer teams I used to follow—the Pumas de la Universidad and the Chivas del Guadalajara—now have players who could be my sons. My school friends have less hair than in my memory, and larger bellies than medically advisable.

Furthermore, certain resentments and hatreds that I took with me from Mexico are no longer valid, particularly in the political realm. To speak of censorship of the press these days is ridiculous. Of course there are pressures, but nothing like what compelled me to leave. In trying to explain now why I left Mexico for the United States almost two decades ago I frequently get suspicious looks. The reasons that at the time weighed so heavily on me have vanished from the daily reality of Mexican society, and new generations are practically unaware of them. The Mexico I left behind—dominated by a single authoritarian, corrupt, omnipresent party—is now found only in textbooks . . . and in my memory.

With every visit I try to bring myself up to date, but in just a few days it's impossible to know what ideas are being debated, what music is being listened to, what restaurants are the best and what expressions are in vogue. When I left Mexico, it was common to say, *"Qué onda?"* Today that's been replaced by *"Cómo ves?"* and the *"cuate"* or *"chavo"* by *"broder."* I continue to say *"órale"* or *"híjole,"* but these words now sound a little outdated.

When I was young, radio stations played a great deal of English-language music; today Spanish dominates. At that time it was also difficult to find a journalist who you could believe; you had to read between the lines. I even recall my fruitless search for a French magazine—*Paris Match*—which in the early 1980s had published a story that was critical of Pres. José López Portillo. You couldn't read those kind of stories in Mexico. The few issues of that magazine that came into the country were quickly collected and confiscated. Today on television, radio and in the Mexican press, it's common to find honest, rebellious, critical journalists.

I try hard not to fall behind the changes occurring in Mexico, but it's a race I can't win. There are more and more things of which I am unaware. What happened to me with *chile* is happening with Mexico; my tolerance for hot sauce has diminished, as has my intrinsic knowledge of the nation where I grew up. Sometimes I think that I have stopped being Mexican.

Mexico City, which I traveled around as a boy by bus, car and subway, is more and more foreign to me. I used to have a sense for the duration of a stoplight, the routes with less traffic depending on the time of day, and where to go on the weekend without having to flip through the newspaper. I still venture to drive there, but I do so now with great caution; I am glued more to the brakes than to the accelerator, and I have lost the habit of honking the horn at the slightest offense.

I'm also now used to living in a society where phone, fax or Internet can resolve things. I don't have to change the license plate on my car every two years or waste an entire morning renewing my driver's license or going to the bank: almost everything can be done by mail. In comparison, Mexico seems to be a society weighed down by bureaucratic obstacles and where the simplest procedures can turn into a nightmare of long waits and setbacks. This is something I don't miss.

In leaving behind the delays, the tricks and the senseless explanations—"The office manager didn't come to work today," "We lost electricity and with it all the information on the system," "You'll have to talk to the boss about that and he's very busy right now, come back tomorrow"—I lost touch with a Mexico that has changed a great deal in the last two decades. The frustration of Mexican society—with its poverty, systematic corruption and abuses by authorities—is palpable. This can be explained, in part, by the defeat of the PRI in 2000 and Fox's victory. Nevertheless, six years is not enough to structurally change a country plundered for decades by the ruling classes.

I missed the process in which Mexicans converted their frustration into action and tumbled the PRI from power. Like many others, I doubted until the last moment that something like that could happen. I was obviously not in touch with how most Mexican voters felt until the results were in. I no longer harbor the hope of bringing myself up to date unless at some point I decide to return to Mexico to live.

Having lived so many years outside of Mexico, I'm sure I have developed an idealized and, therefore, false vision of Mexico. That vision, however, was torn to shreds on March 23, 1994, when PRI presidential candidate Donaldo Colosio was assassinated in Tijuana.

I was in Miami when I received a phone call from Porfirio Patiño, the head of the Univision bureau in Mexico City. "Colosio was shot and I think he's dead," he said. "Cut it out," I replied laughing, thinking it was another one of the jokes he used to test my weak knowledge of the country. Porfirio, though, ever steady in difficult moments, kept on. "He was shot at a meeting in Tijuana."

Immediately we interrupted our programming and went on the air with the story of the attempt on Colosio's life, not saying that he was dead, however. I wouldn't report his death until I had independent confirmation. Porfirio turned out to be right.

Those who saw me on air that day say that I lost my composure; my voice was nervous and choked with emotion, I was about to burst into tears, and I didn't appear focused. The truth was that the news broke my mental stability for a moment, along with the preconceptions I had about my own country. I never imagined that a presidential candidate, especially one as popular as Colosio, would be killed like that in Mexico. I immediately recalled the disbelief of Americans when they found out about the death of John F. Kennedy. For Mexicans, what happened to Colosio was something similar.

1994 was one in which Mexico should have celebrated its entry into the first world with the signing of the Free Trade Agreement. Instead, that year all the contradictions, vices and defects of a political system in effect since 1929 came to light. First there was the uprising of the Zapatista movement in Chiapas, on January 1, in the name of ten million indigenous Mexicans who were being treated as second- or third-class citizens. Then came the assassination of Colosio in March, and in September the assassination of PRI leader José Francisco Ruiz Massieu, former brother-in-law of the Salinas de Gortari brothers. The fear of violence and the possible resurgence of an uncontrollable Mexico was one of the main factors in the presidential elections that year, and it was skillfully and cowardly exploited by Ernesto Zedillo, the PRI candidate who replaced Colosio. In 1994, Mexico exploded.

NO ONE HAD EVER kept me waiting so long for an interview as Subcomandante Marcos did. I arrived in early 1996 with my cameraman, Angel Matos, in the small town of La Realidad, in the Lacandona jungle of Chiapas, which had been turned into a kind of border between the zone controlled by the Zapatista guerrillas and the zone dominated by the Mexican army. We had established contact with Marcos through a sympathizer of the rebel movement in Mexico City, and he had personally accompanied us to Chiapas in order to ensure that no one in Pres. Ernesto Zedillo's government was following us.

Subcomandante Marcos supposedly knew about the interview and had authorized it. When we arrived in La Realidad, however, he was nowhere to be found. I waited thirty hours for him. Every time we were about to give up, the villagers who were putting us up would say, "He'll be here soon." They let us sleep on the floor in one of the classrooms in the village's makeshift school where I wound up getting a serious case of fungus on my hands. Weeks later I still had blisters on my hands. We ate enough beans, tortillas, chile and coffee so that our stomachs were satisfied. One day one of the *señoras* in the village felt sorry for us, and she cooked us some eggs.

The wait was a good lesson. The indigenous *chiapanecos* are among the poorest people on the continent, and spending two days with them made me understand why they were rebelling. After centuries of discrimination and being marginalized, they no longer had anything to lose, and with an income below a dollar a day they would never be able to secure a better life for their children. It was a cycle of poverty passed down from generation to generation.

During one of the many quiet moments, I played soccer with some of the guerrillas. It was Sunday, and even the guerrillas rest from time to time. Not counting the leaders, there was hardly anyone over the age of twenty-five. During the week they spent their time helping their families in the fields and training in the art of guerrilla warfare in the mountains. On Sundays, though, they played soccer. It was easy to identify them; I had never played soccer against a team that wore black boots that came to the knee.

It was hard to believe that these dark-skinned boys with indigenous features had the government of Mexico up against a wall when they began their armed rebellion on January 1, 1994, the same day the Free Trade Agreement between Mexico, the United States and Canada went into effect. What did they want? To overthrow the government? Promote their leftist ideas? Or did they simply want to let out a desperate cry to cry to escape poverty and marginalization?

From the very beginning it was the skillful management of the media that put the Zapatistas on the map, forcing first the government of Carlos Salinas de Gortari and later that of Ernesto Zedillo to listen to them and negotiate with them. Their charismatic leader, Subcomandante Marcos, also surely had a lot to do with the strong impact they had on Mexican society.

Finally, one afternoon, two guerrillas emerged from the forest and came for us; they wore balaclavas and said, "Now he's coming, follow us." We set off walking, leaving La Realidad behind, crossed through a cornfield, and there, in the middle of a dense wooded area, was Subcomandante Marcos. His pipe was lit; it smelled like maple. He was holding an M-16 and wore a faded green cap over the balaclava. Despite the mask, the reddish, unhealthy bags under his eyes were unmistakable. "I don't sleep at night, and I eat once a day," he told me. His right boot had a huge hole in it, and he was very aware of the dangers of living in such a remote place. "The forest," he said, "begins to make you inflexible. You lose touch with reality, and that's when you become intolerant."

His hands surprised me; they were small, delicate, white, without calluses, and the nails were clean and recently cut. They were not the rough, hardened hands of the peasants. They were the hands of a leader who connected frequently to the Internet on his laptop, the hands of a reader of Shakespeare and the Spaniard Váquez Montalbán, of an inquisitive person who wanted to know if Hong Kong would wind up being like China or vice versa. They were the hands of an interviewee who preferred to ask questions rather than answer them.

In just a short time Subcomandante Marcos had dominated the art of the sound bite. "When people have no voice, they pick up a weapon," he said, justifying his armed movement. In reference to the tactics that he had used in order to introduce his movement to the world, he said. "Revolutions of the twenty-first century are revolutions of words."

"Do you still justify violence in order to achieve your goals?" I asked.

"We maintain that the Zapatista movement is *sui generis* in the sense that it is a war to make people listen," he replied. "It is a war that does not plan destruction, the annihilation of the enemy, nor our taking their place."

"There will never be, then, a President Marcos of Mexico?"

"No, God protects us," the subcomandante responded. "God protects Mexico. God protects Marcos from that problem."

"Some see heroism in the balaclavas," I remarked. "But surely you know that others also see in them opportunism or even cowardice?"

"Yes, there are many people who write me to say that I don't show my face because I'm a coward."

"Don't they have a right to say that?"

"Yes, they have a right to say that, especially because of our history. You aren't a hero, they say, because Mexican heroes have always shown their face, they have always had a face."

"Why don't you take the mask off then, why don't you take it off right now," I urged.

"Because it has become a symbol, independent of us. Those people who until now were without a name, without a face, the common people who aren't important, might now have the chance to take a decisive action toward life and the environment they are in."

"When do you think you'll remove the mask?"

"When we become a civil and peaceful political force, the weapons and the masks will have to disappear.

"I'm not Rafael Guillén," he said, denying the official government version that the guerrilla leader was a former university professor. When I showed him a magazine with a photograph of the academic, he pushed it aside. "This story about Rafael Guillén is just one of many lies." The only admissions he made were that he had not seen his family in fifteen years, and that he had five siblings, not seven as the government claimed.

We really know very little about Subcomandante Marcos's personal life, only that in early 2001, when he led a peaceful march from Chiapas to Mexico City, he publicly admitted that he had a companion whose name was Mar. "What about your nom de guerre?" "Marcos is the name of a colleague who died, and we always take the names of those who have died, with the idea that one does not die but rather keeps on fighting," he said.

"So there will be a Marcos for quite a while then?" I asked, bringing the interview to a close.

"Yes, even if I die, someone else will take the name of Marcos and he will continue, he will continue to fight."

When Vicente Fox ran for president, he said that he would solve the problem of the war in Chiapas in "fifteen minutes." Well, those fifteen minutes have come and gone, and there still isn't any peace in southern Mexico. The fact is that the situation in Chiapas is not an isolated case. Subcomandante Marcos and the Zapatista guerrillas are very important national symbols. Not only do they represent a whole part of the population that historically has been discriminated against, they have also established themselves as an alternative to the worldwide trends toward globalization. The indigenous people who live in this part of the hemisphere have not been taken out of poverty by globalization. Furthermore, the globalization of commerce and the increase in disappearing cultures are a real threat to their indigenous world.

The Zapatistas are a thorn in the side of official Mexico that won't just go away. Every time politicians of all political persuasions make triumphant declarations in Mexico City on the state of the economy and the respect for human rights, all one has to do is look south and see that nothing has changed. That's why when Subcomandante Marcos told me in an interview that even if he died, someone else would fight in his name, it suggests to me that there still is a Mexico that refuses to become invisible. Racism against the Indians is a reality in Mexico that is not officially recognized, nor have useful programs been developed to stop the bigotry.

The Zapatista Insurrection should be understood as a resistance movement against issues that are typically Mexican and that refuse to die out. It's curious to note that in a world that wants to erase borders in order to homogenize cultures, movements such as the Zapatistas, Muslim groups, Palestinians and even Europeans who oppose the European Union, as well as a strong faction in the U.S., represent the strongest argument against globalization.

The interesting thing about this antiglobalization phenomenon, which is criticized by many as anachronistic for attaching itself to the past, is that it is not a priority in the United States. The isolationist cycles that characterize American foreign policy have coincided with the demanding cries for recognition coming from different groups. If the United States would have listened to the alarms and the growing anti-American sentiment in the Arab world, they could have possibly implemented policies that would have avoided terrorist acts like September 11, and the attacks on the embassies in Tanzania and Kenya. Unfortunately no one listened to those alarms.

In the same fashion, the Mexican government did not want to listen to the south, to the Mexico that lives in the jungles of Chiapas, whose cries of anguish would become the most significant armed rebellion since the revolution of 1910. And because we shut our eyes to the situation, the consequences were far worse than anything we could imagine, and it also hindered our ability to solve these conflicts in the short or middle terms. No one can destroy the current of antiglobalization in fifteen minutes. Not even a cowboy with boots like Vicente Fox.

MY FRIEND PORFIRIO PATIÑO, who was very much in touch with a Mexico that had gotten away from me, is the one who most questions my Mexicanness. He doesn't do so in a blatant way, though. On the contrary, after our many conversations about the state of the country I always wind up with the uncomfortable feeling that my distance from Mexico is that much greater. "You aren't Mexican anymore," he says to bother me, and then he bursts out laughing.

I'm much more realistic about my visits to Mexico now. A few years ago I presumed to know as much about the country as any of its inhabitants, but this was a denial of a reality that pained me. The truth was, it was normal that I would feel more distant, but I didn't want to admit it.

A good friend of mine from the university, Ada Carrasco, once told me that I shouldn't expect to know what Mexicans think if I am staying on the thirty-sixth floor of a hotel on Paseo de la Reforma and carrying dollars in my wallet. "You have to know what the coins are worth." Her comment affected me deeply. However, even when I don't stay in five-star hotels but rather in the refuge of my mother's apartment, and despite being able to tell a one-peso coin from a ten, I have that strange feeling of arriving in a place that's not entirely mine. Yes, sometimes I feel like an exile in my own country.

Ada has never let me lie. And she doesn't know how to lie either. No one that I know writes so well and so much from the soul as she. Her letters, e-mails, everything, comes from inside her. But ironically, she doesn't want to publish anything. Maybe she's afraid to be discovered: vulnerable, sensual and sensible. Our relationship has been characterized by similarities, curiosity and a will to live. We also think that our fathers— both of them architects—fought over the same girlfriend. Ada's father never accepted me. He said that I was nothing more than a figurine. I never did understand what he was talking about, even when he chased me out of his house. He warned me: "Ada is a family girl," before he threw the door on my face. But that only made me want to keep in touch with Ada even more.

Our bonds also go back to a mutual public humiliation. We once participated in the music festival at the Iberoamerican University, and the experience was a disaster. Ada forgot the words to the song, so my lonely voice made the rats scurry, while I tried to muffle its sound behind guitar stokes. When we were finished, the few who heard us applauded a bit because they felt sorry for us. But it took more than that embarrassing event for me to give up on my ephemeral career as a rock-and-roller.

With Ada, I shared never-given kisses, trips that we never took and dreams that never came true. We were always at the margins, on violin strings ready to snap. And since we barely touched one another, we can't forget one another. We put time on pause and we left a whole life waiting. In the end, we would have no other solution but to make up for lost time, as Proust did . . . through the Internet and through a bunch of letters and telegraphs. Like with a soccer game, we are waiting for overtime in order to break the even score of two suspended lives.

Ada knows perfectly well why I left Mexico. "When I look at how fast you live, I get vertigo," she tells me. But not all friends understand one another.

It hurts when I am constantly asked in Mexico, "why did you go to *gringolandia* and to the *unai esteits?*" It's clear that the circumstances that drove me to leave Mexico and those that pulled me toward the United States have changed, but despite my detailed explanations to family members, fellow journalists and friends, my experience—the painful departure, the confusing arrival, the chaotic effort to adjust and, at times, my success abroad—is impossible to communicate. We are living in different worlds.

When I return to Mexico City to promote my books or to cover a news story, other journalists from Mexico treat me poorly. From time to time, when I receive some recognition abroad for my journalistic work, it is more likely to be of interest in Bogotá, Managua or San Salvador than it is in Mexico City. I'm not a prophet in my land; I am the outsider, the other.

My mother and siblings always make an effort to see me when I'm in

Mexico City, but getting together once a year in a summer house or going out to dinner every three or four months is not the same as living the everyday life of a large family like ours. That is what I miss most. I am not part of their daily lives, and that hurts.

I am not from here nor am I from there.

The distance has allowed me to look at my country from a very different perspective than someone who has never lived abroad. Maybe the Mexicanness was exacerbated precisely because of the distance. Every time I return, however, I never feel like I truly fit in. There is always something that comes up to remind me I am not from here.

The contrasts that I never understood and still don't also jump out at me.

México me duele when I see that the promises to put an end to the poverty of sixty million people is renewed every six years, but every day there seem to be more poor people. *México me duele* when I realize that the country has one of the worst distributions of income in the world. *México me duele* when I see how poor (and corrupt) politicians wind up with millions in their bank accounts, when you have to fear a policeman more than a criminal, when the indigenous people are treated like third-class citizens, when priests, businessmen and journalists abuse their power with impunity, when racism causes laughter and not indignation, when a nation with so much natural beauty and so many resources cannot manage to break away from its prejudices and economic burdens. My view, however, has lost the freshness of someone who soaks up Mexican reality on a daily basis.

Just as I feel strange when I visit Mexico, I also feel out of place in the United States. The United States has been extraordinarily generous to me. It was here I was able to achieve what in Mexico was unthinkable: to be a success in a competitive profession, live comfortably, report and write freely without fear of consequences, travel the world and have an influence on the region of the world where I was born. That is to say, the United States gave me what Mexico could not, but it is still a nation that is not mine. Despite my having lived here for two decades, it hasn't gotten under my skin; I still feel Mexican.

I like *tacos al pastor* more than hamburgers, avocadoes from Michoacán more than those from Florida, and *agua de Jamaica* more than Kool-Aid. I prefer an afternoon at Malinalco to one at Disney World, and a night of rumba in Acapulco over one in Atlanta. I wouldn't trade a single game of World Cup soccer for two Superbowls, three World Series games and four Stanley Cup finals. I can speak Spanish without thinking, and I can't dream in English. Now I listen to Sting but I understand better Bosé and Serrat and groups like Mecano and Maná.

I am far away, but Mexico is always with me. The Nobel peace prize recipient Adolfo Pérez Esquivel said that someone who disappeared in the dirty war in South America is the "absent present" among his family members; he's not there but they always think about how he might have disappeared, the meals he liked, the books he used to read, the music he used to listen to and the circumstances that culminated in his death. Something like that happens to me with Mexico.

For me, Mexico is the "absent present." When I'm not there, memories from the years I spent there are constantly with me. I can't help it. It would be much easier if the process of adapting to the United States had been more complete, if I had forgotten about Mexico; then I would feel free to become an American citizen. Things, however, are more complicated in one's inner world.

My sense of identity is composed of many more things than those that presently surround me, and an important part of it is Mexico, the country that calls to me as much when I am awake as when I am dreaming, but that no longer knows how to welcome me. It doesn't know if I'm a Mexican or a foreigner. I am, in fact, a little of both.

CUBA OF THE NORTH

Miami is the most vilified city in the world . . .
a warm but dangerous city.

—ZOÉ VALDÉS (MILAGRO EN MIAMI)

It was a stormy Saturday. It rained all day long. So just as those who skin chickens for a living almost never eat chicken and mechanics don't want to see nuts and bolts on the weekend, journalists who make a living reporting information sometimes also like to distance themselves from the news—for their mental health.

So, that Saturday, June 23, 2001, I hadn't read the newspapers or turned on the TV. I played soccer in the morning and then took my son, Nicolás, for a hamburger and french fries with green ketchup and a Coke.

"Did you hear about Castro?" asked the man who was waiting on us.

"No," I replied, imagining the typical ritual of insults and diatribes against the Cuban dictator.

"He fainted this morning in the middle of a speech in Havana," he told me emphatically. "You didn't hear about it?"

This Cuban American, who knew me from the

frequent visits with my son to the restaurant and who had spent seven years in Castro's jails, couldn't believe that someone like me who makes a living from the news did not know what for him was the most important piece of news coming out of his country in the last four decades. The possibility that Castro could die, with thousands of people to witness it, was without precedent.

The debate in Miami that afternoon was endless. *"El Viejo* is going to die," said many in the Versalles restaurant on Calle Ocho. It's cerebral ischemia, the beginning of Alzheimer's, one neurologist on TV said. The official version, however, was much simpler: sunstroke. The Cuban leader, who was about to turn seventy-five, got tired due to the excessive heat and not enough liquids. Hundreds of those attending the event apparently also passed out because of the sun, just like Castro. A well-made-up Castro, however, appeared that very night on a television program in which he joked about the incident; he wanted "to play dead" to see what kind of funeral was planned for him. The bottle of rum and celebrations in Miami, Castro said, would have to wait. Once again.

It's impossible to understand Miami without thinking about Cuba. The island is the reference point for most of the exile community. Whoever comes here has to undergo what I call the baptism of exile. "What do you think of Castro, *chico?"* is the initiation question. From the response it is clear which side you are on.

MY BRUSH WITH FIDEL

It was the perfect hunt. The animal holed up in a luxury hotel. All I had to do was take aim and shoot. What I could not have imagined was that this cornered animal was going to be so dangerous and that he would use all his resources to defend himself, including the physical force of his bodyguards.

In July 1991, the first Latin American summit was held in Guadalajara with the participation of all the presidents and heads of state of Latin America, Spain and Portugal. Castro, despite being the only dictator in the region, was also invited. The organizers decided to put all those invited on a single floor of the Camino Real Hotel, with large gardens separating the rows of rooms and suites. It was a veritable political zoo. In one wing of the hotel were the presidents of Argentina, Uruguay and Chile; in another those of Honduras, El Salvador and Guatemala, and so on. It was, in fact, very comfortable for the leaders; they only had to take a few steps to see their colleagues.

The organizers made the mistake, however, of allowing journalists to enter the same area of the hotel where the heads of state were, without any restrictions whatsoever. They would not commit the same error in subsequent Latin American summits. The result was that the journalists became hunters in a zoo. No prey was too difficult to catch.

Fidel Castro was and still is, without a doubt, one of the most difficult interviews to get. First, because he grants very few, and a dictator was a rarity among the democratic fauna of the continent. Second, because his loyal assistants made sure that the interviewer sympathized with the revolution or, at the very least, that he asked a fair number of easy questions. Last because there is a long list of blacklisted journalists who will never be allowed to interview the dictator.

Because I worked at Univision—an American television network based in Miami, home to the Cuban exile community—I fell into the category of journalists who would never have access to Fidel, ever. Nevertheless, in Guadalajara, for just a few hours, the rules of the game changed.

I entered the Camino Real Hotel as if it were my home, and I headed straight for Castro's suite. I waited for a few minutes along with several other journalists and then the Cuban leader appeared. It was the first time I had ever seen him. He looked taller and his beard whiter than on TV. His olive-green uniform and black combat boots looked comical and out of place in the warm Jaliscan summer. He greeted us in a fatherly way. This hunchbacked old man is the one who has seized the democratic will of Cubans? I wondered. Some journalists began to throw out easy questions that Fidel batted away with the grace of a major-league baseball player, and then he left to see his friend Joaquín Balaguer, president of the Dominican Republic.

I followed him to the room where the Dominican president was staying and I camped out. I wasn't going to leave that spot until I got an interview with Fidel. It was now or never. Never in my career as a journalist would I have such an opportunity again. For years I had made formal requests to interview Castro and not once had I even received confirmation that my request had been considered. Silence. I hadn't even received a no. For them, the Cuban bureaucrats of the island, I didn't exist.

I told my cameraman, Iván Manzano, what our plan of attack was. "When you see Castro, don't stop filming," I told him. "I am going to rush at him with the microphone." Half an hour later, Fidel came out of Balaguer's room, surrounded by his bodyguards. I counted eight; three in front of him, one on each side, and three behind. I stood in the middle of the hallway as they walked toward me. The bodyguards tried to push me aside, but I brushed them aside and threw out the first question for the dictator. It was just a lure. If he bit, if he began to reply, it would be easier to continue the conversation.

"*Comandante,* we spoke with the president of Argentina [Carlos Menem], and he said that Marxism was a museum piece," I said.

"In my opinion, it's too new to be a museum piece. Capitalism, however, is three thousand years old," Castro replied, taking the bait.

His bodyguards remained calm. Castro kept walking slowly, and he touched my left shoulder with his hand, as if he wanted to hug me. As soon as I felt his arm on my shoulder, I moved back. He lowered his arm.

"I can't let Castro hug me," I thought as I listened to the words of the dictator; first, because I didn't want him to think I sympathized with him, and second, because the Cuban exile community in Miami and my fellow journalists would never forgive me.

I asked him a couple of questions about the future of Communism after the fall of the Berlin Wall. Castro avoided as best he could the suggestion that the next country to fall would be Cuba. As he was answering he again tried to put his arm around my shoulder.

I know it sounds improbable that while you're walking, asking Castro questions, you're also thinking about other things. However, I couldn't stop thinking about what Fidel was trying to achieve by putting his arm around me. Discredit my questions? Have viewers identify me with his regime? Have the exile community in Miami reject me because of his gesture? What did he want? No one I had ever interviewed had tried to hug me in the middle of a conversation.

Once again, as soon as I felt his arm, I stepped back. When I did so, Castro gave me a look of reproof, and his bodyguards began to approach us. I knew I had only a few seconds left, so I threw out a question that was sure to hurt, since it touched on the very essence of his dictatorial system and his long stay in power.

"Many people believe that this is the time for you to call for an election," I said.

"I respect the opinion of those *señores*," he replied, annoyed, "but they really have no right to demand elections in Cuba."

Election was the key word. The idea had been circulating at the Latin American Summit to pressure Castro to democratize the island, and Castro had not commented. When I said the word, however, one of his bodyguards stuck his elbow in my stomach, coming between Fidel and me. As soon as Castro had finished speaking, the same bodyguard shoved me aside with another elbow, this one stronger, throwing me to the ground. The microphone went flying. Castro said nothing; he just kept walking, not even turning around to look at me.

AY, MIAMI! How difficult it is to understand you!

I'm always cold in Miami. The air-conditioning is on full blast in movie theaters, restaurants, malls and office buildings. Furthermore, they put huge amounts of ice in the drinks. Miami, the most tropical city in the United States, can also be the coldest. Beyond its contrasts, though, Miami is a challenge; a challenge to nature, politics and often to common sense.

My arrival in Miami was much more turbulent than my arrival years before in Los Angeles. Moving from Mexico City to Los Angeles felt almost natural; I went from the city with the most Mexicans in the world to the city with the second greatest number of Mexicans. Miami, on the other hand, was different.

In Miami I was part of a minority—the Mexican one—within another minority: the Cuban American one. Simply identifying myself as Mexican brought me face to face with various sectors of the Cuban exile community who have always been suspicious of the closeness of Mexican administrations with Fidel Castro's dictatorship.

No matter how I tried to explain to these Cubans that I never shared most of the policies of the PRI—including the close relationship with the Cuban tyranny—doubt always seemed to be present.

That initial rejection slowly transformed into insults. One of the worst insults one can receive from an exiled Cuban is for him to call you a Communist. Simply because I was Mexican, some members of the exile community accused me of being leftist. If in fact I were a Marxist, I would say to my critics, I would never have decided to come to the United States, the land of capitalism. My explanations, however, were of no use. I was just a Mexican in a Cuban sea, and any signs of tolerance were buried beneath unfounded accusations and stereotypes.

The Cuban exile community in Miami in the mid-eighties was ideologically controlled by a small group of politicians and supporters from the far right. The irony of their position was that their unyielding attitude toward any reconciliation with Cuba and their blind support of the embargo against the island sometimes turned out to be counterproductive and only ended up strengthening the regime in Cuba.

Many, many years would have to pass before the Cuban community would understand that I was not a leftist. The change in perception began with the birth of my daughter, Paola, who carries Cuban blood in her veins, and it was finally confirmed with my critical and relentless coverage in Cuba during Pope John Paul II's visit in January 1998.

IT TOOK ME SEVERAL YEARS to get a visa to enter Cuba. On three occasions—in Washington, Lima and Mexico City—I applied unsuccessfully for a visa. What's more, they would never even confirm that they had received my application. Suspicions that I would be critical of the Cuban government because I lived in Miami and worked for Univision, a member of the independent media, were understandable, but with the pope's visit I had another chance.

After many conversations with high Cuban officials and multiple warnings, they approved visas for a group of journalists from Univision, which included me. The emphasis of our coverage would of course be John Paul II's visit and the apparent beginning of religious tolerance in Cuba. For me, however, it was quite clear that I had to deal with Cuba for what it was: a dictatorship.

So as soon as I arrived on the island I made contact with a group of dissidents and independent journalists. Their vision of the island was devastating. Just by speaking with the foreign press, they were running an extremely high risk. Not only could they lose their jobs, but they also could be thrown in jail. However, the papal visit was an extraordinary opportunity for the world to see the repression in Cuba.

For example, I met a journalist who barely had enough money to buy a couple of pencils and a few sheets of paper because he'd been fired from his job. On the faces of the dissidents I interviewed in the outskirts of Havana, I learned what fear was: bloodshot eyes, trembling voices and ears on the alert.

Havana is a dark, silent city. At night it invites you to discover it on foot, and let the breeze from the breakwater spray your face. It's also, however, a city that hides its fear. On the streets of the capital—Santiago, Camagüey and Santa Clara—I spoke with many Cubans who became deaf and dumb when asked a simple question about Fidel. I also saw how the hookers who milled around the hotels for foreigners—teenagers, practically little girls—would prostitute themselves for a dinner, a chocolate bar or even a Barbie doll.

Since my arrival on the island I had been carefully watched. The compact car we had reserved somehow magically became an enormous black Mercedes with a chauffeur. "So you'll be comfortable, Mr. Ramos," they said. One of the many car antennas could have been transmitting the intense conversations I was having with producer Rafael Tejero and cameraman Raúl Hernandez. Both Rafael and Raúl are Cuban exiles, and in their characteristic spontaneity, they railed against the island and Castro every chance they could, in front of our wide-eyed chauffeur/spy.

The masses at which the pope officiated were filled with *"segurosos,"* or members of the state security. This explains the absence of protests. It was easy to spot the undercover police; some compassionate official had instructed them to buy sunglasses, and many of them had not bothered to remove the sticker with the letters "UV" that was stuck to the lens.

My reports, conversations and television presentations via satellite were monitored and recorded by the Cuban government. I was told this by a couple of midlevel officials who were concerned about my news coverage and who paid me a "courtesy visit" at the hotel where I was staying. The second "courtesy visit" was anything but courteous. A higher ranking official warned me that if I continued to interview dissidents and independent journalists I would never be allowed to return to Cuba. "Dissidents are .02 percent of the population," he assured me without citing his sources. "There is no reason to talk to them."

Naturally, I continued reporting on Cuba as I would any other dictatorship; pointing out abuses, the lack of freedom, the poverty, the fear of authorities and the sophisticated systems of surveillance and repression. And the Cuban government kept its promise. Since then I have not been allowed to return to Cuba. They have treated me as they did before the pope's visit; despite my having applied for a visa a couple of times, Cuban officials have not even bothered to return my phone calls.

In my news coverage it was clear that I had no sympathy for Castro and his regime. "You were right," I said to several Cuban journalists upon my return to Miami. "The repression and lack of freedom in Cuba is exactly like you told me long ago."

I have never sympathized with any dictatorship or authoritarian regime, whether it is of the right or the left. My antipathy has been well divided between Pinochet and Castro. When I returned from Cuba, however, it seemed like the honorable thing to publicly recognize that the Cuban exile community was not exaggerating the atrocities and constant violations of human rights that were being committed on the island.

That "you are right" that I expressed to the Cuban community in Miami was enough to transform their sometimes cold or suspicious treatment toward me. From that moment on, I think they understood that you can be Mexican and a journalist and still oppose a dictatorial regime. "The

Mexican government," I often told them, "does not speak for me." In Miami, though, it took years for them to believe me.

All exile communities are strengthened when they sense they are confronting the rest of the world. That's just what happened with the Cuban exile community during the Elián González crisis.

On Thursday, November 25, 1999, two fishermen found a five-year-old boy floating in an inner tube off the coast of south Florida. He had been floating in the shark-infested waters for about fifty hours. Eleven other people lost their lives in their attempt to travel from Cuba to the United States, including Elián's mother, Elisabet, and her boyfriend.

As soon as the Elián case came out in the press, a custody battle began that would involve Juan Miguel González, Elián's father, Lázaro González and his exiled family in Miami, the U.S. and Cuban governments, numerous civil and religious organizations and an army of lawyers and opportunistic hangers-on.

The debate in Miami was the following: with the mother gone, who should get custody of the boy; his father living in a dictatorship or his family members who live in a free country? A survey conducted by the *Miami Herald* and published on April 9, 2000, indicated that 83 percent of Cubans in Miami wanted Elián to stay in the United States. That sentiment, however, went against the international practice of reuniting minors with a surviving parent, several national surveys and a countless number of editorials and articles worldwide.

During the 150 days Elián spent in south Florida until he was forcibly taken from Lázaro González's house on Saturday, April 22, 2000, Miami isolated itself from the rest of the world. What was valid in other parts of the world was not valid in Miami. Many accused the Cuban exile community of being uncompromising. One reporter from *El Mundo* wrote that, "The Elián soap opera has hung the label of Banana Republic on Miami again."

During the crisis sparked by Elián, who shortly after his arrival turned six, international public opinion launched its strongest attacks on the position of the Cuban exile community in Miami. Nevertheless, they did not waver in their support of Lázaro González's family, who wanted Elián to remain in the United States.

From a distance it was practically impossible to understand the position of Cubans in Miami. How could they not want to hand the boy over to his father? many wondered. The explanation was quite complicated. For many Cubans it was unthinkable to force a boy to return to Castro's dictatorship. During the so-called Peter Pan Operation, thousands of Cuban children left the island without their parents so they wouldn't have to grow up in a Communist regime. That's exactly what most in Miami wanted for Elián—a future without Communism or repression. Other younger and more liberal Cubans understood that the boy's place was with his father, regardless of where he lived, but they didn't dare publicly criticize the position of their elders. This would have been interpreted as a betrayal of the efforts of their parents and grandparents to give them a better life in a free country.

As a journalist, I found the Elián case to be one of the most complicated stories I have had to cover. The neutral position that journalists must maintain was viewed with suspicion by both sides. If we reported Castro's statements on Noticiero Univision, we were criticized in Miami, and if we emphasized the position of Lázaro González and his daughter Marisleysis—who was acting as a substitute mother to Elián—we were accused of being infiltrated by "the Mafia in Miami."

The Elián case brought out the best and the worst of journalism in Miami. Inside the newsroom room at Univision, people were divided. I work with several Cuban journalists who also had opposing views on Elián. Even though we made a tremendous effort to be objective and accurate during our coverage of Elián, I'm not so sure that our reporting was balanced. The news touched many of the journalists in very personal ways. There were times when it was hard to differentiate their personal opinions from their suggestions about what to cover and how to cover it. We all, I believe, came out of the Elián experience tarnished in one way or another.

Naturally, I, too, had my dilemmas. As a father I would want my children to stay with me in the event they didn't have their mother. I wouldn't want either of my two children, however, who by the way have Cuban blood in them, to live in a dictatorship, much less for them to have been treated with the force and abuse of authority that Elián had to experience the morning he was snatched from the home of his family members in Miami. The photograph of a heavily armed policeman aiming at the fisherman who is holding Elián inside a closet is fitting of a tyranny, not of the oldest democracy in the world.

In the end, others made the decision about Elián, not his father or his family members in Miami. There were no clear winners. However, the main loser was Elián. It bothered me a lot how Elián was continuously manipulated by important figures of the Cuban exile community—taking photos, making political statements, frequently speaking for him, filming him with ulterior motives—in the same way I find it revolting to see Fidel Castro and his ministers hugging the boy in demonstrations and other large events in Cuba.

Castro, in my point of view, lost a lot. Even though he managed to have the boy returned to Cuba, never before had his dictatorship been so brutally attacked on an international level. Nowadays there is no one who can say they don't know that human rights are constantly being violated in Cuba. No one. Elián enabled the last veils of false legitimacy that were covering the Cuban regime to be removed. In the face of the many criticisms for refusing to return a boy to his father in the absence of his mother, the exile community unmasked Castro's regime.

Another loser of this crisis was Al Gore. His ambiguous position with respect to Elián did not enable him to distance himself from the Clinton administration when it ordered that the boy be removed from his uncle's house in Little Havana by force. George W. Bush, on the other hand, capitalized wonderfully on the incident, so much so that in his own view he owes the 2000 presidential election to the Cuban vote in Florida. Elián led Bush by the hand to the White House.

One Saturday afternoon, when Elián was still at Lázaro's house in Little Havana, I went to see him, but not as a journalist. That day I didn't have to do the newscast, but I wanted to see with my own eyes the boy who had caught the world's attention. I saw him three times: playing in the yard at the house and flirting with the many guests and television cameras. There was a spark in his eyes, alive and alert. I thought his easy initial smile, however, hid the pain of a very confused boy who had just lost his mother. (On one occasion, in fact, he called Marisleysis "Mamá.") What made me saddest was that that boy who was running around the yard and being fought over looked like the loneliest soul on earth. I couldn't bear it for long, and I left.

The Elián case might have reinforced some the image of intolerance of the Cuban exile community; it has, as have all exile communities, certainly been intolerant of Castro's abuses of power. That explains the U.S. embargo against the island, the constant criticisms of nations who do business with the dictatorship and the indignation toward journalists who go to the island and do not report on the political repression and child prostitution.

With respect to Cuba, generally speaking there are two approaches to handling the situation there, although both have the same objective: the democratization of the island. The United States believes that the way to promote democracy and the end of the Castro era is by strengthening the embargo and limiting the tourist, diplomatic, academic, cultural and commercial contacts with the island. Most countries in the world believe the exact opposite; that more commerce, more diplomatic and cultural contacts and more tourism would eventually have a negative effect on the dictatorship. In the absence of an agreed-upon international strategy against Castro, however, little has changed politically on the island in the last forty years.

There are great contradictions in U.S. foreign policy; it does not treat all dictatorships the same way. China, like Cuba, is a Communist dictatorship where human rights are continuously violated. However, the United States has diplomatic relations with China and there are practically no trade restrictions. In fact, China is one of the main commercial partners of the United States. That is not the case with Cuba.

Former President Clinton told me that the disparity in treatment between China and Cuba could be explained by the shooting down of two small airplanes from the Hermanos al Rescate group by the Cuban government. The Chinese have not shot down any U.S. plane, Clinton insisted. George W. Bush explained it to me by saying that U.S. trade with China is fundamentally carried out with individuals and not the government, and that in the case of Cuba, trade would only strengthen Castro's power. Whatever the reason, the United States has a black hole in its foreign policy.

If the embargo had not overthrown the Castro regime, why not try some other formula? For many exiles the embargo is more than an economic issue, it is a moral question. It pains them to even think about doing business with someone who has done them so much harm. I suspect that this policy won't change anytime soon, and that the embargo will be enforced while Bush is in the White House. Nevertheless, I don't know if a coherent international policy to isolate the Cuban dictator can be achieved. Castro cannot continue to be treated like a legitimately elected leader in global forums. The Latin American nations should lead this effort. An isolated Castro, without a microphone to the world, can be made irrelevant, and thus forced from power.

A specified policy applied to Castro has not been used and could end with the dictatorship. The Cuban people should be bombarded with foreign products, contacts and ideas, while Castro and his henchmen are isolated on the international level. I doubt that Castro can survive that kind of offensive. But are Cuban exile leaders ready for something new, or are they willing to wait until Castro's death, as the Spanish did with Franco?

The insistence of the Cuban exile community on maintaining and strengthening the U.S. embargo against the island, regardless of the fact that it has not succeeded in overthrowing Castro, has led to the creation of an image of intolerance surrounding Cuban Americans. That image, though, is a stereotype that is not supported by reality. To begin with, the Cuban exile community is not monolithic nor does it express itself with just one voice.

I live alongside Cubans who listen to my opinions and who may not agree with them but who respect them. I have a good friend, Felipe Mourín, who has been with me since my early days as a journalist in Miami, and we speak every day. Often our exchanges are contentious and emotionally charged, but he has opened my eyes to things that may be difficult for someone who is not Cuban to see.

The Cuban American community sets an example for what other Latino groups in the United States could achieve in politics. In Miami, the most important political positions are held by Cubans; from the mayor to less important offices. When elections are held, Cubans generally get out and support their candidates. Cities with a high percentage of Hispanics in California, Texas, Illinois, Colorado, Arizona and New York could (and should) follow this example. If Mexican Americans had understood this in time, Los Angeles would have already had a Latino mayor in 2001 and Houston in 2002.

If Miami were as intolerant as they say, why have so many international companies set up operations here? Why have Latin Americans made this port their second home? Why can Spanish be spoken in this city without fear of discrimination? Why are the most powerful Latino radio and television stations in Miami? Why is south Florida one of the areas experiencing the greatest growth in the country? Why do Hispanic politicians control some of the most important offices in the city and the county? Why are Latinos in Miami in such influential positions in the media and in the art and business worlds? Why? Because Miami is a city that knows how to welcome outsiders, and the change they bring with them. Joaquín Blaya, the Chilean executive who transformed the Spanish-language television and radio industry in the United States, used to say, rightfully so, that Miami is a place that treats Latinos like first-class citizens, something that cannot be said of many U.S. cities.

Furthermore, instead of Americanizing me, Miami has Latin-Americanized me. My dear friend Rosaura Rodríguez, in line with her Bolivarian spirit, is convinced that living in Miami has allowed her to understand the totality of the Latin American problem—the poverty, the corruption, the hopes for democracy and the challenges of globalization—and to develop a clear sense of solidarity and belonging. If she had remained in Cartagena, as many of her friends did, her world would be, well, a small one. Instead, her books and novels reflect a free woman open to mixtures and convergences. Miami expanded her universe.

My experience in Miami is similar to hers; Miami has made me more Latin American and has freed me from the vices of nationalism. However, at the same time I have to admit that Miami has a fixation with the Cuban theme. This is impossible to deny.

Miami is often referred to as Cuba of the North. Cubans have transformed this city politically, economically and culturally, and when they get something into their heads, it's hard to stop them. Mexico is an "absent present" for me, just as Cuba is an "absent present" for Cubans in Miami. The difference is that with Cuba, just ninety miles from the Florida Keys, it often seems you can even smell it.

I read a study some years ago that stated that only 5 percent of Cubans in Miami would return to a free Cuba. I don't know about that, but what is clear is that the ties between Cuba and south Florida are indissoluble, with or without Castro. There will always be a Cuba of the South and a Cuba of the North, and that of the North has been my home for more than a decade.

Living in Miami has not been easy for me. The suspicions of critics became insults, but I was able to put up with it because I always found that most people were not suspicious and didn't criticize or insult me. And, at the end, they also know how to love, embrace and protect you. I soon learned that the Cuban American community is not a homogeneous block either, and that the constant flow of immigrants from other countries, like Colombia, Venezuela, the Caribbean, Central America and Mexico, has made it a prototype of multiethnic and multicultural diversity that the United States is experiencing. Miami, like Los Angeles, is the future of the United States, and the future tastes like a well-blended coffee.

GRAY HAIR, AIRPLANES, TRIPS AND SMELLS

If I could live my life again,
in the next one I would try to make more mistakes.
I wouldn't try to be so perfect, I would relax more.
I would be sillier than I was; in fact,
I would take very few people seriously.

—JORGE LUIS BORGES (INSTANTES)

GRAY HAIR

My first problem in front of the camera is that I have a baby face. One smart-aleck executive even suggested I add gray to my hair to make me more credible. That wasn't necessary, since soon after, I detected my first gray hair. It was a few days after my daughter left for Madrid to live with her mother. I'm convinced that that gray hair, and the hundreds that followed, appeared because of the sadness of being so far away from her. Thanks to friends like Sergio Saavedra and his family, I got back on my feet. The delicious Mexican breakfasts I would have at their house in Mission Viejo, California, on Sundays were fundamental to my not losing my mind. The gray hairs, nevertheless, multiplied.

Years later, my problem is that so much gray hair

makes me look older than I really am. Another television executive, who has more gray hair than I, suggested I dye my hair. I paid no attention to him either. I have always found something false about men who dye their hair, and as I'm in a business where falseness does not sell, I prefer to be gray and believable rather than dye my hair.

I have literally aged in front of the television camera. I was twenty-eight years old when I began my first Univision newscast. Now, at forty-four, the change is visible. The ease in front of the camera is now accompanied by crow's-feet and uncontrollable gray hair. Journalistically speaking, this stage is better than when I had chestnut-brown hair, smooth skin and butterflies in my stomach every time I was on air.

All things considered, it's better to have gray hair than no hair at all, and on television that is a fundamental difference. I have always suspected that my bosses would be able to put up with all the gray hair in the world, but not baldness.

Currently, there isn't a single national anchorman on U.S. television who is bald. This is a clear indication to me that I work in a business where aesthetics are extremely important. No respected television executive would dare say that he hired a person simply because he or she looked good. He would expose himself to multimillion-dollar law suits from better qualified candidates. Hiring decisions are always accompanied by sensible explanations: he has a lot of experience, he comes from a bigger market and he has covered wars . . . But the reality is that part of our job depends on our bosses liking the way we look in front of the camera. I would like to be able to say that things are different, but I would be lying.

The world of television is not necessarily full of the most intelligent people I know, but it certainly has some of the most persistent— reporters, writers, producers and technicians alike. Competition is so tough that only those who make that extra effort, the extra phone call, those who wait until someone will see them, those who work for free until a position opens up, those who take the early morning spot just to get a foot in the door—only those who want it most make it to the end.

There are also a lot of shy people on television. Though it may seem hard to believe someone who is seen by millions of people a day, I'm a shy person. Sometimes it is a real effort for me to speak before a large group. That shyness is something I have overcome but that is always, in some way, present. A sociology teacher of mine at the university told us that people choose the careers they do in order to compensate for their weaknesses. My shyness has certainly been more than compensated for by being seen by millions every night on the newscast, being heard on the radio and being read in newspapers, the Internet and these very pages.

Along with the shyness, however, comes independence. My main qualities and defects are tied to independence. As a young boy I learned to manage on my own, take responsibility and not blame anyone, ever, for what happened to me. In my case, the formula worked. One tends to repeat successful behaviors, and, with or without gray hair, and with a shyness that is well managed, I will continue to do things my way, with the greatest degree of independence possible. I wouldn't know how to do it any other way.

It's inevitable that people who see me every night on TV have some kind of interest in knowing a little more about me. I consider this to be part of my job. I have always said, however, that they only know me from the waist up; my secrets, my relationships and my dreams are not for public consumption. Despite all the time I spend in front of the television camera, I try to maintain a personal life that is not readily available on the weekly gossip magazines.

When people recognize me on the street, especially in Miami, there is always someone who says, *"Mira que chiquitico!"* or someone who says he thought I was taller, bigger or younger. "It's the makeup, the high chair and the lights," I usually reply when the image they had of me does not match the reality. Regardless of whether they think I look better or worse on television, I have never stopped being grateful to them for letting me into their homes every night for half an hour.

AIRPLANES

Flying is something almost magical for me. I'm still surprised by the magic of getting on a plane in Miami for fourteen hours and then arriving in Sydney, Australia. When I was a student and worked part-time in Mexico City, some of my days extended for fourteen hours, only instead of on a Boeing 747, those hours were spent on an endless number of subways and buses, which didn't get me anywhere.

A million miles. That's what the card I just received from one of the airlines says. On a map on my desk I mark off the countries I have visited. I just recently reached the milestone of setting foot on five continents.

I think my obsession with traveling and getting to know distant and interesting places has its origin in the impossibility of doing so when I was young. For a while it was absolute torture working in a travel agency organizing trips for others that I would have loved to take. Once I was able to fly, though, a fear of airplanes became my new challenge.

My fear of flying, however, is justified. It all began on a two-engine Air Sinai plane crossing the desert with my parents from Cairo to Tel Aviv. Shortly after we took off, I realized that the air I was feeling on my legs was not from the air-conditioning system but rather from a hole in the fuselage. The noise drowned out all conversation. One of the passengers, who may have been a diplomat and was used to this flight, had put cotton in his ears. I was inside a flying blender, a piece of scrap metal.

Later on I would find out that it was one of the first commercial airplanes to be built, the kind that have been around the world and that end up in third-world countries like Egypt. The flight was uneventful, but it was the first time I was scared in an airplane. Never before had I thought about the possibility of dying in an airplane crash. In fact, an Air Sinai plane crashed in a sandstorm shortly after our trip. I never found out if it was the same two-engine plane in which I had flown; it wouldn't have surprised me.

During the Persian Gulf War, my experience on the C-130 made the danger much clearer. I am doubly concerned when I have to get on a plane piloted by the military, especially because they are forced to make decisions in the air unrelated to the safety of the flight. That's just what happened to me when I was flying to Venezuela to interview Pres. Hugo Chávez.

EVEN THOUGH TWO of his closest associates had assured me I could interview the president in Caracas, it was Chávez who decided at the last minute that I would have to follow him to the town of Guarumita, near the Colombian border.

The presidential plane was full, so we got on a small propeller plane so we could get to the interview in the state of Táchira. I was traveling with two cameramen, Angel Matos and Martín Guzmán, and with the producer, Marisa Venegas. In the eight-seat plane there were other reporters and a public official. Shortly after we left Caracas, Martín detected white smoke filtering into the cabin. It was the first sign that something was wrong.

"Smoke, smoke," one of the journalists said, but the pilot and the copilot, both young servicemen who were barely twenty-five, did not seem to be aware.

"Heeeey, pilot," I shouted, worried, "they're saying there's smoke." "We heard," replied one of the pilots seriously, "we're checking the instruments." They shut off the heating system, the cabin grew cold and the smoke disappeared.

The small plane continued its ascent until it reached twenty-four thousand feet. We had been in the air twenty minutes. All of a sudden, the cabin began to fill with white smoke again. *"Hijole,"* I thought, "now we're screwed."

"That's dust," the public official said.

"Dust my foot," responded one of the journalists. "I smoke, and that's not dust."

No, it wasn't dust.

The pilot descended to ten thousand feet and announced, "I'm going to depressurize the cabin; you're going to feel some pain in your ears. If anyone feels dizzy or needs air, let me know so I can give you an oxygen mask." As soon as he had depressurized the cabin, the smoke disappeared.

Most of the passengers, though, were asking the pilot to land as soon as possible, but the pilot didn't want to. "We have to get to La Fría," he told us. "We have a mission. That's my recommendation, and there'll be no discussion about it."

The pressure on the military pilot was obvious. Pres. Hugo Chávez, head of the armed forces in Venezuela, had given him the order to take us to the Colombian border, and not even an emergency like this would convince him to abort the mission. By refusing to land, however, he was endangering our lives.

I was scared. My jaw was moving involuntarily and uncontrollably, and the muscles in my chest were dancing to their own beat. The palms of my hands and my forehead were sweating profusely.

Not even five minutes after the pilot's explanation, smoke began to fill the cabin again, making it difficult for us to breathe. I was seated behind the pilot, and I saw he was pale. I asked him to make an emergency landing at the military base in Barquisimeto, but he didn't say anything until after he had landed the plane.

I'm not a religious person, but when we landed a Catholic priest came over to us—what was this man of the cloth doing on a military base?—and handed each one of us a card of the Virgin of the Good Shepherd. I still have it today.

Regardless of the inevitable risks, flying is not what it used to be. I remember perfectly how my father and my mother would get ready for a flight for days, and how they would wear their best clothes. Nowadays, flying has lost its magic. It's a business for the masses that forces us to sit in a seat designed for children, eat food with the consistency of plastic and suffer the humiliations of some airlines that refuse to give us credible explanations with respect to frequent delays and price increases, and to this we have to add the endless security checks after the terrorist attacks of September 11.

Without airplanes, though, my life would be that of a frustrated man from the provinces resigned to dreaming about the photographs of the faraway places hidden in magazines. I prefer the imperfect present of modern aviation—with its many inconveniences—to the days when I was sadly anchored to the ground.

TRIPS

I recall the sun coming up over the Ganges River in India, an afternoon waiting on line to see a short, white Lenin in the Red Square, a bicycle ride through Beijing, rainy afternoons in Kyoto, and an interminable night in Managua waiting for the results of the elections that did away with eleven years of Sandinista rule. I'm still haunted by the silence and darkness of Havana, the eyes of a dead Kuwaiti, and the children lost during the war in Kosovo. I smile when I remember a flight in a hot-air balloon over Tanzania and another in a helicopter over the Great Barrier Reef in Australia. I can still smell the wonderful concoctions from the markets in Oaxaca and Marrakech. I can vividly recall a romantic candlelight dinner in Santorini, a lunch in Barcelona, fried fish in bread in Istanbul, and the marathon sessions of *tacos al pastor* in Mexico City. The beaches of Virgin Gorda, Turks and Caicos, Cancún, and the island of Hayman and Moyo in Indonesia are like mental postcards and provide escapes from every stressful situation. There are no cities that are geographically more beautiful than Rio de Janeiro, Capetown or Sydney. There are two trips, though, that I have fixed in my mind and in my heart. The fall of the Berlin Wall in November 1989 was my confirmation that journalism is the privilege of recording firsthand how history changes. I was on a trip to Miami when I saw the images on TV of young Germans destroying, little by little, the Berlin Wall before the impassive eyes of soldiers from both East and West Germany.

I obtained an emergency passport from the Mexican consulate in Miami and left so quickly for Berlin that I didn't even have the chance to buy a coat. It was freezing that first morning when young Berliners reclaimed their liberty with pick and shovel, but activity there was frenzied; there were hundreds, thousands of people, banging away at whatever piece of the Berlin Wall they could reach.

It didn't take long for the wall to start to crumble to pieces. The first stones and rocks gave way to large chunks of concrete that thundered as they hit the ground. The impressive thing was that the East German soldiers, who on other occasions had shot to kill anyone who attempted to cross the wall or destroy it, just stood there, their rifles hanging motionless at their sides.

Freedom had finally come to East Germany. I couldn't resist destroying a piece of that wall with my own hands, hammer and chisel. The little stones I recovered, stained with red, yellow and green graffiti, have come with me through all my many moves.

I have never witnessed a more impressive spectacle. The destruction of the Berlin Wall, blow by blow, tear by tear, had no equivalent in the mountain of stories I have covered in more than two decades. An era had come to an end. History was changing before my eyes, and, excited, I said to myself. "This is why I am what I am! This is why!"

THE TRIP I MADE TO INDIA with my mother and my Uncle Armando to see the religious leader Sai Baba was very different in nature from seeing the fall of the Berlin Wall. One was a political matter, the other spiritual, but both experiences were liberating. India had always intrigued me, but it wasn't until I began to toy with the idea of taking my Uncle Armando, who was eighty-seven at the time, to see Sai Baba, that the plan took shape. I was excited to put my uncle on a plane and take him out of Mexico for the first time. Sure, it would be a vital, unforgettable experience for him, getting to know the avatar, who he considered to be the incarnation of God, the spiritual leader of more than fifty million people, but personally it would be a challenge to my growing religious incredulity.

As a child and an adolescent, the Catholic Church had left me frustrated and angry, for its abusive behavior by some of the priests as well as its refusal to openly discuss hundred-year-old dogmas. That's why the trip to India opened up for me the possibility of getting in touch with my spirituality without the need to be part of an institutionalized and paralyzed religion.

The trip turned out to be an extraordinary lesson. The poverty did not shock me; I have seen it all over Latin America. The poverty in India, though, is particularly noticeable because the caste system, although diluted, hampers social mobility. The poor in India have few ways out; their parents were poor, and their grandparents and great-grandparents were poor. It's a poverty that is passed down from generation to generation, and few can escape the weight of a thousand-year-old system accustomed to corralling millions, separately.

In order to reach the ashram of Sai Baba in the rural town of Putta-parthi, we had to travel from Delhi to Bangalore and from there take a car until we reached the spiritual refuge of Prashanti Nilayam. We were re-ceived with a typical greeting—*Sairam, Sairam*—and given a room for three dollars a night. And that was just what it was—a room. It had no beds or furniture or mirror or towels or anything. We rented some small mattresses, a couple of sheets, and we bought the essential mosquito net.

After our arrival we got ready to see Sai Baba, who made two public ap-pearances daily in a ceremony known as *dharsans.* My skepticism would not leave me in peace. Would Sai Baba be a divine being like Rama, Krishna, Jesus Christ, Muhammad, Buddha and Zoroaster? We dressed in white, and with twenty thousand others entered an enormous hall with a roof sustained by columns but without walls. We were not allowed to take photos of Sai Baba, and before the men and women were separated, we had to pass through a metal detector. There was an eerie silence for such a large crowd as we waited. Some were meditating and others were reading one of two books that were in vogue about the curative powers of urine: *Auto-Urine Therapy* and *The Water of Life.* The event was surreal.

Soon after it began to smell of incense, we could hear music. A figure with an afro and dressed in an orange tunic appeared in the distance. Two gold buttons were his only adornments. At that time, in 1995, he appeared much younger than his seventy-two years. He seemed to float. After a few *bhajans* or religious chants, Sai Baba began his three-hour speech in Tel-ugu, his native language. Fortunately there was an instantaneous transla-tion into English.

I was trying to explain to my Uncle Armando what Sai Baba was say-ing: "God is like the fire that is underneath the ashes . . . the ego is a ser-pent we must destroy . . . the body is not ours, it is lent to us," and a question he threw out that seemed to be directed at me, "How is the eye going to see God when it can't even see itself?" My uncle, though, didn't need my linguistic juggling act from Telugu to English and then into Spanish. He had read it all before.

As Sai Baba was walking across the enormous hall, I saw two tears run down my uncle's face. Sai Baba was close enough so that we could make visual contact with him, and apparently that's what happened. In an instant, my Uncle Armando's eyes met Sai Baba's. They connected, and my uncle interpreted that visual encounter as the tacit approval by his spiritual leader of the road he had decided to take in life. He didn't need anything else.

We saw Sai Baba three more times, but my Uncle Armando could have returned to Mexico after that very first encounter. My mother and I spoke endlessly about the words of Sai Baba, his intention to teach "the essence of all religions," the inexplicable creation of the *vibhuti*—ash that he seems to produce by moving his hands—and the experience of spending several days without a mirror and on a strict vegetarian diet. The peace that my uncle emitted after locking eyes with his spiritual leader, though, had more of an impact on us than anything else.

Sai Baba did not convert me into a religious person. I still have my doubts. However, never before had I been so in touch with my internal being or so aware of the nonmaterial universe. The look of peace that Sai Baba transmits—something that I had witnessed on other occasions in Pope John Paul II and in the Dalai Lama—continues to intrigue me. I don't know where it comes from, but when I recall it, I can't help but smile.

In the end, I learned the most important lesson from the moral integrity and spiritual strength of the eighty-seven-year-old man whom I accompanied to India and who today believes more than ever in the divinity of Sai Baba.

SMELLS

The writings of Marcel Proust influenced me greatly as a young boy because of the link between smell and memory, his search—like mine in this book—for lost time, and because of the reaction of a university teacher when I told him that Proust's novel was the best I had ever read.

Few have linked the nose so clearly to the past like Proust. The famous madeleines sent Proust back to his French childhood in the same way a *bolillo caliente* sends me back to the Mexico of the 1960s. It shouldn't come as a surprise either that one of my favorite novels is *Perfume* by Patrick Suskind, in which he describes the life of a man in the Middle Ages who is almost blind and who uses his sense of smell as an infallible guide.

The sense of smell is very important to me, due to the fact that my ability to smell is very limited. I'll explain. I have had three noses; that's right, three. I was born with forceps, and everything seems to indicate that the obstetric surgeon who was attending to my mother used my nose to pull me into the world. According to my mother, the marks on my nose from the forceps remained on my face for several days.

As I grew up, my nose took on a notable curvature toward the left, which prevented me from breathing correctly. I was always very aware of the irregularities of my nose. I didn't do anything about it, though, until I was fifteen or sixteen, when I decided to have my nose operated on. After that first operation I noticed that food didn't taste the same, but I was able to correct everything with a little more salt and hot sauce. My new, straight nose justified everything.

One day, however, a basketball game at our preparatory school ended in a fight, and the referee—a student from the opposing team's school—hit me from behind and destroyed my nose with one swift blow. The expression of horror on my mother and my grandfather Miguel when they saw my squashed nose was enough to garner the courage to return to the operating room.

I returned for my second operation in 1978, smack in the middle of the World Cup. That was my first mistake. I remember vividly how I woke up in the middle of the operation—the anesthesia had worn off—to find the doctors who were working on me watching a World Cup match. "Who's winning?" I asked. They quickly increased the anesthesia, and I missed the end of the game. My nose came out all right, but not as perfectly as I had hoped. "It's very banged up," the doctor told me by way of an explanation. I wanted to tell him that if he hadn't been watching the soccer match while he was operating on me things might have turned out better, but I didn't dare. The World Cup was the World Cup.

I learned to live with one side of my nose narrower than the other. I snored like a lion, causing my brother Alejandro (with whom I shared a room) countless sleepless nights. My sense of smell was reduced even more this time. There were now certain smells that I couldn't make out. Eating became an almost entirely visual and digestive exercise. Food had very little flavor.

In the United States I had yet another accident. In a soccer scrimmage my nose wound up getting flattened by the shoulder of a teammate, and as icing on the cake, seconds later I took a blow to my face from the ball. This was a time to put the best plastic surgeons in the world to the test. I looked for one in Beverly Hills, and I found Ronald Matsunaga, who achieved the impossible job of reconstructing a nose that had been smashed to smithereens. "Mother Nature is going to push your nose to the side," said a concerned Matsunaga about the tendency of my beat-up nose to curve, "but we have to beat Mother Nature." The result, I'll admit, is quite satisfactory, but I can barely smell anything.

My olfactory cells were either destroyed or injured after so many blows and three operations. I am the last one to know if there is a bad odor, and I have to be extra careful so that I am not the object of strange looks. I can detect very strong smells, and once my nose picks up an odor I can smell it for weeks. It's as if my brain were celebrating the capture of a smell and won't let it escape.

For a long time I carried around with me the smell of the dead soldiers I saw in Kuwait, the combination of garlic and onion that plagues the Moscow subway, the halitosis of former Venezuelan president Rafael Caldera and the damp smell of some old cardboard boxes from my last move. That smell, curiously, was very similar to the one I carried around with me in Afghanistan. I can't do anything about it. Once my nose captures an odor it won't let go, and as long as that odor is present in my mind, it's almost impossible to enjoy the smell of a stimulating perfume or an especially tasty dish.

While my olfactory memory may be diminished, it is well defined. The first few months of my children's lives are still present in my nose. I can remember the skin cream my first girlfriend used and the smell of the grass after it had rained and the sun had come out again at my house in Mexico City. My father had the unmistakable smell of a mixture of ciga-rettes with lotion, a smell that for me was comforting and warm; for any-one else that very combination would have been unbearable. The smell of my father's new cars also makes me smile, and, like Proust, when I conjure up those smells as if they were spirits, I return to my past. How wonderful it is to smell the grass from my childhood, my father and my country!

I have more of Mexico in my olfactory memory than I do of the United States. The main smells I carry in my mind found their way in before my nose was fractured the third time, so those are the ones that have been with me my whole life. Since 1985, after recovering from the last opera-tion, very few smells have found their way in. Therefore, for me, the United States is an odorless country, neutral, and so, my nose is always pointed toward Mexico.

THE ETERNAL RETURN

I am not from here,
Nor am I from there.

—FACUNDO CABRAL

There are days when I am consumed by the overwhelming desire to return to Mexico, days when nostalgia overcomes me. It's the sadness of being where I don't want to be. Milan Kundera, in his extraordinary novel *Ignorance,* said that "nostalgia is the suffering caused by the unfulfilled desire to return."

This is true. Sometimes, though, returning is impossible because our home (that is, where we have accumulated our memories, where we are loved, where we feel safe and protected, where we dream) is no longer where it was. That happens to many immigrants. We think our home is in our country of origin, but when we return we realize that things have changed; we no longer feel so protected, so safe, so loved, nor do we feel like such dreamers. We become homeless.

I like the word *homeless* more in English than in its limited translation in Spanish: *desamparado.* A homeless person is one who has no home, one who can't find his place in the world. It has a broader connotation in English than in Spanish. For a long time I thought that my home would always be in Mexico, but several things happened. First, the house I grew up in was sold. Second, Mexico City slowly but surely became a foreign place for me, and third, I began to form new ties in the United States that put an even greater distance between me, my house and Mexico City.

My children tether me to the United States. They were both born in Miami, and even though legally they are considered Mexicans and have Mexican passports, their lives have little or nothing at all to do with the country where their father was born. Therefore, as the song that was interpreted by Facundo Cabral and Alberto Cortez goes, "I am not from here, nor am I from there."

Despite the affection that ties me to the United States, returning to Mexico continues to be a central theme in my life, and this, of course, is an old theme. Ulysses in Homer's *Odyssey* implored, ". . . I continuously want and long to go home." But the "damaging winds" from the north prevented his boat from heading to Ithaca and he couldn't return. Ulysses spent twenty years away from home.

The main theme in *The Odyssey* is not returning home, but the journey itself. "For twenty years he thought about nothing else but returning," says Kundera in his analysis of Ulysses. "But once he had returned, he realized that his life, the very essence of his life, his center, his treasure, was not in Ithaca but rather in his twenty years of adventures around the world." That contradiction is what many immigrants and refugees experience, including Kundera. We want or we say we want to return home, even though deep down, we suspect we may never return. Why not? Because we are not the same people we were when we left; the journey changed us.

Furthermore, by leaving, we put a distance between ourselves and those who remain behind that is not easily overcome. I fear, for example, that my siblings will never really understand exactly why I left. After all, they decided to stay, and they are all very happy. "Everyone thinks we leave so we can enjoy an easier life," said Kundera, who left Czechoslovakia seeking refuge in France. "They don't know how difficult it is to make your way in a strange world."

When I speak with some of the more than twenty million people of Mexican origin who live in the United States, I don't have to explain how complicated it was to get ahead. They too have had the same experience; we understand each other. On the other hand, when I go back to Mexico, there is always someone who suggests that I chose the easy road. Those who stayed behind sometimes reproach us for having left. We are, as Kundera suggests, "the Great Traitors." In his view, they are the ones who chose the easy road, not us.

That difference is often insurmountable, and this is not true just of Mexicans or Czechs. I'm sure that the Cuban exiles in the United States will have very similar experiences of rejection and isolation when Cuba becomes free and they return to the island either temporarily or permanently.

Even though we may not be understood, those of us living abroad continue to remember. "Memories vanish if they are not recalled from time to time in conversations with friends," Kundera said. "Groups of fellow countrymen tell the same stories until they are sick of them, and in this way they become unforgettable." Nothing is truer. I can recall vividly the intense and nostalgic conversations I had in California and Florida with my good friends from Mexico—José Luis, Benito, María Amparo, Marco Bracamontes, Marco Mendoza, Sergio Saavedra, Miguel Angel Tristán—and the way in which a single verse of music or just a bite of Mexican food would take us back, south of the border. Nostalgia begins in the mouth, spreads to the ears and finally overpowers the mind.

"Everyone is mistaken about the future," declared the Czech immigrant in *Ignorance*. I am no exception. The year I planned to spend outside of Mexico turned into two, and has now been extended to twenty, the same number, oddly enough, that Ulysses spent away from Ithaca and Gandhi from South Africa. Could twenty years abroad be a vital mark that makes returning impossible?

There exists, without a doubt, a point of no return, and that is when our lives in our new country are more intense than the memories nourished by nostalgia. Finally, the accumulation of experiences abroad causes our memories to lose the importance they once had when we first left, and they become yet another chapter of an odyssey.

IN THE UNITED STATES I became more organized or less spontaneous, depending on how you look at it. I have been more successful than I could ever have imagined being in Mexico. Insofar as it is possible, I control my destiny. I have earned enough to assure that my children will have a better life than the one I had. I save out of fear of suffering the shortages I experienced when I was young.

I am terrified by the thought of opening my checkbook and realizing that I barely have enough to survive, like during those difficult days in Los Angeles. That's a nightmare that I often have, with my eyes wide open. I am very conservative with my money, and I invest it every month. I save for rainy days. I buy only what I can afford to pay in cash, and every month I pay off my two only credit cards. I don't owe anything to anyone.

I have more things than before—I can't carry them all in two hands anymore as I did when I arrived in Los Angeles—but much less time to enjoy them. Yes, I have more—isn't that part of the American dream? But I am also a more complete man than when I left, and that's important; I know how to walk alone, and with my eyes closed I can separate what is trivial and superfluous from what is essential.

What I have yet to resolve is the matter of returning to Mexico.

It is from the United States that I leave to cover stories and conduct interviews around the continent, and it is here I return with the confidence of knowing that nothing will happen to me because I asked tough questions. This nation protects freedom of speech as one of its principal values as set forth in the First Amendment to the Constitution, and for a journalist like myself, who has seen and experienced all kinds of censorship, self-censorship and pressure in both the workplace and from governments around the continent, it's comforting to be able to work with complete freedom. The United States is my journalistic trench, and I am extremely grateful. But I am still struggling with the idea of making the United States my one and only country.

It has welcomed me for twenty years, given me a job, helped me get ahead both professionally and economically, protected my freedom of speech and given me my two greatest joys: my two children. At the same time, I hope I have given something back through my effort, with my reporting, with my vision of what it means to be Latino and an immigrant, and by my example (and with my taxes, of course) of improving the place where I live as much as possible.

The United States, though, has yet to become my only country. And I still don't know if it ever will be. It's possible, but many things would have to happen first, among them, forgetting once and for all about returning to Mexico.

Just as at one time there were some things that drove me from Mexico and others that pulled me toward the United States, now there are times when the roles are reversed. There are days when the idea of returning to Mexico is more appealing and interesting to me than a secure retirement in the United States, but as soon as I begin to explore the possibility, doubts begin to fly. I'm sure that if I were to return to Mexico I would miss my life in Miami more than I can imagine.

Furthermore, my leaving Mexico hurt others. Why did you go? Why did you leave us? The "we" turned into "I" and "they." They—my parents, siblings, friends, coworkers and classmates—stayed in Mexico. I left. This is what separates us most.

The Ramos family organizes a family reunion at least once a year, and it is paradise for me. It's like returning halfway. I am back in touch with what I left behind and with those people I love the most and who love me. For my children and their cousins—scattered between Madrid, Miami, Saltillo and Mexico City—those reunions give them a feeling of continuity and belonging. For me, it is a way of returning.

Not long ago, as I was shooting a special for television, I swam the Río Bravo (or Rio Grande, as they call it in the United States), so that I could experience on my own what immigrants suffer when they come North. But I did the crossing backward: I went from the American to the Mexican shore of the river. I really didn't cross all the way. I stayed right in the middle of the river so that the U.S. border guards who were accompanying me in two launches wouldn't get in trouble. For me, that experience, being in between two countries, shaking from the cold, having a hard time staying up because of the weight of my wet clothes, and having my sense of direction confused by the currents, is full of symbolism for me. Sometimes I feel like I am fighting to define myself.

Or maybe this is all an artificial and unnecessary dilemma. Maybe I belong to both countries simultaneously: made in Mexico and developed in the United States. It's impossible to give quantitative value to these types of experiences. Where do I belong more, here or there? There's no way of really knowing.

On a bureaucratic level, I've tried to solve this contradiction by keeping my Mexican passport along with my U.S. Resident Alien Card, or Green Card. This way I don't betray anyone, although I am sure that my position may exasperate the most nationalist souls in both countries. It's a legal juggling act that doesn't always reflect the "we" that I feel.

For example, after the terrorist attacks of September 11, I felt like I was more a part of the United States than ever before. Even though I am an immigrant, I felt like I belonged to a country that was attacked, that will not allow itself to be threatened and that will move on. The present and the future were more important to me than the past during those crucial moments during the autumn of 2001.

The United States is one of the few countries in the world that allows anyone to become a citizen. That would not be possible in Germany or Japan. In other words, the essence of American society is its acceptance of diversity, and its willingness to accept immigrants. The whole American family has its roots in another country. But more powerful than tolerance and acceptance of foreigners is the unique fact that in this country, one can reinvent one's life. Self-determination—the right of each individual to choose his or her destiny—is what makes this country so special. The stories about the success known as "the American dream" are repeated countless times in small towns and big cities of this country, because wherever one may be, this country affords one the right to choose as one pleases. A woman who would be forced into an arranged marriage in Africa or Asia can marry whom she pleases here. And a journalist such as

I, in Latin America, would probably end up poor, censured, frustrated and under pressure, while in the United States I have achieved a level of success after having traveled through half the world, and with great journalistic experiences under my belt. The United States allowed me to reinvent myself. I wonder if I could have done the same thing in Mexico.

Now this might resolve any identity issues. But the question Where do I belong? remains unanswered. I am looking for my house, my home, a place where I feel completely comfortable, where I have everything; a place where I don't miss anything and I am not missed, where I don't feel like a foreigner or like I just arrived, where I will always be welcome, where I don't have to introduce myself all the time, where I can say *"nosotros"* without forcing it, where I don't have to explain my accent or apologize for who I am; where I can be myself, without masks. I don't know if I will ever find that home.

An important part of my life has been formed with will, effort, desire and a good dose of resistance and rebelliousness. All this has marked my destiny. But this part is not complete. It is rooted in my profession, in my passion—journalism—but it has not yet dropped anchor and that is why I often wander aimlessly.

Maybe there's no reason to think about it, and it bothers me to do so anyway, but there is no reason why I should return to a place that only exists in my mind. Returning to 10 Piedras Negras Street, the house where I spent my childhood, is a very pleasant thing to do . . . in my dreams. And maybe this search for a home is destined to fail, since it is really a search for balance and internal peace. Since I was a child, I never stayed still. Wherever I arrived, I was ready to leave.

I haven't arrived yet. Or better yet, maybe I have arrived many times and I have left many times too. I am still a journalist crossing borders, a man looking into a mirror, an immigrant without a home.